HABERMAS AND PRAGMATISM

There are few living thinkers who have enjoyed the eminence and renown of Jürgen Habermas. His work has been highly influential not only in philosophy, but also in the fields of politics, sociology and law. This is the first collection dedicated to exploring the connections between his body of work and America's most significant philosophical movement, pragmatism.

Habermas and Pragmatism considers the influence of pragmatism on Habermas's thought and the tensions between Habermasian social theory and pragmatism. The collection contains superb essays by leading pragmatists and a postscript by Habermas on his relationship to pragmatism. The essays range over pragmatic themes found in law, social theory, developmental psychology and aesthetics. Some of the most compelling recent issues in philosophy and social theory are addressed in the process, as well as the relationship to Habermas of Kant, Peirce, Mead, Dewey, Piaget, Apel, Brandom, and Rorty.

Habermas and Pragmatism offers original insights into both pragmatism and Habermas's philosophy, and reveals the rich work that is currently taking place in those fields. Along the way it addresses the nature of objectivity, transcendentalism, pluralism, relativism, democracy, and ethics. It will prove an invaluable collection to anyone in the fields of philosophy, social theory, political theory and sociology.

Contributors: Jürgen Habermas, Karl-Otto Apel, Myra Bookman, David Ingram, Cristina Lafont, Lenore Langsdorf Joseph Margolis, Frank I. Michelman, Tom Rockmore, Sandra B. Rosenthal and Richard Shusterman.

Editors: Mitchell Aboulafia is Professor of Philosophy, **Myra Bookman** is Senior Instructor in Humanities and Philosophy, and **Catherine Kemp** is Assistant Professor of Philosophy at the University of Colorado at Denver.

D0143887

HABERMAS AND PRAGMATISM

Edited by
Mitchell Aboulafia, Myra Bookman
and Catherine Kemp

London and New York

First published 2002
by Routledge
11 New Fetter Lane, London EC4P 4EE

Simultaneously published in the USA and Canada
by Routledge
29 West 35th Street, New York, NY 10001

Routledge is an imprint of the Taylor & Francis Group

Typeset in Garamond by Taylor & Francis Books Ltd

Printed and bound in Great Britain by MPG Books Ltd, Bodmin

British Library Cataloguing in Publication Data
A catalogue record for this book is available from the British Library

Library of Congress Cataloging in Publication Data
Habermas & pragmatism / edited by Mitchell Aboulafia, Myra Bookman &
Catherine Kemp.
p. cm.
Includes bibliographical references and index.
1. Habermas, Jürgen. 2. Pragmatism. I. Title: Habermas and pragmatism. II.
Aboulafia, Mitchell. III. Bookman, Myra Orbach. IV. Kemp, Catherine.
B3258.H324 H193 2002
193–dc21
2001048826

ISBN 0–415–23458–1 (hbk)
ISBN 0–415–23459–X (pbk)

CONTENTS

CONTENTS

CONTRIBUTORS

Mitchell Aboulafia is Professor and Chair of the Philosophy Department, and Director of the Graduate Interdisciplinary Programs in Humanities and Social Science at the University of Colorado at Denver. He is the author of *The Cosmopolitan Self: George Herbert Mead and Continental Philosophy* (University of Illinois Press, 2001); *The Mediating Self: Mead, Sartre, and Self-Determination* (Yale University Press, 1986); and *The Self-Winding Circle: A Study of Hegel's System* (W.H. Green, 1982); and the editor of *Philosophy, Social Theory, and the Thought of George Herbert Mead* (SUNY Press, 1991).

Karl-Otto Apel is Professor Emeritus at the University of Frankfurt am Main and has held professorships at the Universities of Saarbrücken and Kiel. Among his numerous articles and books are *Towards a Transformation of Philosophy* (Routledge and Kegan Paul, 1980); *Charles Peirce: From Pragmatism to Pragmaticism* (University of Massachusetts Press, 1981); *Selected Essays: Towards a Transcendental Semiotics* (Humanities Press, 1994); and most recently, *The Response of Discourse Ethics* (Peeters, 2001).

Myra Bookman is Assistant Director of Graduate Interdisciplinary Studies and Senior Instructor of Philosophy at the University of Colorado at Denver. She worked as a Visiting Scholar at Harvard University from 1991 to 1993. Professor Bookman's interdisciplinary background is extensive, connecting ideas from developmental psychology, cognitive science and linguistics to contemporary discussions in philosophy and social theory. Her recent articles have appeared in philosophy, law and interdisciplinary journals.

Jürgen Habermas is Professor Emeritus at the University of Frankfurt am Main. Among his numerous books: *Knowledge and Human Interests* (Beacon Press, 1971); *Communication and the Evolution of Society* (Beacon Press, 1979); *The Theory of Communicative Action* (2 volumes, Beacon Press, 1984, 1987); *Moral Consciousness and Communicative Action* (MIT Press, 1990); *Postmetaphysical Thinking: Philosophical Essays* (MIT Press, 1992); *Between Facts and Norms: Contributions to a Discourse Theory of Law and Democracy* (MIT Press, 1996).

David Ingram is Professor of Philosophy at Loyola University. His major publications include: *Habermas and the Dialectic of Reason* (Yale, 1987); *Critical Theory and Philosophy* (Paragon House, 1990); *Reason, History, and Politics: The Communitarian Grounds of Legitimation in the Modern Age* (State University of New York Press, 1995); and *Group Rights: Reconciling Equality and Difference* (University of Kansas Press, 2000). He has also edited *Critical Theory: The Essential Readings* (Paragon House, 1991) and *The Political: Blackwell Readings in Continental Philosophy* (Blackwell, 2002).

Catherine Kemp is Assistant Professor of Philosophy at the University of Colorado at Denver. She has published articles in the areas of legal theory and modern philosophy, including "Habermas among the Americans: some reflections on the common law" (*University of Denver Law Review*, 1999) and "Two meanings of the term 'idea': acts and contents in Hume's *Treatise*" (*Journal of the History of Ideas*, 2000). She specializes in common law theory and the philosophy of David Hume.

Cristina Lafont is Associate Professor at Northwestern University. She has studied extensively at the University of Frankfurt and specializes in German philosophy, particularly hermeneutics and critical theory. She is the author of *The Linguistic Turn in Hermeneutic Philosophy* (MIT Press, 1999) and *Heidegger, Language, and World-Disclosure* (Cambridge University Press, 2000).

Lenore Langsdorf is a Professor at Southern Illinois University, Carbondale. Her research is based in hermeneutic phenomenology, Deweyan pragmatism, and process metaphysics, and is concerned with issues in the philosophy of communication.

Joseph Margolis is Laura H. Carnell Professor of Philosophy at Temple University. He is the author of numerous books, including *Historied Thought, Constructed World: A Conceptual Primer for the Turn of the Millennium* (University of California Press, 1995); *Life Without Principles: Reconciling Theory and Practice* (Blackwell, 1996); *The Flux of History and the Flux of Science* (University of California Press, 1993); *Interpretation Radical but Not Unruly: The New Puzzle of the Arts and History* (University of California Press, 1995). With Jacques Catudal he has recently edited an anthology, *The Quarrel Between Invariance and Flux: A Guide for Philosophers and Other Players* (Penn State University Press, 2001), which serves as a companion to *Historied Thought, Constructed World*.

Frank I. Michelman is Robert Walmsley University Professor, Harvard University, where he has taught since 1963. He is the author of *Brennan and Democracy* (Princeton University Press, 1999), and has published widely in the fields of constitutional law and theory, property law and theory, local government law, and jurisprudence. Professor Michelman is recent past President of the American Society for Political and Legal Philosophy, and a fellow of the American Academy of Arts and Sciences. Over the past several years, he has consulted on matters of constitutionalism in South Africa.

Tom Rockmore, Professor of Philosophy at Duquesne University, is the author of numerous books, including *Before and After Hegel: A Historical Introduction to Hegel's Thought* (University of California Press, 1993); *Hegel's Circular Epistemology* (Indiana University Press, 1986); *Fichte, Marx, and the German Philosophical Tradition* (Southern Illinois University Press, 1980); *Habermas on Historical Materialism* (Indiana University Press, 1989); *Irrationalism: Lukács and the Marxist View of Reason* (Temple University Press, 1992); and *On Heidegger's Nazism and Philosophy* (University of California Press, 1997).

Sandra B. Rosenthal, Provost Distinguished Professor of Philosophy at Loyola University of New Orleans, has published eleven books and approximately 200 articles on pragmatism and its relation to various issues and movements, and has presented invited formal lectures on pragmatism in China, Poland and Germany, among other places. She is on the editorial boards of several journals and books series, and has served as president of various professional organizations, including The Charles Peirce Society, The Society for the Advancement of American Philosophy, and The Metaphysical Society of America, and on the executive committee of the American Philosophical Association, Eastern Division. Her more recent books include *Speculative Pragmatism* (Open Court, 1992); *Charles Peirce's Pragmatic Pluralism* (SUNY Press, 1994); and *Time, Continuity, and Indeterminacy: A Pragmatic Engagement with Contemporary Perspectives* (SUNY Press, 2000).

Richard Shusterman is Chair of Philosophy at Temple University and Directeur de Programme at the Collège International de Philosophie, Paris. His more recent books include *Pragmatist Aesthetics* (Blackwell, 1992); *Practicing Philosophy: Pragmatism and the Philosophical Life* (Routledge, 1997); *Performing Live* (Cornell, 2000); and the edited collection *Bourdieu: A Critical Reader* (Blackwell, 1999).

ACKNOWLEDGMENTS

Work on a project as ambitious and wide-ranging as this inevitably incurs many debts for its editors. We are grateful to our colleagues in the Philosophy Department at the University of Colorado at Denver. We owe a special debt to our colleague Rob Metcalf, for his graceful and timely translation of Professor Habermas's "On John Dewey's *The Quest for Certainty*," and to Andrew Barber, our Administrative Assistant, who was helpful in too many ways to enumerate. We also wish to thank our non-university supporters: Joyce Aboulafia, Irving Aboulafia, Kelly Bookman, Raggio Colby, Joe Esposito, Hill Kemp, Margaret Kemp, and Harper Louden.

We are thankful for the encouragement, persistence, and patience of our editor, Tony Bruce, and for the efforts of the team at Routledge, Muna Khogali and Zoe Drayson. Without their efforts this volume would not have been possible.

Our contributors deserve special thanks for their efforts both at their own articles and toward sustaining a conversation within these pages. We are grateful to Jürgen Habermas for permission to translate his article, "On John Dewey's *The Quest for Certainty*," which originally appeared in *Die Zeit*, 23 July 1998. We also wish to thank Karl-Otto Apel for translating and revising his article, "Zum Verhältnis von Moral, Recht und Demokratie. Eine Stellungnahme zu Habermas Rechtsphilosophie aus transzendental-pragmatischer Sicht," which originally appeared in Peter Siller and Bertram Keller (eds) *Rechtsphilosophische Kontroversen der Gegenwart* (Baden-Baden, Nomos, 1999), pp. 27–40. This article is reprinted by permission of the author. An earlier version of Richard Shusterman's article, "Habermas, pragmatism, and the problem of the aesthetic," appeared in his *Practicing Philosophy: Pragmatism and the Philosophical Life* (New York, Routledge, 1997), ch. 4, and is reprinted by permission of the author and Routledge Press. A shorter version of Cristina Lafont's article, "Is objectivity perspectival? A comparison of Brandom's and Habermas's pragmatist conceptions of objectivity," appeared in German as "Kann Objektivität perspektivistisch sein? Ein Vergleich der Objektivitätskonzeptionen von Habermas und Brandom," in

K. Günther and L. Wingert (eds) *Die Öffentlichkeit der Vernunft und die Vernunft der Öffentlichkeit* (Frankfurt, Surkamp, 2001).

Finally, we wish to express our gratitude for the contributions made by Professor Habermas to this volume. His responses to specific questions regarding his relationship to pragmatism provide an invaluable context for the remarks of the other contributors.

INTRODUCTION

Mitchell Aboulafia

For much of the world, and for much of its history, the United States has been known as a champion of *laissez-faire*, a midwife to redemptive individualism, and a guardian of private property. So it is indeed one of the small ironies of the American experience that pragmatism, which champions social and collective life, will be remembered by future generations as America's philosophy. Some mischievous quirk of fate has ordained that America's envoys to posterity should be advocates of a philosophy that often stridently promotes the importance of collective life, and which at times even echoes the sentiments of a seemingly foreign tradition, namely, left-wing Hegelianism. Why this should have come to pass is, of course, a historical question, and historians will tell us that along with the claims of the private sphere, America has almost always produced those who privileged collective and communal life, from the days of its earliest religious communities, the utopias of the nineteenth century, to the communes of the 1960s. America is a complex place. And pragmatism is a complex tradition, for not all pragmatists have concerned themselves with the communal and social, and no two have addressed the latter in exactly the same fashion.

There are indeed many different types of pragmatism, perhaps at least the thirteen that Arthur O. Lovejoy noted.[1] Yet, in spite of the different paths taken by individual pragmatists, it is difficult not to see a concern with the social – along with fallibilism and an infatuation with novelty – as the lifeblood of a tradition that embraces Peirce's community of inquirers, Dewey's Idea of Democracy, Mead's social self, and recent social democratic voices, such as those of Cornel West, Nancy Fraser, Richard Bernstein, and even, in his own ironically informed liberal way, Richard Rorty. If linking pragmatism so deeply to the social offends, because obvious counterexamples can be found, one might ask if either of the following alternatives rings true: pragmatism is a philosophical tradition that is neutral with regard to social and collective life; pragmatism is positively hostile to collective experience. Jürgen Habermas is surely someone who would not find much merit in either suggestion.

Habermas has had a long-standing interest in pragmatism, dating from

1

the early 1960s and his exposure to Charles Sanders Peirce by Karl-Otto Apel, a friend since Habermas's university days.[2] He tells us in an interview,

> Encouraged by my friend Apel, I also studied Peirce, as well as Mead and Dewey. From the outset I viewed American pragmatism as the third productive reply to Hegel, after Marx and Kierkegaard, as the radical-democratic branch of Young Hegelianism, so to speak. Ever since, I have relied on this American version of the philosophy of praxis when the problem arises of compensating for the weaknesses of Marxism with respect to democratic theory.[3]

And in a statement from the same interview, Habermas clarifies an intuition that he believes links him to Rorty and to pragmatism.

> As far as Richard Rorty is concerned, I am no less critical of his contextualist position. But at least he does not climb aboard the "anti-humanist" bandwagon, whose trail leads back in Germany to figures as politically unambiguous as Heidegger and Gehlen. Rorty retains from the pragmatist inheritance, which in many, though not all, respects he unjustly claims for himself, an intuition which links us together – the conviction that a humane collective life depends on the vulnerable forms of innovation-bearing, reciprocal and unforcedly egalitarian everyday communication.[4]

There are commentators who support Habermas's own identification with pragmatism. One of the most consistently sensitive to Habermas in this regard has been Richard Bernstein, who Habermas tells us was the first "real" pragmatist he had ever met.[5] In commenting on Habermas's words regarding the intuition that he shares with Rorty, Bernstein provides the following admirable summary of some of the links between Habermas and pragmatism.

> For Habermas is profoundly right in recognizing that the basic intuition or judgment that stands at the center of his own vision is also central to the pragmatic tradition. Both share an understanding of rationality as intrinsically dialogical and communicative. And both pursue the ethical and political consequences of this form of rationality and rationalization. It was Peirce who first developed the logical backbone of this thought in his idea of the fundamental character of a self-corrective critical community of inquirers without any absolute beginning points or finalities. It was Dewey who argued that the very idea of such a community, when pressed to its logical extreme, entails the moral ideal of a democratic community .... And it was Mead who saw that the linkage of

2

dialogic communicative rationality and the institutionalization of democratic forms of life require a new understanding of the genesis and development of practical sociality. ... I vividly recall my own shock of recognition when I first started reading Habermas in the 1960s. For I realized that he, who was primarily intellectually shaped by the German tradition from Kant through Hegel to Marx and by his own creative appropriation from the Frankfurt School, was moving closer and closer to the central themes of the American pragmatic tradition.[6]

In spite of the affinities that Habermas's thought may have to pragmatism, there are those who remain skeptical about affiliating Habermas too closely with this tradition. Questioning Habermas's credentials as a pragmatist, for example, is Hans Joas – the author of a major work on Mead – who notes,

> What prompted my taking issue with Jürgen Habermas's *Theory of Communicative Action* was my surprise at how little this author had adapted from pragmatism for his theory as a whole. After all, Habermas had repeatedly documented his orientation toward the pragmatists Peirce and Mead and had, in the above work as well, justified the fundamental paradigm shift "from purposive action to communicative action" by citing Mead and (albeit problematically) Durkheim. For me it was a matter of describing the relative poverty of Habermas's theory of action.[7]

And a number of the contributors to this volume also question Habermas's credentials as a pragmatist. Joseph Margolis and Tom Rockmore are concerned that in spite of the distance that Habermas places between his work and traditional forms of Kantian transcendentalism, there is still just too much of the transcendental in his thought to make a pragmatist rest easy; Richard Shusterman and Lenore Langsdorf argue that Habermas's notion of communication remains too restrictive to do full justice to aesthetic experience, especially of a Deweyan sort; and Sandra Rosenthal claims that from the vantage point of pragmatism, Habermas's model cannot provide a sufficiently rich account of the self. Apel, on the other hand, believes that in recent years Habermas has moved too far from the transcendental ground necessary to support discourse ethics, which Apel and Habermas developed in light of Apel's interpretation of Peirce. Although in his article for *Habermas and Pragmatism* Apel speaks to Habermas's philosophy of law, he spends a good deal of time explaining just how his views differ from those of Habermas.

Pragmatists often take a turn to the contextual and have been known to be moved by communitarian impulses, even if they are moved by them to different degrees and in different ways. This is a direction that Habermas finds problematic, for it runs the danger of relativism, reveals an insufficient sensitivity to the distinction between justice and ethical life, and often entails an unwillingness or inability to differentiate sufficiently between strategic and communicative action, that is, the purely instrumental from that which is truly rational. Habermas in general worries about the unwillingness of pragmatists to make distinctions that are often necessary, a concern that is apparent in his response to a question about pragmatism's greatest weaknesses in the "Postscript" to *Habermas and Pragmatism.*

> The message that only differences that make a difference should count is often mistaken for advice to blur even relevant distinctions. And just as often the anti-Platonic distrust in an ideological misuse of abstract ideas is misunderstood as the denial of the transcending force and unconditional meaning of claims to truth. There is an empiricist undercurrent in Dewey's and an emotivist undercurrent in James's thought. Both threaten the Kantian heritage that is saved, in pragmatist translation, by Peirce – and, by the way, by Brandom. My friend Dick Rorty is most Kantian in the seriousness of his ambition to turn those weaknesses into philosophical strengths.[8]

Habermas has in fact struggled for years with the problem of how to maintain a Kantian bent toward universality in questions of justice, which entails maintaining a distinction between justice and the habits of ethical life, while at the same time questioning traditional Kantian transcendentalism. Fallibilism and dialogical interaction are not properly addressed in traditional transcendentalism for Habermas, but they are privileged in the pragmatist tradition. And yet the Kantian framework for addressing questions of justice and truth cannot be abandoned. According to Margolis, this unwillingness to fully abandon transcendentalism is symptomatic of a latent Cartesianism in Habermas's thought, and Cartesianism is the antipode of pragmatism.[9] (Margolis also argues in his contribution that Apel has profoundly misinterpreted Peirce by not realizing that the transcendental in Peirce must be understood in terms of transcendental hope.)

I once asked Habermas in a public forum what was the most difficult aspect of his philosophy to defend. He didn't hesitate to answer: quasi-transcendentalism. And when I then asked why he thought that he had to defend it – not an unusual question from a pragmatist vantage point – his answer was straightforward: the Holocaust. This, he wanted to make clear, was not to be interpreted as a psychological motive. It is imperative that we have some sort of intellectual ground, even if only a quasi-transcendental one, in order to counter irrationalism and the moral barbarism that follows in its wake. According to Bernstein, Habermas fears "'irrationalism'

[in] whatever guise it takes – whether ugly fascist forms, disguised neo-conservative variations, or the playful antics of those who seek to domesticate Nietzsche."[10] While it appears that Habermas has put a greater distance between himself and the transcendental *a priori* over the years – for example, by emphasizing the fallibilistic nature of even the presuppositions of argumentation – he cannot yield to what he views as relativism and irrationality.[11]

The bottom line in this for Habermas is that communicative action – which is grounded in the universalistic pragmatics of language – must be nurtured and protected from forces that seek to overwhelm it, forces that often appear in the guise of another form of "rationality," that is, strategic rationality. Even if we cannot guarantee that the validity claims of linguistic interaction – truth, truthfulness, and rightness – are *a priori* in a strictly Kantian sense, the current evidence points to their universality, and we must act as if they are universal until proven otherwise. We need just this universality to avoid the slippery slope of contextualism, for no contextualism can ever provide a ground for cross-cultural appeals to justice. Justice is concerned with proper procedures and is not to be confused with the virtues of particular forms of ethical life. Unfortunately, for Habermas, pragmatism often fails to make this distinction properly and runs the danger of conflating claims of justice with those of the good life, leaving any pretensions of justice to universality mired in the dynamics of a particular cultural constellation. And we are also told that we must not conflate validity with genetic considerations, for there clearly can be different routes to that which is valid.[12] Pragmatists, however, are unlikely to be troubled by these criticisms, for where Habermas sees conflation and confusion, pragmatists often find justifiable and illuminating connections.

R.G. Collingwood and Hans Georg Gadamer would have us believe that philosophers cannot be fully appreciated unless the questions that they ask are understood. If we modify this claim in light of the pragmatic mindset, we arrive at the following: we never really understand a philosopher unless we can understand the problem(s) that he or she is addressing. I have not raised the issue of Habermas's "motives" in defending even a weakened version of transcendentalism or universalism simply to psychologize, for no sophisticated philosophical theory should be reduced to one set of motives or causes. I have raised it to highlight the nature of what might be construed as the central problem of his thought: namely, how to disarm the advocates of fascism and barbarism. I have also raised it in order to begin to suggest why Habermas can never fully become a pragmatist, at least a pragmatist of the Deweyan variety. For all the similarities between Habermas and certain pragmatists, there are often different problems and interests at play, and these are rooted in divergent historical and sociological conditions. The Holocaust and fascism were clearly the defining "events" in Habermas's personal and intellectual development, in a way that perhaps the American Civil War was for the early pragmatists, as we will see below.

For all of Habermas's commitment to "the people," he has seen what can happen when anti-constitutional (fascist) forces and "local" concerns hold sway. Communitarianism and contextualism are impossibly dangerous in this regard. Morality and critique must have some lasting ground, some principle or principles that make riding roughshod over the interests and rights of others morally reprehensible, and not just here, but everywhere, throughout the whole community of nations. It is worthwhile noting in this context that there had been a fascist appropriation in Germany of pragmatism in the work of figures such as Arnold Gehlen and Eduard Baumgarten. (Habermas refers to Gehlen in the above quotation linking his own thought to Rorty's.) That pragmatism as a philosophy of action could be distorted in this fashion, specifically by evading its intersubjective and democratic dimensions, would be a deeply troubling proposition to Habermas.[13]

In Habermas's view acknowledgment of the fact that no such distortion took place in America, that American pragmatists typically viewed pragmatism as an inherently democratic philosophy, is no substitute for a sustained justification of the cross-cultural superiority of constitutional democracy. For this sort of justification democracy must be related conceptually to the rule of law, in an account that appeals to the principles of communicative action. Consider how Habermas links law, the legitimacy of democracy, the presuppositions of communication, and proceduralism in the following passage from *Between Facts and Norms*.

> The argument developed in *Between Facts and Norms* essentially aims to demonstrate that there is a conceptual or internal relation, and not simply a historically contingent association, between the rule of law and democracy ... [T]he *democratic process* bears the entire burden of legitimation. It must simultaneously secure the private and public autonomy of legal subjects. This is because individual private rights cannot even be adequately formulated, let alone politically implemented, if those affected have not first engaged in public discussions to clarify which features are relevant in treating typical cases as alike or different, and then mobilized communicative power for the consideration of their newly interpreted needs. The proceduralist understanding of law thus privileges the communicative presuppositions and procedural conditions of democratic opinion- and will-formation as the sole source of legitimation.[14]

It is precisely this sort of proceduralist vision of the law that is in turn challenged by pragmatists or pragmatically inspired thinkers. In his article for this anthology, Frank Michelman, a friend and a friendly critic of Habermas, questions whether the constitutional contractarian approach embodied in Habermas's work on the law can adequately deal with the relationship of norms to their application. Michelman tells us that

> Habermas expressly, repeatedly, and roundly rejects any semblance
> of a *sittlich* foundation for what is after all supposed to be the
> *universal* and *rational* acceptability of the law. *Reason*, as Habermas
> says, "must already be at work" in the construction of semi-perfect
> legal norms such as Günther's "paradigms" or "doctrine."[15]

And it is just such a *sittlich* "foundation," a "foundation" of substantive moral and ethical practices, that pragmatists typically do not wish to yield. One of Habermas's problems with American Legal Realism, a tradition that can be viewed as aligned with pragmatism, is that it leads to a conflation of politics and law, and a privileging of bureaucratic social planning over democratic processes. In very broad terms one might say that this tradition is too contextualist, too *sittlich*. David Ingram's comprehensive article on Legal Realism argues that Habermas underestimates the complexity of this tradition. Progressive Realists did not conflate politics, economics, and law to the degree that Habermas believes that they did. But there is a larger question that is raised by Ingram's chapter, one which ties it to Michelman's. Can Habermas adequately defend his universalistic approach to the law?

There is little doubt that Oliver Wendell Holmes Jr. would not think so. Given the latter's pragmatically informed approach to the law, the rationalism, proceduralism, and universalistic impulses of Habermas's orientation to the law would not be welcome. In his recent book, *The Metaphysical Club*, Louis Menand tells us,

> When Holmes said that common law judges decided the result first
> and figured out a plausible account of how they got there afterward,
> the implication was not that the result was chosen randomly, but
> that it was directed by something other than the formal legal ratio-
> nale later adduced to support it. Holmes announced what this
> "something" was in the famous fourth sentence of the opening
> lecture of *The Common Law*: "The life of the law has not been logic;
> it has been experience."[16]

The passage Menand cites from Holmes is important and worth quoting at greater length.

> The life of the law has not been logic: it has been *experience*. The felt
> necessities of the time, the prevalent moral and political theories,
> intuitions of public policy, avowed or unconscious, even the preju-
> dices which judges share with their fellow-men, have had a good

deal more to do than the syllogism in determining the rules by which men should be governed.[17]

What did Holmes mean by *experience*, perhaps the most ubiquitous and sanctified term in the pragmatists' lexicon? Menand goes on to say:

> It's a word with a number of associations, but Holmes was using it in a particular sense. He meant it as the name for everything that arises out of the interaction of the human organism with its environment: beliefs, sentiments, customs, values, policies, prejudices – what he called "the felt necessities of the time." Another word for it is "culture."[18]

And with "the felt necessities of our time" we are back on precisely the terrain that Habermas wishes to circumscribe in matters of law and justice. This phrase reflects a stress on culture and experience that ultimately cannot be reconciled with a proceduralist and universalistic vision of the law. Pragmatists and the pragmatically inclined seem to find it impossible to rein in their appeals to experience.

Given this recurrent and pervasive concern with experience, pragmatists would be inclined to highlight how different Habermas's world was from the world in which pragmatism arose, and they would want to do so because it might shed light on the interests and problems at play in the various theories.[19] (Not only are pragmatists absorbed with experience, they cannot seem to let interests go unexamined.) Although I have no intention of providing a short history of pragmatism here – far too complicated a story with too many different chapters – I do want to offer in its place the overarching hypothesis of Menand's book to suggest something of the different worlds inhabited by Habermas and the early pragmatists.

Pragmatism arose in New England in the years following the American Civil War. To be more accurate, in Cambridge, Massachusetts, a town that was home to Peirce, James, the polymath Chauncey Wright, and a number of other thinkers who participated in a club, The Metaphysical Club, in 1872. (A generation or so later John Dewey and George Herbert Mead were born in New England.) Menand offers the hypothesis that the Civil War, with its inexorable violence and raging ideologies, was the problem that pragmatism set about solving.[20] In this reading, Oliver Wendell Holmes Jr. left for the war as something of a political radical and returned committed to shunning every sort of ideological or principled certitude, as well as the mentality of those who hold them, because it is just this sort of "dogmatic" mentality that gives birth to rivers of blood. (And Holmes was not the only club member to be affected by the war. William James, for example, was moved by the experiences of his brothers in the war, and he felt continually torn about not serving in it.) Pragmatism, of course, is a

philosophy that has an aversion to all forms of absolute certainty; fallibilism is its totem.

Whether one can in fact locate the motivation for fallibilism in the blood
of the Civil War is far from a proven claim, for certainly one can turn to
other historical conditions – for example, the diversity of cultures in
America – as well as to internal developments in the sciences to help
account for this feature of pragmatism. And, of course, Menand's more
global hypothesis about the Civil War and pragmatism cannot be the whole
answer, because we would want to know why this response to sectional
hatred and ideology and not another. (A reservation of this sort would
equally hold true when examining Habermas's work in light of fascism and
the Holocaust, for here too we can ask: why his response and not another?)
Menand, however, is not saying that pragmatism can simply be accounted
for in this manner. It clearly is a philosophy that moves with many of the
currents of modernity. It is a child of its times. Nevertheless, the Civil War
must be considered a crucial factor in the rise of pragmatism because it
helped cultivate the conviction that viewing ideas as absolutes is an exceed-
ingly dangerous proposition. Better to treat them as tools and not eternal
verities. But Habermas considers himself to be a fallibilist, so what have we
gained by invoking the influence of the Civil War?

Pragmatists are problem solvers, and one might even say that what pragmatists fear is not being able to solve a problem. A problem for a pragmatist is
a conflict, a tension of some sort, a doubt that has arisen and must be
addressed. And in a sense the big problem that must be overcome is conflict
itself, although not permanently but in bits and pieces, for if America has
taught us anything, it is that new conflicts will arise, if only due to novel
events. Pragmatists are instrumental Darwinians, who are not to be confused
with social Darwinians. American pragmatists are also typically inveterate
supporters of tolerance, for in allowing differences to be noted and seriously
addressed – for example, accepting errors in the context of scientific discovery
– tolerance allows us to devise richer solutions to problems. Tolerance is the
condition for the possibility of genuine harmony: that is, a genuinely satisfying (dare we say, authentic) relief of doubt and conflict, as opposed to the
anodyne of half-hearted convictions. But typically for leading American pragmatists, with the possible exception of Peirce, we are dealing with a dialectic
without end. We will never be rid of doubt and conflict, problems will always
arise, differences will always be present, which is indeed a good thing, for
without differences there is no progress. (Pragmatists did believe in progress,
after all.) And this can lead to a further lesson regarding tolerance: we must be
tolerant of tolerance for the sake of making the world a better place, and this
applies to our social and political lives and not just the laboratory.[21]

But isn't tolerance also a basic category of Habermas's philosophy?
When George Herbert Mead – who, with the exception of Peirce, is the
pragmatist to whom Habermas is most indebted[22] – speaks about taking the

perspective of others, is he not laying the groundwork for tolerance, at least in the social world? No doubt Habermas wishes to promote tolerance, and Mead's notion of taking the perspective of others reflects in part a pragmatist penchant for accommodating difference. However, in Habermas's hands Mead's notion is transformed into a resource for an idealized communication community, in which everyone takes the perspective of everyone else.

> The idealizing supposition of a universalistic form of life, in which everyone can take up the perspective of everyone else and can count on reciprocal recognition by everybody, makes it possible for individuated beings to exist within a community – individualism as the flip side of universalism. Taking up a relationship to a projected form of society is what first makes it possible for me to take my own life history seriously as a principle of individuation – to regard it *as if it were* the product of decisions for which I am responsible. The self-critical appropriation and reflexive continuation of my life history would have to remain a non-binding or even an indeterminate idea as long as I could not encounter myself before the eyes of all, i.e., before the forum of an unlimited communication community.[23]

Although this is not the place to provide a detailed examination of the accuracy of Habermas's interpretation of Mead, I would like to make the following suggestion. For Mead, the taking of the perspective of the other is grounded in the sympathy tradition of British Empiricism and given a Romantic twist via the notion of the intersubjective in Hegel.[24] Mead's notion of taking the perspective of others is no doubt a sociological description of how roles develop, but it is also linked to a kind of universalism, one that says: we are better off when we share as many perspectives as possible, for such sharing is not only made possible by sympathetic relations, it also nurtures sympathy – that is, the kind of sympathy we associate with tolerance for others and their unaccustomed ways. For the pragmatist Mead, as for Dewey and assorted kin, tolerance results from the right habits. It is an attitude as well as a conceptual achievement, and it is due to experience and gives birth to experience.[25]

Although Habermas is clearly aware of the importance of habits and practices, there must in addition be a moment of idealization and universality that links his project back to Kant. However, it is just this tendency to appeal to universal conditions as governing factors for certain types of experience that would "scare" the pragmatically inclined such as Holmes and Dewey. In general, idealizations that advance in the direction of the *a priori* would remain suspect, even if they are presented in Habermas's fallibilistic and empirically minded manner. There would, for example, be a suspicion that Habermas wants us to achieve consensus – e.g., via validity claims as presuppositions of communicative action – before we actually wrestle with difference and novelty. For the pragmatist this is tantamount to trying to sidestep conflict and difference via principles, and this is a path that leads to intolerance and violence. Now, of course, Habermas would want to argue that his "principles," given their procedural character, would never place us on such a path. They are not *a priori* in a traditional sense. They only set the stage for a conversation that allows differences to be heard and treated respectfully. And a conversation of this sort is surely one that any good pragmatist would also endorse.

Habermas and Pragmatism is intended to nurture a dialogue between those committed to a Habermasian version of critical theory and those wishing to challenge or clarify some aspect of Habermas's thought via classical or recent figures and themes of the pragmatic tradition. In organizing the volume the editors did not expect that all of the classical figures in pragmatism would be adequately covered, nor that all of the potentially absorbing topics of research and conversation could be addressed in one anthology. The editors were fortunate that contributors of such distinction were willing to involve themselves in the project, furthering one of the main goals for the volume: namely, stimulating an exchange between two vibrant traditions. Thus far in the Introduction a number of the contributors have been mentioned. In addition to the themes of transcendentalism, aesthetics, law, ethics, and politics that they address, Myra Bookman provides an account of the rarely examined relationship among Piaget, pragmatism, and Habermas; and Cristina Lafont addresses the important dialogue between Habermas and Brandom on objectivity. This is dialogue that is all the more interesting because Habermas views Brandom as a figure in the Peircean tributary of pragmatism that he favors.[26] Which brings us to Habermas's contribution.

Habermas has made a number of comments over the years on his relationship to pragmatism. There are sustained treatments of Peirce and Mead in his work, but little general discussion of pragmatism. In the "Postscript" to this volume, after briefly commenting on the contributions to this anthology, Habermas has kindly answered several question posed to him regarding his relationship to the pragmatic tradition. This is followed by a short piece that has been translated for this volume on Dewey's *Quest for Certainty*.

One last note on organization. The anthology is divided into four sections: "Transcendentalism and reason"; "Law and democracy"; "Language and aesthetic experience"; and "Comparative studies." In certain cases the assignment of chapters to specific sections could have followed a different course. This may seem especially apparent in the case of Apel's chapter, "Regarding the relationship of morality, law and democracy: on Habermas's *Philosophy of Law* (1992) from a transcendental–pragmatic point of view," which has been placed in the section on transcendentalism and reason, and not the one on law. However, a good deal of this piece addresses basic questions about Apel's and Habermas's relationship to transcendentalism, and the article connects rather well with the other three papers in the section. But it would clearly also be of interest to those who wish to focus on the philosophy of law.[27]

Notes

1 See Tom Rockmore, Chapter 3 in this volume, pp. 47, 60, n.1.
2 Jürgen Habermas, *Knowledge and Human Interests*, trans. Jeremy J. Shapiro, Boston, Beacon Press, 1971, p. vii.
3 Jürgen Habermas, "A philosophico-political profile," *New Left Review*, 151, May/June, 1985, pp. 76–7.
4 Habermas, *New Left Review*, p. 82.
5 See Habermas, "Postscript" in this volume, p. 226.
6 Richard Bernstein, *The New Constellation; The Ethical–Political Horizons of Modernity/Postmodernity*, Cambridge, MA, MIT Press, 1992, p. 48. See also Habermas's comments in the "Postscript" to *Habermas and Pragmatism* regarding his early exposure to pragmatism, pp. 225–6.
7 Hans Joas, *Pragmatism and Social Theory*, Chicago and London, University of Chicago Press, 1993, pp. 8–9. See also Hans Joas, *G.H. Mead; A Contemporary Re-examination of His Thought*, Cambridge, MA, Polity/MIT Press, 1985.
8 See Habermas, "Postscript," p. 228.
9 See Joseph Margolis, Chapter 2 in this volume, pp. 31–46.
10 Bernstein, "An allegory of modernity/postmodernity: Habermas and Derrida," in *The New Constellation*, p. 208. This quotation by Bernstein is preceded by the following comment, "Iris Murdoch once shrewdly remarked 'it is always a significant question to ask of any philosopher: what is he afraid of?' The answer for Habermas is clear."
11 Apel notes in his chapter for this volume that Habermas,

> Following the tradition of the "Frankfurt School," ... does not accept a principled (foundational) difference between *philosophy* and *critical–reconstructive social science*. And this means that all philosophical propositions are considered to be *empirically testable* and thus *fallible*, as are indeed propositions of general linguistics (e.g. Chomsky's "innateness" thesis). This holds even for the necessary (unavoidable) *presuppositions of argumentation*, which according to "universal pragmatics" as well as "transcendental pragmatics" are the four "validity claims": *meaning* (ability to be understood), *truth*, *truthfulness* (veracity), and *moral rightness*, and the claim to possible discursive *consensus* with regard to these validity claims.
>
> (p. 19)

12 See Myra Bookman, Chapter 4 in this volume, p. 68.
13 Hans Joas, *Pragmatism and Social Theory*, pp. 107–11.
14 Habermas, *Between Facts and Norms*, trans. William Rehg, Cambridge, MIT Press, 1996, pp. 449–50.
15 See Frank Michelman, Chapter 6 in this volume, p. 133.
16 Louis Menand, *The Metaphysical Club*, New York, Farrar, Straus, and Giroux, 2001, pp. 340–1.
17 See Oliver Wendell Holmes Jr, *The Common Law*, New York, Dover Publications, 1991, p. 1, emphasis added. Originally published: Boston, Little, Brown, 1881.
18 Menand, *The Metaphysical Club*, pp. 341–2.

19 Bernstein's shock that Habermas, as someone trained in the German tradition, could share so much with the pragmatists – whose thought was nurtured in another time and place – is something of a "natural" pragmatist response, given the importance of experience in shaping our habits of mind. Of course, in retrospect we know that Habermas was not isolated from American thought, as he notes in his "Postscript." Further, he lived at a time in which American culture was invading nooks and crannies throughout Europe.

20 See, for example, Alan Ryan, "The group," *New York Review of Books,* XLVIII(9), 31 May 2001, pp. 16–20. In this review of *The Metaphysical Club* Ryan writes,

> What, then, is the problem to which pragmatism is an answer? … Louis Menand's answer in *The Metaphysical Club* is both dramatic and persuasive. It is, he thinks, the Civil War to which we must look for the answer. More exactly, it is the Civil War as it was experienced by the young Oliver Wendell Holmes, Jr. and by his teachers, friends, and intellectual antagonists in mid-nineteenth century Cambridge.

(p. 16)

21 See Menand, *The Metaphysical Club*, pp. 439–40.

22 See Habermas, "Postscript," to this volume, p. 227.

23 Jürgen Habermas, "Individuation through socialization: on George Herbert Mead's theory of subjectivity," in *Postmetaphysical Thinking: Philosophical Essays*, trans. William Mark Hohengarten, Cambridge, MIT Press, 1992, p. 186.

24 Mitchell Aboulafia, *The Cosmopolitan Self: George Herbert Mead and Continental Philosophy*, Urbana and Chicago, University of Illinois Press, 2001, ch. 3, pp. 61–86.

25 See Sandra B. Rosenthal, Chapter 10 in this volume.

26 Habermas, "Postscript," p. 228. "Both [James and Dewey] threaten the Kantian heritage that is saved, in pragmatist translation, by Peirce – and, by the way, by Brandom."

27 I want to thank my co-editors, Myra Bookman and Catherine Kemp, for their comments and suggestions on the Introduction.

Part I

TRANSCENDENTALISM AND REASON

1

REGARDING THE RELATIONSHIP OF MORALITY, LAW AND DEMOCRACY

On Habermas's *Philosophy of Law* (1992) from a transcendental–pragmatic point of view[1]

Karl-Otto Apel

Introduction

In his recent major work *Faktizität und Geltung*[2] (in the following noted as *FuG*) Jürgen Habermas has for the first time presented a "philosophy of law," and has tried to determine its relationship to *moral philosophy* and *theory of democracy* within the framework of his long-standing *discourse philosophy*. In this context, however, a novel "architectonics" of *discourse differentiation* has resulted, which from my point of view is very problematic. The problematic features, in my opinion, concern two points:

1   In his Tanner Lectures of 1986,[3] the preliminary stage of *FuG*, Habermas still pleaded for the foundational priority of *morality to law*, but in *FuG* he introduced a new top position in his "architectonics": the foundational principle of the whole of "practical philosophy" is now to be constituted by a *discourse principle* that is "morally neutral" (*FuG*, 138), rather than by the principle of "discourse ethics." The "principle of morality" (*Moralprinzip*) and the "principle of law" (*Rechtsprinzip*) are now considered to emerge "equiprimordially" (*gleichursprünglich*) with regard to their normative status from the morally neutral "discourse principle" – analogously to their historical differentiation out of "*substantielle Sittlichkeit*" (in the sense of Hegel) (*FuG*, 138).

2   The second problematic point of the novel architectonics of discourse differentiation concerns the following circumstance: the *principle of law* – which is said to be equiprimordial to the *principle of morality*, according to Habermas – is at the same time "identical with" the "principle of democracy," the latter being the normatively foundational principle of politics (*FuG*, 136ff.). For Habermas, this normative equation obviously

results from the following implication of his *discourse theory*: in an ideal form of democracy, the discourses of free and equal citizens can ensure by their procedures that the legislators both make and submit to the laws; or, in other words, that the human rights of citizens can be guaranteed by these same citizens as autonomous legislators (*FuG*, 122ff.).

In *FuG* the scheme of a normatively founded *discourse differentiation* turns out to be as shown in Figure 1.1:

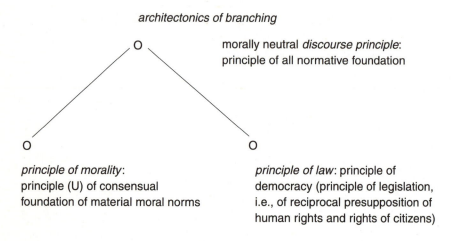

architectonics of branching

O   morally neutral *discourse principle*: principle of all normative foundation

principle of morality: principle (U) of consensual foundation of material moral norms

principle of law: principle of democracy (principle of legislation, i.e., of reciprocal presupposition of human rights and rights of citizens)

Figure 1.1   Architectonics of branching

Now what is problematic about this *branching architectonics*?

I have worked out an extensive commentary on Habermas's *FuG* in my book *Auseinandersetzungen* (1998) under the subtitle *Third attempt at thinking with Habermas against Habermas*, together with two similar attempts in other essays.[4] Given this, I should say something in advance about my long-standing relationship to Habermas in order to clarify the motives and perspective of my comments on *FuG*.

On the early history of "discourse philosophy"

Since about 1970, Habermas and I have been developing a foundation for practical philosophy and the critical social sciences via a conception of communicative or discourse rationality which we developed in a constant exchange of thought. Until recently we both used the term *discourse ethics* as a designation for the basic discipline of *practical philosophy*.[5] But despite strong common concerns, there were also differences between our approaches from the beginning, differences which appeared as early as 1976 when we published the basic conceptions of our approaches in a discussion volume, *Sprachpragmatik und Philosophie*.[6] In this volume we each took up John Searle's elaboration of *speech act theory* (and inspirations from Noam Chomsky), but Habermas used the title "*Universalpragmatik*" and kept close to social science and generative linguistics,[7] whereas I used the title "*Transzendentalpragmatik*" in an attempt to continue a project of the "transformation of transcendental philosophy" which I first propagated in 1973.[8] What is the significance of this difference?

Common to us both is a certain – positive and critical–transformative – connection with Kantian philosophy: for example, a transformation of Kant's philosophy of the "transcendental subject" or "consciousness" in terms of a philosophy of *language* and *intersubjectivity*. In this respect we each take up the "pragmatic turn" of *language-analytic* philosophy. However, Habermas distances himself not only from *metaphysics* in general (as I do), but also from *transcendental philosophy* (which he does not distinguish from metaphysics). Following the tradition of the Frankfurt School, he does not accept a principled (foundational) difference between *philosophy* and *critical–reconstructive social science*. And this means that all philosophical propositions are considered to be *empirically testable* and thus *fallible*, as indeed are propositions of general linguistics (e.g. Chomsky's "innateness" thesis). This holds even for the necessary (unavoidable) *presuppositions of argumentation*, which according to "universal pragmatics" as well as "transcendental pragmatics" are the four "validity claims": *meaning* (ability to be understood), *truth, truthfulness* (veracity), *moral rightness*, and the claim to possible discursive *consensus* with regard to these validity claims. Although for Habermas these presuppositions of argumentation are conditions for the possibility of empirical testing, they are said to be subject to empirical testing and are thus considered to be *contingent*: they could change, according to Habermas, since they belong to social forms of life. Thus there is no *transcendental apriori*.

All this sounds quite plausible to most prominent philosophers today. For, along with surmounting "transcendent" (Kant) metaphysics, "de-transcendentalization" (Richard Rorty) is also demanded,[9] but for me this latter demand ultimately entails a step into the *nonsensical*. Thus, for example, the unavoidable presuppositions of argumentation (which cannot be denied without committing a *performative self-contradiction*) cannot be fallible and subject to empirical tests, because in case of falsification they would simultaneously be presupposed in their transcendental function.[10] For the same reason it makes no sense, I suggest, to imagine that one fine day the presuppositions of argumentation could change, for the question would be: from where – i.e. under which presuppositions – could we think of these presuppositions as being *contingent*? Habermas may try to think this from a *historico-sociological* perspective, and in doing so he may understand himself as a modest and self-critical philosopher. But I would assert that he simply forgets to reflect on *his own* necessary presuppositions of argumentation and thereby falls back to "transcendent" metaphysics, for he takes, as it were, a *divine point of view* outside the world, from which (he tries) to conceive of everything, including transcendental conditions of thought, as being just contingent – that is, as historical facts.

From these remarks it may have already become clear why I could not follow Habermas and the Frankfurt School in abolishing the difference between empirical social science and philosophy; why I insisted instead on the *post-metaphysical* function of *transcendental philosophy* as a *transcendental pragmatics* of argumentative discourse.

For the same reason I always held on to the possibility of, and need for, an *ultimate transcendental foundation of discourse ethics*. Due to the undeniable presuppositions of argumentation (even according to Habermas's original conception of "universal pragmatics"), there must be a dimension of "moral rightness" in acts of argumentation as acts of communicative action. In my *transcendental–pragmatic* interpretation this means primarily that in serious argumentation we have always necessarily acknowledged that all possible members of the argumentation community have *equal rights* in using speech acts in proposing validity claims, and they have *equal co-responsibility* for identifying and solving morally relevant problems of the lifeworld.

(This comprises the primordial solidarity of the discourse partners as such.) Now for me it makes no sense to think that the necessary acknowledgment of these fundamental moral norms, which are the *conditions for the possibility* of serious discourse and thus for all justifying and criticizing of material norms, could change. And this reflection, I suggest, points to the possibility of an *ultimate transcendental foundation* of ethics as *discourse ethics*. So, the first main point of the difference between Habermas and myself centers on the status of the transcendental, and this difference is highlighted in the changes in Habermas's "architectonics" of discourse differentiation in *FuG*.

In this book Habermas not only disputes, as he has done before, the possibility of an *ultimate* foundation of ethics, but for the first time he explicitly denies the immediate implication of the *principle of morality* by the *discourse principle*. This principle is now called "morally neutral" (although it is still considered to be *normatively foundational*), thereby making *discourse ethics* no longer the basic discipline of *practical philosophy*. The claim to "moral rightness" obviously no longer belongs to the necessary presuppositions of argumentation as a form of communicative action, for it is said to be *not yet thematizable* on the level of the primordial discourse principle (see Figure 1.1). Thereby the original conception of "universal pragmatics" has also been abandoned. But for me, above all, the possibility of an *ultimate transcendental–pragmatic foundation of ethics* by reflective recourse to the undeniable presuppositions of argumentation has been lost (and for me no other *foundation* of ethics is possible at all, as still must be shown).

In order to assess the significance and bearing of this point we have to try to understand the motives behind Habermas's new architectonics of branching. First there is a problem that is surely shared by Habermas and myself: the *norms of law* must be distinguished from the *norms of morality* in a specific way. *Historically* both types of norm emerged equiprimordially from "*substantielle Sittlichkeit*" (in the sense of Hegel); *normatively* they must be foundable, precisely with regard to their essential differences, by discourse philosophy. Thus far I can easily agree with Habermas. But for me the question arises: does it follow from the fact that moral norms and norms of law must be *different* that they must be (or even can be) derived from, i.e. grounded by, a primordial discourse principle that is "morally neutral?" This claim – prima facie, perhaps – seems to be a consequence of the assumption that otherwise the principle of *positive law* must be derived from that very principle of *morality* from which it has differentiated itself in the course of history. This is indeed an old aporia of the *philosophy of law* which, I think, Habermas rightly tried to avoid in his new approach.

On the other hand, however, after the emancipation of positive law from the metaphysical doctrine of "natural law," there was and still is the intuitional belief that *law* somehow must be grounded by morality, lest it be surrendered to political power interests. Habermas previously, and still in the Tanner Lectures, obviously shared this latter intuition. However, how can it be made compatible with the insight into the necessary *difference* between the norms of law and the norms of morality in the sense of historically differentiated systems of rules?

Let us first return to the problem of grounding *discourse ethics*. In the years when Habermas and I shared the program of *discourse ethics*, we were always in agreement about the following point: the material norms of morality cannot be *deduced* – say, by philosophers – from principles. Philosophy can and ought to ground only the *procedural* principle for *real* practical discourses (only by substitution for those that have to be carried through in *foro interno*), through which the affected persons themselves – or their advocates – can ground norms that are acceptable to all affected persons and ultimately applicable to concrete situations. As a regulative principle for those discourses, a *universalization* principle (U) is set up which, in a sense, has to prescribe the procedure for the *discursive concretization* of the Kantian principle of universalization.[11]

Now, with regard to those material norms that can be grounded through discourses, certainly a *difference* between the norms of *morality* and those of *law* has to be envisaged (as was supposed already by Kant's distinction between the principles of "morality" and "legality"). One may even affirm that we can only speak of *moral norms* if and when there exist also *norms of law*: that is, those norms that concern only *external actions* (and not mental motives that were not realized by actions), norms whose observation can be enforced by sanctions through the constitutional state (*Rechtsstaat*). This necessary differentiation and reciprocal complementarity for Habermas is obviously a sufficient reason for postulating a *discourse principle* that – according to the *branching architectonics* – is at the same time "morally neutral" and normatively basic for morality and law.

How to ground the procedural principle of discourse ethics

But for me, according to the demand for a *transcendental–pragmatic foundation of discourse ethics*, the following supplement becomes necessary: the *procedural principle* of discourse ethics – the principle of grounding material norms of morality through practical discourses according to the discursive universalization principle (U) – does not lack all morally obligatory content. On the contrary, it must *a priori* ensure the equality of rights and also the co-responsibility of all discourse partners. These *procedural basic norms* of discourse ethics cannot be the result of *practical discourses*, since they make these discourses possible, but nevertheless they need to be grounded with regard to their moral content.

What are we to say, then, about the philosophical foundation of *the procedural basic norms of discourse ethics?* Since they cannot be grounded by *practical discourses*, they obviously must be grounded by the *discourse principle* itself, insofar as this principle prescribes the formation of all material moral norms by practical discourses according to the basic procedural norms. But this foundation through prescribing procedural norms obviously cannot be provided by a *morally neutral* principle. How, then, could this be possible without a *petitio principii*, i.e. without presupposing already what has to be grounded? Indeed, no ultimate foundation by *deduction* is possible without such a *petitio*. But an ultimate foundation is possible through *transcendental reflection on what in argumentative discourse we cannot deny without committing a performative self-contradiction*. Now, precisely this *reflective* foundation is possible in the case of *discourse ethics*, since the *discourse principle*, which cannot be circumvented by argumentation, implicitly contains those basic procedural norms that make possible and prescribe practical discourses in all cases of morally relevant conflicts or differences of opinion. (The methodologically revolutionary point of the foundation of *discourse ethics*, in my opinion, has been prepared by *two changes* in the presuppositions of a rational foundation: first, by the replacement of the "methodical solipsism" of Descartes' and Husserl's *ego cogito* by the transcendental *a priori* of discursive intersubjectivity,[12] and, second, by the replacement of the traditional (rationalist) conception of *grounding* (or foundation) through deduction by grounding through reflection.[13]

However, if this is correct with regard to *discourse ethics*, how then should the primordial *discourse* principle provide the foundation not only for the principle of *morality* but also for the *principle of law*, which after all has to be different from the *principle of morality*? (At this point the motive of Habermas's *architectonics of branching* becomes relevant again, and I must show a transcendental–pragmatic alternative to his program.)

How to ground the necessary supplementation of the principle of morality by that of (positive) law

First, I want to emphasize the fact that I agree with Habermas's tenet that the *ideal principle of morality* – in the sense of (U) – stands in need of a "supplementation" if, under the lifeworld conditions of a post-traditional society, "social integration" of the society is to be possible. Although I would not admit – as Habermas recently has suggested[14] – that the "cognitive" foundation of the moral principle contains no capacity of motivation or "obligation" whatsoever, I would indeed agree that it cannot ensure the obeying of moral norms in practice. Furthermore, it has to be realized that human beings are overburdened in many respects by the demands of a *discursive foundation* of material norms and their applications. Therefore, it is a functional demand to *supplement the principle of morality by a principle of law*, which can afford to abstract to a great extent[15] from the actual moral motivation of human actors, and thereby ensure the regulation of external actions according to what can and must be expected socially. For, as I have already remarked, by the restriction to the regulation of external actions, it becomes possible for the law to enforce obedience to its norms through the sanctions of the constitutional state (*Rechtsstaat*).

But it is precisely this last insight – the realization of the necessity of *the power monopoly* of the *constitutional state* – which also shows that it is not possible to ground the *law* immediately – according to Habermas's *branching architectonics* – by recourse to the primordial *discourse principle* (as, indeed, is possible with regard to morality, if the discourse principle is not considered to be morally neutral.) By this statement I do not wish to deny that there is an internal relationship between the *primordial discourse principle* and the principle of the *democratic constitutional state*. (I shall come back to this point.) But I want to state that the principle of *positive law* or, respectively, the *constitutional state*, in contradiction to the ideal principle (U) of *morality*, cannot be grounded solely on the basis of the *primordial discourse principle*. For through this avenue alone one could not ground the need for a power monopoly of the constitutional state. (At this point a further foundational argument is needed against those philosophers who – like the classical *anarchists* – plead for *freedom from domination*.)

One may elucidate this point through examining the early history of Habermas's version of discourse philosophy. In the 1960s, in the context of the "philosophy of emancipation," there was much talk about "domination free communication" or "discussion" (and the students of 1968 often gave the impression that they wished to eliminate all structures of *domination* whatsoever). Now I wish to emphasize that even today the *ideal of domination-free communication* or *discourse* can indeed be justified as a necessary presupposition of the *ideal principle of discourse morality*. But, on this presupposition, one cannot *ground a constitutional state*, which has to put its *power monopoly* into the service of enforcing obedience to norms of law. In order to ground such a *constitutional state*, and hence *positive law*, it must be possible to ground norms that are at the same time capable of consent by free citizens and – by their form as norms of law – capable of being passed and put through by the *power-based* authority of a particular state. Thus far, Hobbes' verdict is still valid: *"auctoritas, non veritas, facit legem."*

But then the question arises: how can the normative legitimation of the *constitutional state* be a task of *discourse* philosophy? And this question is especially relevant with regard to *democracy*.

I thoroughly agree with Habermas that the legitimation of the norms of law in a democracy has to be based not only on political power but also on "communicative power": that is, on *discursive procedures* as well. But, in contradistinction to Habermas, I do not believe that this problem can be solved analogously to the normative foundation of morality by immediate recourse to a (morally neutral) *discourse* principle (as is suggested by the "branching" architectonics). It can only be ultimately solved, I suggest, by recourse to a *discourse principle* that by its primordial moral content – i.e. *its content of history-related co-responsibility of all discourse partners* – can justify not only the ideal principle (U) of justice by universalization, but also the necessary *supplementation* of ideal discourse morality by (positive) *law*. And, this means, by political power of the state in the service of enforcing law.

Now, to elucidate this contention I obviously must show how the principle of (positive) law or the constitutional state can be grounded by *discourse ethics as a primordial ethics of co-responsibility*. At this point, I have once more to take recourse to the development of *discourse ethics* by Habermas and myself.

From the beginning, in particular from around 1986, my approach to *discourse ethics* was different from that of Habermas not only in its insistence on a *reflexive, ultimate transcendental–pragmatic foundation* but also in its tenet of *primordial, history-related moral responsibility (or rather co-responsibility)*, a tenet that later found its expression in my distinction between a foundational *part A* and a foundational *part B* of discourse ethics.[16] With regard to our problem of a *supplementation* of morality by positive law or, respectively, the constitutional state, the *A/B* distinction arose from the following consideration: *the primordial principle of morality*, which in my account is implicitly contained in the *discourse principle*, implies not only a "rule of argumentation" on the lines of the universalization principle (U), but also the moral demand that discourse ethics has to be applied to the lifeworld, i.e. that all morally relevant problems – for example, conflicts of interest – should be solved by following the principle (U) of discursive consensus formation. However, what should we do when we cannot expect our opponents (i.e. the needed partners of cooperation) to be prepared to enter a practical discourse in order to settle conflicts in accordance with the principle (U)? They might prefer *strategic negotiations* or even *open war*. In these cases it would probably be *irresponsible* to try to follow the norms, or even the principle, of *ideal discourse morality*. Nevertheless, there remains the primordial responsibility for finding a moral solution to the problems. What then is to be done? In considering these problems, I think we have to *supplement* – on the foundational level of discourse ethics – part A, i.e. the *ideal* basic norm of following the principle (U), by a part B, which obviously cannot be *ideal* in the sense of A. What does this mean?

For a long time I treated the problem outlined so far only as a problem of "ethics of responsibility (*Verantwortungsethik*)" in contradistinction to "ethics of good intention (*Gesinnungsethik*)" in the sense of Max Weber[17]: that is, as a problem of political actions of individuals, especially in existential "limit situations" (in the sense of Karl Jaspers and Jean-Paul Sartre). Up to this point the problem turned out to be one of mediating *consensual* and *strategic* rationality under the guiding principle of a *moral strategy*. But I have arrived at a more general and more radical conception of the problem of part B of ethics: a conception that takes into account not only the situation of personal action under conditions of reciprocal interaction, but also that of acting under conditions of the "functional constraints (*Sachzwänge*)" of *institutions* or *social subsystems* – for example, those of politics or economy.[18] Let me explain.

In ordinary life it is not the case, and cannot be the case, that we act solely on the decision basis of an immediate response to the morally relevant claims of our fellow human beings, say, according to the *I–thee* relationship. This limit case of human encounter is often taken as the paradigm case of moral action by an existentialist ethics of Jewish–Christian provenance, for example by Martin Buber and Emmanuel Levinas. And, no doubt, this is a profound source and focus of moral duties. But in most situations, even those of helping in case of emergency, people must act in accordance with their professional competences: that is, so to speak, by mediating their ways of acting through the conventional possibilities and duties that are pre-given by institutions. Now, in very many situations people act – without much reflection – in accordance with more or less *strategic* routine considerations that are suggested by their belonging to a family, a community, a firm, the nation state, etc. These strategic routine considerations are, so to speak, of a *moral–immoral* nature of quasi-duties; in short, they are suggested and even enforced by *functional constraints* ("*Sachzänge*") of *institutions*. What, then, is the relationship between these constraints and part B of discourse ethics?

If we could suppose that all morally relevant problems of human interaction could be solved on the basis of part A of discourse ethics – by discursive consensus-formation according to the principle (U) – then no *moral legitimation* would be possible for institutions through which *strategic* interaction between human beings would be suggested or even enforced. Since, however, we are always confronted with the problems of part B of discourse ethics (and cannot change this situation through, say, a new beginning of human history), we must derive from this situation a partial moral legitimation – even of institutionalized strategic interaction, for example – of power *politics* and of *economic competition in the service of profit-making*.[19] From a *part A* point of view of ideal morality we may speak of the "functional constraints" of these institutions, whose moral acceptance is enforced by the vital need of political *self-maintenance* and of *material self-preservation*.

Nevertheless, these institutions are *morally legitimizable* only under the condition that, with regard to their release of *strategic* rationality, they can be regulated, and, as it were, domesticated, by *norms of law*. By an order of law that can be enforced at a most universal scale, the *rules* of the strategic game must be subjected to the regulative idea of being acceptable (capable of consensus) to all affected persons. The *systemic order of law* must, so to speak, "sublate" (in Hegel's sense) the political practice of power and the economic practice of competition, whose exertion is prima facie (i.e. in light of part A of discourse ethics) immoral. Thus the *global order of economy* had to make possible the optimal achievement of a provision for all – in the sense of John Rawls' "second principle of justice," which focuses on the weakest – and the *global political order* had to bring about a cosmopolitan order of law and peace, as had already been demanded by Kant in the eighteenth century.[20]

Now, with regard to Habermas's conception in *FuG*, we have to ask the following question: is that functional achievement of a globally valid *order of law* that I have postulated in the light of a *part B of discourse ethics* (already) realized in the present global situation? For only in this case could I agree that the principle of *positive law*, which can be equated with the *principle of democracy*, be considered as an adequate supplement to the ideal *principle of morality* in the sense of discourse ethics. I will, in this context, leave aside the extremely topical and difficult question of a *globalized economic order*, as does Habermas in *FuG*. But then the question that can be related to Habermas's *second main thesis* remains: may the old idea of a universally valid principle of *law* that was and is connected with the idea of "human rights" be *equated* with the *idea of democracy*, which according to Habermas may be traced back to Rousseau and also to Kant's idea of "people's sovereignty?"

Is there a relationship of equivalence between the universal principle of law (as expressed in the idea of "human rights") and the principle of democracy (as expressed in the idea of "people's sovereignty")?

I would, in principle, answer this question in the negative. As I have emphasized already, I do not disregard the *internal relationship* between the idea of democracy and the procedural principle of *legitimizing norms by discourses*, which ensures that the legislators and those who are subject to the law are treated identically. Taking recourse to this fundamental principle, I am even prepared to stick to the *principle of democracy* as a necessary precondition for realizing justice on a global scale. (In this I agree with Habermas and not Rawls, who in his essay "The law of peoples" dropped the condition of a democratic constitution as a precondition of the political realization of justice on a global scale.)[21]

Nevertheless, I would not agree that the principle of democracy, which is expressed by the principle of "people's sovereignty," could in principle stand on the same normative level of legitimation as that principle of law which traditionally finds its expression in the idea of "human rights." It is indeed true, as Habermas points out, that the idea of "human rights" is to be viewed in contradistinction to the idea of *moral norms*, since "rights" from the outset underwent a process of *positivization* and *codification* in the constitution of all constitutional states (*FuG*, 122ff.). Nevertheless, there remains a constitutive difference and tension between the idea of "human rights" that can be grounded *morally* – i.e. by discourse ethics, even under constant recourse to those foundational norms that make moral discourses possible and are thus implied in the procedural norms of practical discourses – and their possible *positivization* through the constitutions of particular constitutional states. And the existing democracies – even the imaginable democracies (in the plural) – are particular states! This is implied by the Rousseauean conception of *"people's sovereignty."*

Habermas has not completely overlooked the difficulty that arises at this point for the *equation* of the *universal* principle of right (implied in the idea of human rights) and the *principle of democracy*. But he believes that the difficulty, which exposed Rousseau's conception to the suspicion of *nationalism* or even *totalitarianism*, can be surmounted in principle. We would only need to dismiss the idea of "political ethics" as that of ethical self-realization of one people or "ethnos," which was indeed connected by Rousseau with the idea of "people's sovereignty," and to replace it by the idea of the *constitutional state* and the pertinent "constitutional patriotism (*Verfassungs-patriotismus*)" (*FuG*, 132). But it seems to me that the difficulty with the Rousseauean idea of democracy is not only, and not even primarily, a consequence of the *ethnic* or *nationalist* dimension of his conception, but rather a consequence of the idea of "raison d'état," which was (and still is) connected with the idea of "sovereignty" since Jean Bodin and Richelieu. Even if the idea of national self-realization, which is still very vivid in the European democracies, could be surmounted and replaced by "constitutional patriotism," in a way similar to what seems to be the case in the United States of America, the simple fact would remain that (at least today) *there are several particular democracies* that relate to each other in *power relations* which are relevant at the level of *foreign politics*. This fact, I suggest, remains a grave obstacle for every attempt at equating the principle of *universal law* with that of democracy.

To overlook this fact, in my opinion, reflects a certain naivety in regard to foreign politics, a naivety that can indeed be found in present-day theories of democracy in the West, in those of the *Liberals* as well as in those of the *Communitarians*.[22] Philosophers are inclined to thematize the moral and juridical aspect of politics primarily from the point of view of – local or even supposed global – *domestic politics*. They are often surprised when this supposition from the perspective of non-occidental cultures is considered to be a symptom of Western *cultural centrism*. (An aggressive confession of this cultural centrism has in fact turned up in Richard Rorty's contention that it is impossible and unnecessary to justify and defend, in an international forum, the legitimacy of Western democracy on the basis of a philosophical principle. Only the opposite, he says, is possible and necessary: that is, to make the acceptability of philosophical principles dependent on one's belonging to the Western cultural tradition and to justify them by appeal to that tradition.)[23]

To be sure, Habermas's universalist position is fundamentally different from that of Rorty. But precisely for this reason one must critically notice that, like the philosophical contestants of the American debate between Liberals and Communitarians, he too shares the tacit presupposition that one may methodically disregard the foreign politics dimension of self-maintenance that belongs to all particular states as power systems (*FuG*, 158). I have to confess that I consider this to be false and naive. In fact, through this abstraction the empirical evidence that testifies against the equation of the universally valid *principle of law* with the *principle of democracy* is made invisible. Evidence against this equation can be seen in the present global discussion about "international law," for instance, in the Security Council of the UN where there is a tension between the idea of the rights of *world citizens*, which is oriented towards human beings as individuals, and the traditional principle (of *jus gentium*) of *non-intervention* into *sovereignty rights* of particular states.[24] This tension shows that we are today not allowed to disregard the moral reservation of "human rights" (traditionally grounded in *natural law*, or the *law of reason*, and today justified by *transcendental pragmatics*, in my opinion) with regard to all possible positivizations through particular constitutional states, even if they are democracies.

The international discussion about human rights must go on. And it must take into account the arguments of developing countries – arguments, for example, of the following type: the lack of material prerequisites of survival can reduce the value of individual rights of liberty, and thus a "human right" of economic development can temporarily deserve preference. But even in the developed democracies of the West there is a tension between the *universal unifiable part of the law* that finds its place in the preambles of constitutions and the *political discourses* that respond to the problems of *raison d'état* of a particular political system, for example in the enduring debates about the rights of foreigners, of those seeking asylum, and of immigration in general, etc. No democratic state has thus far been able to afford to strictly subordinate its particular interests to universally valid human rights.

Therefore, for the time being, an insight still holds which Kant succinctly expressed in the seventh proposition of his essay "Idee zu einer allgemeinen Geschichte in weltbürgerlicher Absicht (Idea for a universal history from a cosmopolitan point of view)": "The problem of establishing a perfect civil constitution depends on the problem of the external relationship between states to be ruled by law and it cannot be solved without the solution of the latter problem."[25]

Notes

1   This article is a translation and revision by Professor Apel of his previously published article, "Zum Verhältnis von Moral, Recht und Demokratie. Eine Stellungnahme zu Habermas Rechtsphilosophie aus transzendentalpragmatischer Sicht," in Peter Siller and Bertram Keller (eds) *Rechtsphilosophische Kontroversen der Gegenwart*, Baden-Baden, Nomos, 1999, pp. 27–40. Reprinted by permission of the author.

2   Jürgen Habermas, *Faktizität und Geltung. Beiträge zur Diskurstheorie des Rechts und des demokratischen Rechtsstaats*, Frankfurt a.M, Suhrkamp, 1992.

3   J. Habermas, "Recht und Moral" (Tanner Lectures of 1986) in *FuG*, 541–99.

4   See K.-O. Apel, *Auseinandersetzungen: in Erprobung des transzendentalpragmatischen Ansatzes*, Frankfurt a.M., Suhrkamp, 1998, pp. 727–838.

5   J. Habermas, *Moralbewußtsein und kommunikatives Handeln*, Frankfurt a.M., Suhrkamp, 1983; *Erläuterungen zur Diskursethik*, Frankfurt a.M., Suhrkamp, 1991; K.-O. Apel, *Diskurs und Verantwortung*, Frankfurt a.M., Suhrkamp, 1988; *Auseinandersetzungen*, Frankfurt a.M., Suhrkamp, 1998; *The Response of Discourse Ethics to the Moral Challenge of the Human Situation As Such and Especially Today*, Leuven, Peeters, 2001.

6   K.-O. Apel (ed.) *Sprachpragmatik und Philosophie*, Frankfurt a.M., Suhrkamp, 1976.

7   See J. Habermas, "Was heißt Universalpragmatik?" Frankfurt a.M., Suhrkamp, pp. 174–272.

8   Cf. K.-O. Apel, *Transformation der Philosophie*, Frankfurt a.M., Suhrkamp, 1973, vol. II, part 2, "Transformation der Transzendentalphilosophie"; English translation, *Towards a Transformation of Philosophy*, London, Routledge & Kegan Paul, 1980; reprinted with Marquette University Press, Milwaukee, 1998.

9   Cf. M. Niquet, *Transzendentale Argumente*, Frankfurt a.M., Suhrkamp, 1991.

10 Cf. K.-O. Apel, "Fallibilismus, Konsenstheorie der Wahrheit und Letztbegründung," *Auseinandersetzuingen*, *op. cit.*, pp. 81–194.

11 Cf. J. Habermas, "Uber Moral und Sitllichkeit – was macht cinc Lebensform 'rational'?" in H. Schnädelbach (ed.) *Rationaltät*, Frankfurt a.M., Suhrkamp, 1984, pp. 218–35.

12 Cf. K.-O. Apel, "Das Apriori der Kommunikationsgemeinschaft und die Grundlagen der Ethik," *Transformation der Philosophie*, vol. II, *op. cit.*.

13 Cf. also W. Kuhlmann, *Reflexive Letztbegründung, Untersuchungen zur Transzendentalpragmatik*, Freiburg i.B./München, K. Alber, 1985.

14 See J. Habermas, "Erläuterungen zur Diskursethik," Frankfurt a.M., Suhrkamp, 1991, p. 186f.

15 Kant, by the metaphysical dualism of his doctrine of the two realms, has been misled into affirming that the problem of establishing a *constitutional state* must be solvable "even for people of devils (if only they have intelligence)" (*Akademie-Textausgabe*, VIII, 366, trans. K.-O. Apel). By contrast, Rawls seems to me to be right in his insistence that a "sense of justice" has to be presupposed if the keeping of contracts is to be reliable.

16 See K.-O. Apel, *Diskurs und Verantwortung*, Frankfurt a.M., Suhrkamp, 1988, especially p. 103ff.

17 Cf. M. Weber, "Politik als Beruf," *Gesammelte Politische Schriften*, Tübingen, 1958, p. 493ff.

18 Cf. K.-O. Apel, "Diskursethik vor der Problematik von Recht und Politik," in K.-O. Apel and M. Kettner (eds) *Zur Anwendung der Diskursethik in Politik, Recht und Wissenschaft*, Frankfurt a.M., Suhrkamp, 1992, pp. 29–61; "Can 'liberation ethics' be assimilated under 'discourse ethics'?" in L. Martin Alcoff and E. Mendieta (eds) *Thinking from the Underside of History. Enrique Dussel's Philosophy of Liberation*, Lanham, Rowman & Littlefield, 2000, pp. 69–96; "Diskursethik als Ethik der Mitverantwortung vor den Sachzwängen der Politik, des Rechts und der Wirtschaft," in K.-O. Apel and H. Burkhart (eds) *Prinzip Mitverantwortung*, Würzburg, Königshausen & Neumann, 2000, pp. 69–96.

19 Cf. K.-O. Apel, "Institutionenethik oder Diskursethik als Verantwortungsethik? Das Problem der institutionellen Implementation moralischer Normen im Falle des Systems der Marktwirtschaft," in J.R. Harpes and W. Kuhlmann (eds) *Zur Relevanz der Diskursethik*, Münster, LIT, 1997, pp. 167–209.

20 Cf. I. Kant, "Zum ewigen Frieden," *Akademie-Textausgabe*, VIII, pp. 341–86.

21 See John Rawls, "The law of peoples," in S. Shule and S. Hurley (eds) *On Human Rights, the Oxford Amnesty Lectures*, London, HarperCollins, 1993, pp. 41–81.

22 Cf. K.-O. Apel, "Das Anliegen des anglo-amerikanischen 'Kommunitarismus' in der Sicht der Diskursethik," in M. Brumlik and H. Brunkhorst (eds) *Gemeinschaft und Gerechtigkeit*, Frankfurt a.M., Fischer, 1993, pp. 149–72.

23 See Richard Rorty, "The priority of democracy to philosophy," in *Objectivism, Relativism and Truth*, Cambridge, Cambridge University Press, 1991, pp. 175–96; and for a critique, see K.-O. Apel, *Diskurs und Verantwortung, op. cit.*, p. 397ff.

24 Cf. K.-O. Apel, "On the relationship between ethics, international law and politico-military strategy in our time: a philosophical retrospective to the Kosovo conflict," *European Journal of Social Theory*, 4/1 (2001), pp.29–40.

25 I. Kant, *Akademie-Textausgabe*, VIII, 24 (trans. K.-O. Apel).

2

VICISSITUDES OF
TRANSCENDENTAL REASON

Joseph Margolis

I

There is an unguarded note in one of Hilary Putnam's remarks, close to the
end of his much-admired little book *Reason, Truth and History*, that captures
what may be the fatal *pons* of his entire philosophical labor. Countering a
criticism of Richard Rorty's, which appears in Rorty's Presidential Address
before the American Philosophical Association (1980), urging us to abandon
all absolutes and accept the fact that "there is only the dialogue," Putnam
asks:

> Does this dialogue have an ideal terminus? Is there a *true* conception
> of rationality, a *true* morality, even if all we ever have are our *concep-*
> *tions* of these? [Rorty says there is "only the dialogue," there is "no
> ideal end" to our inquiries about truth and right conduct.] But how
> [asks Putnam] does [this] differ from [a] self-refuting relativism?

The implication is that there must be "a true conception of rationality";
but there is nothing in the entire corpus of Putnam's publications to tell us
what it is or what it must be. Putnam answers his own question this way:

> The very fact that we speak of our different conceptions as different
> conceptions of *rationality* posits a *Grenzbegriff*, a limit-concept of the
> ideal truth.[1]

I find it difficult to believe that Putnam did not *suspect*, in putting this
thought forward, that it was impossible to defend, and, moreover, impossible to defend on his own or any pragmatist assumptions: he simply leaves
the cognizing power of Reason hanging in the air! I single Putnam out, not
to batter his views but to isolate the most telling clue we have about the
futility of recent tendencies, particularly among the friends of pragmatism,
to rely on Reason in both theoretical and practical matters. There *is* no
faculty of Reason and there are no necessary truths of Reason that can direct

31

us productively in science or morality. If there were, pragmatism would be utterly untenable.

Our remarkable appetite for the dictates of Reason, which already appears at the beginning of Western philosophy, is a dreadful trap that has siphoned off our energies from the better prospects of what to believe and do under the conditions of practical life. Putnam is, transparently, a victim of a deep longing that apparently will not subside, that takes the form (in him) of worrying whether our grip on objectivity could possibly survive accommodating any form of relativism. At the very least, it is a little startling to find that he senses no incongruity between the ideal function of his *Grenzbegriff* and the standard pragmatist resistance to invariances of any kind. I mean to justify a conjectural leap from Putnam to Jürgen Habermas and, by that, to compare the recent German and American uses of pragmatism. Bear with me, please: a similar weakness occurs in both.

By "Reason" (written with a capital "R"), I understand a would-be faculty apt for discerning or judging what, invariantly, universally, or necessarily, is true or right – or rightly constrains whatever may be judged to be true or right. Putnam is no partisan of Reason conceived so baldly, but his question leads in Reason's direction: he offers no qualification of any kind.

He opposes admitting any faculty said to guide us in choosing the best of all possible conjectures[2] or to serve the inexorable tendency of intelligence to converge on the laws of a perfected natural science.[3] He plainly takes these to be false leads, and he counters with a pluralist proposal. But with the best will in the world, one cannot really say where Putnam stands on the matter. For example, he repudiates "the *externalist* perspective," "a God's Eye point of view," objectivism – which claims that

> the world consists of some fixed totality of mind-independent objects. There is [it says] exactly one true and complete description of 'the way the world is.' Truth involves some sort of correspondence relation between words or thought-signs and external things and sets of things.[4]

Putnam rejects this view, as well as what he calls the "*criterial* conception of rationality" according to which "there are institutionalized norms which define [as by necessary and sufficient conditions] what is and what is not rationally acceptable,"[5] which he associates (somewhat tenuously) with Wittgenstein, with the positivists, with the Oxford ordinary language philosophers. He finds the idea fraught with insuperable difficulties. Nevertheless, precisely in saying all that, although he undermines the prospects of his own *Grenzbegriff* thereby, he *does* affirm the *Grenzbegriff* but offers no conceptual grounds for his convictions. The question nags, therefore: are there any favorable arguments to call on? I know of none that are decisive.

Putnam's avowal rests with an uncertain compromise, which he presses (elsewhere) in a pluralistic direction. "We must [he says] have criteria of rational acceptability to even have an empirical world ... these reveal part of our notion of an optimal speculative intelligence."[6] The remark poses a troublesome complication (possibly not central to the question of rationality, possibly quite central) that depends on Putnam's having recently rejected his well-known "internal realism" (his own version of pragmatism), which he advances in the book *Reason, Truth and History*),[7] the very text in which the concept of the *Grenzbegriff* is launched. There certainly is a role for "speculative" criticisms of whatever we now presume is rational or reasonable – but "an *optimal* speculative intelligence"? Not (at least) until we are able to confirm Kant's transcendentalism or convert Charles Peirce's "transcendental Hope" into something more robust in the Kantian manner!

The truth is, there is an insuperable difficulty in the attempt to defend a strong view of rationality without the baggage of a privileged faculty or an absolute rational *telos* or something of the sort – which, in any case, is flatly incompatible with the classic forms of pragmatism. For pragmatism is best construed as committed to the doctrine of the flux: not chaos but the postulate that there are no inviolably necessary structures in nature at large and that human cognizing powers are practical, *ad hoc* habits at best, not changelessly apt faculties that evolve effectively within nature itself.

I begin with Putnam, therefore, for the sake of an economy: frankly, to isolate the nerve of Putnam's failure as a quick clue to isolating a cognate weakness in Jürgen Habermas's not dissimilar exertion. The flaw they share may (unceremoniously) be put this way: first, that what they seek is flat-out incompatible with the pragmatism they embrace; but, second, that, at a deeper level, the argument each favors founders on an elementary *non sequitur* that threatens to reinstate what they themselves are at pains to disallow. If either had succeeded – *per impossibile* – he would have reconciled pragmatism and Cartesianism or pragmatism and Kantian transcendentalism or something of the sort, converted an irreconcilable opposition (the same that has engaged the West for nearly four hundred years) into a pleasant harmony. Instead, what their efforts betray is a peculiarity of late twentieth-century pragmatism (and allied European movements) to save what can be saved of the original Cartesian vision by co-opting the best arguments of its opponents.

Before proceeding further, let me offer another clue from another American source – Donald Davidson's criticism of Thomas Kuhn, which has the merit of sketching a minimal argument of precisely the sort Putnam and Habermas must be seeking – which Davidson realizes would, if confirmed, reconcile at a stroke the contemporary forms of objectivism that descend from Descartes (without explicit appeal to epistemic privilege) and the play of historically contingent, divergent beliefs that would otherwise scuttle the objectivity the first means to secure. It is a clue drawn from what Putnam calls the "externalist perspective." Here is what Davidson says – I leave it unanalyzed: I offer it only to leaven what I shall shortly say about Putnam and Habermas:

> The dominant metaphysics of conceptual relativism, that of differing points of view, seems to betray an underlying paradox. Different points of view make sense, but only if there is a common co-ordinate system on which to plot them; yet the existence of a common system belies the claim of dramatic incommensurability [that is, betrays the unintelligibility of incommensurable "conceptual schemes"].[8]

This is a notorious, even cleverly worded, charge, which Davidson nowhere shows bears directly on *any* well-known philosophical position – relativism, in fact, or incommensurabilism: specifically, the views of Thomas Kuhn and Paul Feyerabend. I ask you only to bear in mind the similarity between what Davidson says here and what Putnam says about his *Grenzbegriff*. The two agree (with almost nothing in the way of argument) that relativism is incoherent. But Davidson explicitly affirms that if (impossibly) relativism were viable, it could be defended by reference to a "Cartesian" conceptual grid that would permit us to plot all non-paradoxical conceptions together! Read in the sense Davidson intends, that would be completely incompatible with the conditions of "conceptual relativism's" or "incommensurabilism's" ever being eligible at all. I see in Putnam's *Grenzbegriff* an abbreviated appeal to something similar. The argument's extension (which I have in mind) is caught in the same Cartesian (or Kantian) net. Were there space enough, I would apply the charge to Karl-Otto Apel as well, for related, but not quite the same, reasons.

II

The principal thing to grasp about Putnam's and Davidson's enthymematic clues is that they represent the attenuation of a grand argument that, in endlessly diverse forms, has threaded its commanding way from the very beginnings of Western philosophy down to our own time – which I have in a way caught in mid-stream, labeling it "Cartesianism" or Cartesian realism or Cartesian rationality: because modern philosophy has found its most congenial theme in the interval that spans Descartes and Kant rather than the interval (say) between Heraclitus and Parmenides (including Anaxagoras, for instance). But the theme is the same in both; and Putnam and Davidson have cast their versions of the same doctrine – the necessity of invariance in thought and/or reality in all intelligible change – in the leanest possible way that seems to give flux its due.

That, I suggest, is the unvoiced aim of the general self-deception the sternest minds at the end of our century dream of rescuing from the threatening flux. Putnam's contest with Richard Rorty and Davidson's warning about the incoherence of Kuhn's and Feyerabend's historicizing of science are first cousins to one another, second cousins to Habermas's conviction, third cousins to Descartes and Kant, and direct descendents of Heraclitus's *Logos* and Aristotle's *nous*. Pragmatism, which Putnam embraces (or did recently embrace) and which Rorty foists on an unwilling Davidson, is perceived to be, in its contemporary voice, an American-born strategy for opposing any such union (say, something akin to the union of the Cartesian and post-Kantian), which (that is, the opposition to Cartesianism) took more extreme forms, in continental Europe, in the poststructuralisms (for instance) of Jacques Derrida and Michel Foucault.

What Putnam and Davidson isolate, very differently of course, is an argument of Reason masquerading as a reasonable argument: an argument that in the heyday of "Cartesianism" (or its more ancient forms) would have required a privileged faculty or a sense of telic convergence in the play of contingent conjecture, but now needs no more (it seems) than to be remembered – to be vindicated. There may be a "Peircean" thread in Putnam and Davidson, despite Putnam's demurrer and affinity for Dewey and William James and despite Davidson's objection to any pragmatist connection of any kind. Habermas makes a likelier and livelier addition within the terms of this invented troika, because he *is* a genuinely sanguine champion of the telic constancy of Reason itself.

Charles Peirce palpably hovers behind Putnam and Habermas: Peirce, who may be thought to have nearly redeemed the Cartesian (or Kantian) *telos* without the threat of Cartesian (or Kantian) privilege. That may indeed be the ultimate irony of Peirce's evolutionary pragmatism – the agapasm, the synechism, the fallibilism – by which the radical contingency of inquiry (tychism, in Peirce's idiom) is led back, in the infinite long run (which can never be pragmatically reached), to the final invariant "habits" of reality. Peirce makes it clear enough that he is prepared to abandon Kantian transcendentalism (which he obviously admires) in favor of a regulative Hope (still transcendentally invoked but without cognitive pretensions of any kind) that proves so robust in Peirce's hands that we are tempted to refuse the textual standing of Peirce's own demurrer. One way or another, the theme persists in Putnam and Davidson and Habermas. But how would one know, in a world denied all substantive necessities, that the contingencies of fallible inquiry would lead to objectivism or to a pluralism of variously perspectived accounts of reality that never seriously threaten to be irreconcilable or epistemically incommensurable? As far as I can see, there is no answer in either Davidson or Putnam. Peirce plausibly excuses himself since he still holds fast to convergences justified by transcendental Hope alone.

This last, of course, is the dubious Schellingian trace of Peirce's huge undertaking, which, though more and more demanding in Peirce's later work, is surgically discarded in John Dewey's spare optimism. It does catch up (at considerable cost) the sense in which pragmatism extends the post-Kantian opposition to the kind of "Cartesian" privilege that runs from Descartes to Kant, includes Kant, and then gymnastically recovers (in Peirce himself) what remains of Cartesian objectivity *within* deliberately blind terms. Peirce makes explicit within the boundaries of "transcendental Hope" (plainly misread by Apel) the Cartesian traces of post-Kantian philosophy. The same traces surface in Putnam and are cleverly erased in Davidson's naturalism (in avoiding an explicit epistemology, without yet abandoning objectivism):[9] hence, also, in Richard Rorty's double game of playing post-modernist subversive and Davidsonian naturalist at the same time.[10] One way or another, all of these features re-enact a thinned-down version of the persistent contest between "Cartesianism" (now to include Kantian transcen-dentalism) and late eighteenth- and early nineteenth-century post-Kantian philosophy. It was Dewey who decisively exorcised the Cartesian vestiges in Peirce's pragmatism, which spring up again in our own day. But the traces were there, in Peirce.

It is not strange, therefore, that Habermas, *via* Karl-Otto Apel, who of course provides the first sustained European appreciation of Peirce's immense labor[11] (out of Frankfurt–Critical sources, mind you), should occupy a somewhat Deweyan-like role (relative to Apel – and to Peirce). Not quite, of course, since Reason claims strong facultative powers in Habermas but not in Dewey. I can afford no more than the briefest piece of evidence of Peirce's equivocation (which, in a way, Kant also betrays, perceived from the post-Kantian vantage).

Here is a passage from Peirce's well-known "A guess at the riddle" (*c.* 1890), which confirms, as well as any short passage can, Peirce's attempt to bring together in a pragmatist spirit an evolutionary treatment of Cartesian realism (if I may characterize it thus) and the fluency of contingent inquiry and reason. Bear in mind that, for Peirce, "Law is *par excellence* the thing that wants a reason" (1891); and "A reason has its being in bringing other things into connection with each other [firsts and seconds, in Peirce's idiom]; its essence is to compose: it is triadic, and it alone has a real power [that is, either as law or thought]" (1909):[12]

> Nature herself [Peirce conjectures] often supplies the place of the intention of a rational agent in making a Thirdness genuine and not merely accidental; as when a spark, as third, falling into a barrel of gunpowder, as first, causes an explosion, as second. But how does nature do this? By virtue of an intelligible law according to which she acts ... what makes the real forces really there is the general law of nature which calls for them, and not for any other components of the resultant. Thus, intelligibility, or reason objectified, is what makes Thirdness genuine.[13]

If you read this in the spirit in which Peirce specifically says he favors "objective idealism" according to the formula "matter is effete mind" (1891),[14] you see at once the sense in which Peirce points the way to treating objectivity in a vestigially "Cartesian" spirit by explaining it in terms that join pragmatism and post-Kantian idealism – an idealism more like Schelling's than Hegel's (which – that is, the latter – is no idealism at all). For Peirce, "rationality" (and Thirdness and the taking on of "habits" in the evolutionary sense) is primarily *not* human; or it is human only where it manifests itself cognitionally.

What I mean is that, for all their would-be economy, Putnam, Davidson, Rorty, and Habermas yield implicitly to something akin to the inherent "rationality" of the larger processes of independent nature (which Peirce champions) – without, of course, betraying any attraction to post-Kantian idealism. Otherwise, what they claim would never entirely escape the charge of arbitrariness (or privilege). But to argue as they do (however innocently) *is* to invoke once again the vestigial Cartesian element in Peirce and Kant and even (at times) Hegel. Peirce forever teeters on the edge of reclaiming transcendentalism. His scruple is to resist it, but the seeds of the duality are plain enough. Apel is glad enough not to resist; Habermas resists, but not convincingly. Dewey will have none of Peirce's temptation; Davidson is an out-and-out objectivist (whom Rorty palms off as a pragmatist); Putnam seems not to have grasped at all the deeper import of having advocated his *Grenzbegriff*. And none of these figures – running from Peirce to Rorty – hits on the idea of a constructive realism. Had Peirce favored that option, he would have anticipated Dewey, seen the advantage of James's (often muddled) theory of truth, and escaped the ambivalent Cartesianism of his own account of Thirdness in nature.

My point is simply that, although it is indeed true that the post-Kantian tradition affords the best resource for defeating Cartesianism, it is risked on its own terms: telic, evolutionary, transcendental regularities are, by way of commonsense projections, all eligible (it seems) to Cartesian recovery. There you have the grand irony of late twentieth-century American philosophy and, by a parallel route, late German philosophy. Nearly every important American philosopher of the last thirty or so years is a crypto-Cartesian of one kind or another. Davidson, Rorty, and Putnam are the most interesting of these because they are so explicitly anti-Cartesian in their arguments and so stubbornly Cartesian in the doctrines they ultimately defend. You will find the same duality in Kuhn and W.V. Quine and Wilfrid Sellars – and, more recently, in John McDowell and Robert Brandom. And, of course, it makes more than a strong appearance in Habermas and Apel.

III

I come now to a complicated part of the story. Complicated, because it is well-nigh impossible to characterize Habermas's conception of rationality without comparing its treatment (in Habermas) with the treatment it receives in American pragmatism and Kant. In fact, one cannot rightly understand Habermas's thesis except as a modification of Karl-Otto Apel's; one cannot understand Apel's except as an analogue of Charles Peirce's account of the relationship that holds between the logical, ethical, and aesthetic forms of goodness; one cannot understand Peirce's account except as an intended improvement on Kant's analysis; and one cannot understand this entire sequence except in terms of the remarkable similarity between the differences that hold between Peirce and Dewey on the one hand and Apel and Habermas on the other.

I economize here, because I have now sketched the lesson of the classic pragmatist sources and the most recent American treatment of the Cartesian issue, and because Apel (hence, also, Habermas, though at a remove) commits a fatal mistake in reading Peirce – not merely a textual mistake, though it is at least that – for Apel strays into a *non sequitur* that defeats his pragmatized version of the Kantian theme both he and Peirce address. The result is a gap in Apel's argument that Apel does not see. The explication calls for a bit of patience. But the quickest way to identify the flaw in Habermas's account is to review Apel's argument about rationality; and the quickest way to isolate the flaw in Apel's argument is to recall what Peirce says more carefully about the same issue.

In "The three kinds of goodness," the fifth of seven lectures on pragmatism given at Harvard University in 1903, possibly the most influential of Peirce's papers in the formation of Apel's pragmatized or semiotized version of the Kantian treatment of practical or normative reason, Peirce argues that just as there are necessary laws of nature (if there are!), there are necessary normative laws ensuring the "conformity of things to ends" – which are, however, only synthetically linked to phenomena, *not* derivable from any perceptually grounded sources ("not within those phenomena").[15] Peirce means, of course, that *if* the scientifically factual, the ethical, and the aesthetic *were* transcendentally grounded in terms of theoretical or practical reason, there *would be* necessary laws: it's here that he substitutes a purely regulative Hope for Kant's constitutive conditions of cognitive "possibility."

About ethics specifically, Peirce goes on to say:

> [E]thics is the normative science *par excellence*, because an *end* – the essential object of normative science – is germane to a voluntary act in a primary way in which it is germane to nothing else. For that reason I have some lingering doubt as to there being any true normative science of the beautiful. On the other hand, an ultimate end of action *deliberately* adopted – that is to say, *reasonably* adopted

– must be a state of things that *reasonably recommends itself* aside from any ulterior consideration. It must be an *admirable ideal*, having the only kind of goodness that such an idea *can* have, namely, esthetic goodness. From this point of view the morally good appears as a particular species of the esthetically good.[16]

It's here that Apel goes awry. For Apel makes a point of approving Peirce's remark: "The only moral evil is not to have an ultimate aim" – that is, an end which is "possible," "ultimate" (at least in the sense specified as "esthetic"), "absolute" (that is, "what *would be* pursued under all possible circumstances"), and not such as might (*contra* Kant) be "reduced to a mere formalism."[17] Peirce means to hold to the general Hegelian objection to Kant's formalism in ethics. He *does not* mean to reclaim any transcendental constitution of moral judgment: there's no necessity in having "an ultimate end," though it is still "evil" not to have one, according to the purely regulative (never necessary) function of transcendental Hope! Apel reads the notion as *a pragmatically necessary constraint on practical reason.* But that is neither Peircean nor anywhere secured. Without the missing argument, Apel's entire theory collapses. (In fact, it is nowhere supplied.)

Peirce held that an "ultimate end" entails an "infinite hope"; yet, although he obviously believed that "we all have" that hope ("that what is Best will come about"), *there can be no evidence and no compelling reasons for so believing!* Infinite *hope*, Peirce says, "is something so august and momentous, that all reasoning in reference to it is a trifling impertinence."[18] There is no necessity in phenomenal matters, and one can only hope that there are necessities in ethical and aesthetic matters. True necessity obtains only in the space of strict "logical goodness" (in effect, in deduction);[19] and infinite Hope raises practical difficulties similar to the theoretical difficulties of the "long run" in the sciences.[20]

If you grasp the limitations Peirce imposes on "ethical science," you see at once the extraordinary simplification Dewey produced in his ethics and aesthetics, relieved, as in *Art and Experience* and *Human Nature and Conduct*, of any teleologism or evolutionism or constitutive transcendental Reason.[21] On Peirce's view, Dewey would have had to count as an "anthropologist" of sorts.[22] But *Apel* means to restore (and improve) *Kant's* transcendentalism by way of *Peirce's* pragmatist eclipse of Kant himself.[23] Extraordinary!

The whole of Apel's fatal error – not merely in the textual sense but in the way of advancing a transcendental argument – is adumbrated in the following pronouncement:

Anyone who engages in argument [Apel affirms] automatically presupposes two things: first, a *real communication community* whose member he has himself become through a process of socialization, and second, an *ideal communication community* that would basically be capable of adequately understanding the meaning of his arguments and judging their truth in a definitive manner.[24]

The phrase "automatically presupposes" clearly signifies that we are (in the second clause) in the presence of a constitutive transcendental condition that is not merely "postulated" in Peirce's sense[25] but affirmed by an exercise of Reason. Unfortunately, we have the dictum but not the supporting argument. Apel wrongly interprets Peirce's dictum − "logic presupposes ethics"[26] − as a definite transcendental constraint. Peirce himself always concedes that "an ultimate aim" − truth or rightness, say − may well be "essentially *unattainable*,"[27]: hence, also, impossible to approximate. In any case, it cannot be discerned by any rational means. Apel's claim fails, therefore: he nowhere supplies the supporting grounds he requires.

IV

In the early 1980s, at the time of the translation of his *Transformation* volume, Apel was certain that he and Habermas held similar views regarding the pragmatic grounding of "communicative competence."[28] Both accepted (for different reasons) the validity of Habermas's important essay "What is universal pragmatics?" as well as the successor arguments of "Discourse ethics" and *The Theory of Communicative Action*.[29] Habermas's early formulation clearly shares the difficulties noted in Apel's doctrine; and even his more recent formulations tend to do little more than affirm the need for a transcendental (or a "transcendental–pragmatic") grounding of the constraints proposed. Apel and Habermas have diverged more and more, however, in their reading and rereading of Habermas's published views; and Habermas himself never quite divests his thesis of the transcendentalizing cast of Apel's influence. Nevertheless, there is good reason to think that pragmatism and Kantian transcendentalism remain completely incompatible, and certainly Habermas has tried to free "pragmatic" necessities of "argumentative" discourse from the doubtful authority of transcendental reason.

In a recent essay, "A genealogical analysis of the cognitive content of morality," for instance, Habermas offers the following rather tortured observation − I think we need the entire evidence of Habermas's caution:

> The point of ... a justification of the moral point of view is that the normative content of this epistemic language game [moral discourse] is transmitted only by a rule of argumentation to the selection of norms of action, which together with their moral validity claim provide the input into practical discourses. A moral obligation cannot follow from the so to speak transcendental constraint of unavoidable presuppositions of argumentation alone;

rather it attaches to the specific objects of practical discourse, namely, to the norms *introduced* into discourse to which the reasons mobilized in deliberation refer. I emphasize this when I specify that (U) [that is, the principle of universalizability] can be rendered plausible *in connection with a* (weak, hence nonprejudicial) *concept of normative justification* ... With (U) we reassure ourselves in a reflexive manner of a residual normative substance which is preserved in post-traditional societies by the formal features of argumentation and action oriented to reaching a shared understanding. This is also shown by the procedure of establishing universal presuppositions of argumentation by demonstrating performative self-contradictions, which I cannot go into here.[30]

Habermas obviously means to distance himself from Apel's formulation, in spite of the fact that he admits the "so to speak" transcendental constraints that remain at the level of "argumentative" discourse. He clings to the notion of "unavoidable presuppositions," the admission of which would be sufficient to justify invoking "performative self-contradictions"; but it is more of a premise than a finding: hence, not yet liberated from the transcendental sources he himself knows to be unconvincing. When, however, Apel trancendentalizes Peirce's dictum — that "logic presupposes ethics" — *he* means his reading to impute transcendental force *to moral judgments directly*. If I understand Habermas aright, he still affirms the necessity of the normative "universals" of "argumentation and action oriented to reaching a shared understanding." But moral norms (as such) are, he admits, "introduced" freely into this or that discourse from contingently relevant considerations — to which, then, indissolubly, the would-be transcendental conditions of rational discourse are applied. Habermas has never quite found a convincing label for his pragmatic universals of discourse; but the true reason may be that the "pragmatic contradictions" said to be produced by their violation are themselves more than merely doubtful. Certainly, Habermas has never really satisfied us on that count.

The adjustment between the discursive and the moral is meant to mark an additional improvement on Apel's and Kant's original moral conception.[31] Plainly, by this time Habermas and Apel had ceased to agree. The difference between them centers on a division between (1) the pragmatically necessary presuppositions of argumentative communication, the violation of which yields "performative self-contradictions" (Apel) and (2) reasonably "introduced" universalizable norms apt for "possible" agreement by "all" in this domain or that, that draw, pluralistically, "weakly," on pragmatic analogues of the "strong" universals of the first kind and yet apply to diverse, pertinently restricted moral proposals (Habermas). Even this demarcation proves uncertain, if we are to judge by Habermas's replies to a series of objections (revolving around apriorism and its alternatives) posed by Apel, Herbert Schnadelbach, and Wolfgang Kuhlmann.[32]

Confessedly, it is not easy to reconcile Habermas's mounting replies in a single statement. But it is clear enough that Habermas opposes Apel's strong disjunction between *a priori* and *a posteriori* (or *lebensweltlich*) reason. Habermas has yet to answer on two scores: on one, as to what kind of rational necessity his "unavoidable presuppositions" can claim if they are not bona fide transcendental conditions of "possibility"; and, on the other, what kind of categorical standing can be assigned his universalizable moral prescriptives (even if they are inseparable from discursive necessities) if there are no substantive moral norms that take precedence over merely formal considerations. On the first, the would-be presuppositions strike me as vacuous or worse – think of what the commitment to truth or validity comes to if either is treated as a relational construction (as it must be), or what sincerity comes to, if sincerity, like loyalty, is never more than a dependent virtue. On the second, universalizability is known (surely known to Habermas) to be almost endlessly manipulable in support of diametrically opposed maxims (this is the point of Hegel's critique of Kant's moral formalism);[33] then, too, there is no evidence that moral intuitions need be, or even can be, plausibly strengthened, in standard cases, by being universalizable – or that there is even a robust practical sense in which "all" persons "affected" in any given instance *could* be pertinently consulted.

The short argument comes to this: there is nothing Habermas provides that is adequate for securing any form of normative universality or pragmatic necessity that Apel has not already failed to secure by *a priori* means. Habermas's "egalitarian universalism,"[34] which exceeds mere consistency of usage, adds nothing that can be counted on. Think of the possibility (which Habermas does not attempt to disprove) that rationality is itself a social construction of some sort, hence hostage to the same normative quarrels Habermas would have it judge. (You see, of course, the parallel with Putnam's *Grenzbegriff*.) What, for instance, of the possibility that relativism and epistemological incommensurabilism (regarding rationality in moral matters, or even truth and validity in science[35]) might prove coherent and self-consistent and pertinent to particular quarrels, and viable and even helpful and instructive? You have only to think of the factions of Northern Ireland or in the Middle East or, indeed, the behavior of political parties anywhere in the world, to see the ideal's faulty charm. Habermas has no answer: he has effectively abandoned the pertinence of historicist and constructivist (that is, contexted) objections *by* insisting on universality and universalizability; for they bind him to a Kantian resolution even where he means to resist specifically transcendental fixities.

What both Habermas and Apel miss is the full significance of Peirce's account of fallibilism: Apel fails to see that Peirce transforms *a priori* truths into articles of transcendental *Hope*,[36] by which he subverts every epistemic form of Kantian necessity; and Habermas fails to see that fallibilism applied in short-run practices cannot approximate to any universal or necessary long-run norms beyond formal consistency.[37] In that plain sense, pragmatism cannot be reconciled with any Kantian-like project, whether aprioristic (as in Apel) or *lebensweltlich* (as in Habermas).

Here, now, is another longish passage that helps to pinpoint Habermas's shortcomings more precisely:

> We understand the expression "justify" [in grounding all argumentative discourse] when we know what we have to do in order to redeem a universal, i.e. trans-spatio-temporal and in this sense unconditional validity claim by deploying reason. This can be the case just as much with regard to the truth validity of an assertoric statement as it can with respect to the validity a normative statement has as being right. We understand the term "justify" when we know the rules for an argumentational game within which validity claims can be redeemed discursively ... Justification must always be provided in one and the same place – there are no meta-discourses in the sense that a higher discourse is able to prescribe rules for a subordinate discourse. Argumentational games do not form a hierarchy. Discourses regulate themselves ... The fallibilist meaning of an argumentational game takes into account only that universal validity claims have to be raised factually – namely, in our respective context, which does not remain stationary but rather will change ... The presumption of fallibilism refers solely to the fact that we cannot exclude the possibility of falsification even given convincingly justified theories which are accepted as valid.[38]

This is as clear a statement of Habermas's recent views as I have been able to find. (We need the entire text.) But you cannot fail to see the telltale traces of the insuperable defects already adduced: first, that "universal" (or "unconditional") validity invokes the term "all" only in the sense of consistency of usage – it has nothing whatsoever to do with obligating "all" rational participants in any actual discourse (hence, fails to secure the ground that's needed);[39] second, that, on a Wittgensteinian reading of the "lifeworld" (which Habermas appears to favor), there *are*, *in* following the "rules" of "validity," literally no determinate rules that we follow (which *is* of course Wittgenstein's point[40] but not Habermas's); and, third, that, on Habermas's rejection of the "hierarchical" disjunction between "final" (or *a priori*) justificatory reasons and any local, provisional validation of first-order (practical) claims under the conditions of history, the admission of the first two findings precludes any possible recovery of universal or necessary pragmatic conditions *via* fallibilistic approximation (hence, also, fails to strengthen the rational force of universalizable moral maxims).

But to admit all that *is* to defeat both Habermas's and Apel's Kantianisms – certainly, any presumption in favor of detecting "pragmatic self-contradictions"[41] robust enough for the substantive work of moral discourse. It is, to be honest, very hard to see how (U) – the universalizability principle – could possibly provide, in any operationally convincing way, either a necessary or a sufficient condition for the validity of any substantive norm in practical life or theoretical inquiry: either literally *"generalized, abstracted, and free from all limits"* or capable of answering to "the interests and value-orientation of *each individual* [so that it] could be *jointly* advanced by *all* concerned without coercion."[42] I shall have to leave the matter there, without for instance touching on the enormous question (both Marxist and Freudian, at least) of self-deception and the true interests of human agents.[43] It is perhaps enough to say that no purely formal conception of Reason could reassure us on that score.

Notes

1 Hilary Putnam, "Values, facts and cognition," in *Reason, Truth and History*, Cambridge, Cambridge University Press, 1981, p. 126.
2 See Hilary Putnam, "Wittgenstein on religious belief," in *Renewing Philosophy*, Cambridge, Harvard University Press, 1972, particularly the discussion of David Lewis's *Counterfactuals*, Princeton, Princeton University Press, 1973.
3 See Hilary Putnam, "Bernard Williams and the absolute conception of the world," in *Renewing Philosophy*.
4 Hilary Putnam, "Two philosophical perspectives," in *Reason, Truth and History*, p. 49.
5 Hilary Putnam, "Two conceptions of rationality," in *Reason, Truth and History*, p. 110.
6 Hilary Putnam, "Facts and value," in *Reason, Truth and History*, p. 134.
7 See Hilary Putnam, "Sense, nonsense, and the senses: an inquiry into the powers of the human mind," (The Dewey Lectures, 1994), *Journal of Philosophy*, XLI (1994), pp. 445–517.
8 Donald Davidson, "On the very ideas of a conceptual scheme," in *Inquiries into Truth and Interpretation*, Oxford, Clarendon, 1984, p. 184.
9 See Donald Davidson, "A coherence theory of truth and knowledge," in Ernest LePore (ed.) *Truth and Interpretation: Perspectives on the Philosophy of Donald Davidson*, Oxford, Basil Blackwell, 1986.
10 See Richard Rorty, "Pragmatism, Davidson and truth," in LePore, *Truth and Interpretation*; and Joseph Margolis, "Richard Rorty: philosophy by other means," *Metaphilosophy*, XXXI (2000), pp. 529–46.
11 See Karl-Otto Apel, *Charles S. Peirce: From Pragmatism to Pragmaticism*, trans. John Michael Krois, Amherst, University of Massachusetts Press, 1981.
12 *Collected Papers of Charles Sanders Peirce*, 6 vols, edited by Charles Hartshorne and Paul Weiss, Cambridge, Harvard University Press, 1931–5, 6.12, 6.343.
13 *Collected Papers of Charles Sanders Peirce*, 1.366.
14 *Collected Papers of Charles Sanders Peirce*, 6.25.
15 *Collected Papers of Charles Sanders Peirce*, 5.121, 5.126.
16 *Collected Papers of Charles Sanders Peirce*, 5.130; see also 5.128–9.
17 *Collected Papers of Charles Sanders Peirce*, 5.133–4. See Karl-Otto Apel "The *a priori* of the communication community and the foundations of ethics: the

problem of a rational foundation of ethics in the scientific age," in *Towards a Transformation of Philosophy*, trans. Glyn Adey and David Frisby, London, Routledge and Kegan Paul, 1980, p. 287, n. 23.

18 *Collected Papers of Charles Sanders Peirce*, 5.357.

19 See *Collected Papers of Charles Sanders Peirce*, 5.133, 5.142, 5.145–50.

20 *Collected Papers of Charles Sanders Peirce*, 5.134–6; see also 5.13–126, 5.142, 5.145.

21 See John Dewey, *Art as Experience*, New York, Minton, Balch, 1934; and *Human Nature and Conduct: An Introduction to Social Psychology*, New York, Random House, 1922, 1930.

22 *Collected Papers of Charles Sanders Peirce*, 5.130.

23 Karl-Otto Apel, "From Kant to Peirce: the semiotical transformation of transcendental logic," in *Towards a Transformation of Philosophy*, pp. 79–80. See also *Collected Papers of Charles Sanders Peirce*, 5.382n; and Joseph Margolis, "Peirce's fallibilism," *Transactions of Charles S. Peirce Society*, XXXIV (1998), pp. 535–69.

24 Apel, "The *a priori* of the communication community and the foundations of ethics," p. 280.

25 See *Collected Papers of Charles Sanders Peirce*, 6.36; see also 5.382n.

26 Apel, "The *a priori* of the communication community and the foundations of ethics," p. 262.

27 *Collected Papers of Charles Sanders Peirce*, 5.135–6 (italics in original), which implicitly questions the coherence of Apel's line of reasoning.

28 See Karl-Otto Apel, "Noam Chomsky's theory of language and contemporary philosophy: a case study in the philosophy of science," in *Towards a Transformation of Philosophy*, pp. 203–6, 222–4, n. 101–4. Apel effectively confirms that Habermas still held (at least up to the translation of *Transformation*) to the theories of his (Habermas's) early influential paper, "What is universal pragmatics?" in *Communication and the Evolution of Society*, trans. Thomas McCarthy, Boston, Beacon Press, 1979.

29 See Jürgen Habermas, "A genealogical analysis of the cognitive content of morality," in *The Inclusion of the Other: Studies in Political Theory*, edited by Ciaran Cronin and Pablo De Greiff, trans. Ciaran Cronin and others, Cambridge, MIT Press, 1998; "Discourse ethics: notes on a program of philosophical justification," *Moral Consciousness and Communicative Action*, trans. Christian Lenhardt and Shierry Weber Nicholsen, Cambridge, MIT Press, 1990; *The Theory of Communicative Action*, 2 vols, trans. Thomas McCarthy, Boston, Beacon Press 1984.

30 Habermas, "A genealogical analysis of the cognitive content of morality," p. 4. Here, Habermas defers to Apel's account of "performative self-contradictions" but avoids an explicit transcendentalism. For Apel's objections (in advance), see Apel, "The *a priori* of the communication community and the foundations of ethics," p. 262.

31 See Habermas, "What is universal pragmatics?" pp. 21–5: "A genealogical analysis of the cognitive content of morality," pp. 6–7.

32 See, particularly, Jürgen Habermas, "A reply," in Axel Honneth and Hans Joas (eds) *Communicative Action: Essays on Jürgen Habermas's* The Theory of Communicative Action, trans. Jeremy Gains and Doris L. Jones, Cambridge, MIT Press, 1991. The most accessible versions of the apriorist objections to Habermas appear in Karl-Otto Apel, "Normatively grounding 'critical theory' through recourse to the lifeworld? A transcendental–pragmatic attempt to think with Habermas against Habermas," in Axel Honneth, Thomas McCarthy, Claus Offe and Albrecht Wellmer (eds) *Philosophical Interventions in the Unfinished Project of Enlightenment*, trans. William Rehg, Cambridge, MIT Press, 1992; and

Herbert Schnadelbach, "The transformation of critical theory," in Honneth and Joas, *Communicative Action*.

33 See, for instance, G.W.F. Hegel, *Natural Law*, trans. T.M. Knox, Philadelphia, University of Pennsylvania Press, 1975, pp. 75–8.

34 Habermas, "A genealogical analysis of the cognitive content of morality," p. 40.

35 See, for instance, Thomas S. Kuhn, *The Structure of Scientific Revolutions*, enlarged edn, Chicago, University of Chicago Press, 1970, Section X.

36 Apel, "Normatively grounding 'critical theory' through recourse to the life-world?" pp. 128, 142–3. There is an excellent exposé of the *ur*-difficulty one (implicitly) finds in Apel and Habermas, in a very different (textually unrelated) discussion of Husserl's phenomenologized method, in Maurice Merleau-Ponty, "The philosopher and sociology," *Signs*, trans. Richard M. McCleary, Evanston, Northwestern University Press, 1964, Here, late Frankfurt–Critical and Husserlian arguments may be made to converge.

37 See Habermas, "A reply," pp. 232–3.

38 Habermas, "A reply," pp. 231–2.

39 This is also the crucial difficulty in John Rawls appeal to rationality, in *A Theory of Justice*, Cambridge, Harvard University Press, 1971, which Rawls subsequently attenuated (disarmingly) by the substitution of a candid ideological postulate; but he never really abandons the substantive moral universals he advances in *A Theory of Justice* but nowhere vindicates. He says as much in his *Political Liberalism*, New York, Columbia University Press, 1993.

40 Ludwig Wittgenstein, *Philosophical Investigations*, trans. G.E.M. Anscombe, Oxford, Basil Blackwell, 1953, I, §§201–2, 240–2.

41 See Habermas, "Discourse ethics," pp. 82–98; and Karl-Otto Apel, "The problem of philosophical foundations in light of a transcendental pragmatics in language" (revised), in Kenneth Baynes, James Bohman and Thomas McCarthy (eds) *After Philosophy: End or Transformation?* Cambridge, MIT Press, 1987. For Apel's rebuttal, see Apel, "Normatively grounding 'critical theory' through recourse to the lifeworld?" pp. 126–8.

42 Habermas, "A genealogical analysis of the cognitive content of morality," in *The Inclusion of the Other*, pp. 41–2 (italics in original). See also Habermas, "Discourse ethics," pp. 65–6; and Jürgen Habermas, *Between Facts and Norms: Contributions to a Discourse Theory of Law and Democracy*, trans. William Rehg, Cambridge, MIT Press, 1996, p. 556, n. 15.

43 See, for instance, Gayatri Chakravorty Spivak, *A Critique of Postcolonial Reason: Toward a History of the Vanishing Present*, Cambridge, Harvard University Press, 1999, p. 9; see the rest of Ch. 1.

3

THE EPISTEMOLOGICAL
PROMISE OF PRAGMATISM

Tom Rockmore

Unimportant writers and philosophical movements are often grasped correctly in their own time, while important writers and philosophical movements often displace the discussion underway and are more often misunderstood in their own time. These writers and movements are criticized for doctrines they do not hold, but are routinely praised for others they reject. The epistemological promise of pragmatism lies in an understanding of knowledge in practice in the wake of the failure of epistemological foundationalism, the strategy for knowledge, which has largely dominated the modern discussion, and which was understood in diverse ways by the first generation of American pragmatists. But it has been largely misunderstood in the recent emergence of a radical analytic form of pragmatism in such writers as Quine, perhaps Putnam, certainly Rorty, Apel, and now even Habermas. Everything happens as if pragmatism, which in the meantime had lost any identifiable set of doctrines, had finally come to mean all things to all people so that in one form or another it had now become acceptable to everyone and not unacceptable to anyone at all. If that is the case, surely different observers have very different kinds of pragmatism in mind.

For present purposes, it will be useful to distinguish between "pragmatism" and "radical pragmatism." By "pragmatism" I will mean classical American pragmatism, the movement which begins in Peirce, then develops in James and Dewey, and which is being redeveloped in such more recent figures as Quine, Putnam, Rorty, Rescher, Margolis, and many others. Pragmatism, as Lovejoy points out, is a very diverse movement, which reflects not the disunity but rather the vitality of this tendency.[1] It is a mistake to think of pragmatists as holding to a single credo, set of ideas, doctrine, or point of view. Nonetheless, there is certainly a conceptual core, which can be identified in terms of the genesis of the movement.

Peirce, pragmatism and knowledge

"Pragmatism" means different things to different observers, who, from their respective angles of vision, discern different writers as belonging to the fold.

In order to discuss the interpretation of pragmatism, I will need to characterize it in at least a minimal, incomplete manner, which should not be taken as representing anything like a complete interpretation.

I will focus on the classical American pragmatic approach to theory of knowledge, or epistemology, two terms which I shall understand as synonyms, in Peirce, James and Dewey, the three main figures of the first generation of American pragmatists. This means that I will arbitrarily leave to one side Schiller, Mead, according to some observers Emerson, and others who have legitimate claims to be considered pragmatists, even members of the initial generation.

It is not easy to characterize pragmatism. According to the pessimistic Schiller, there are as many pragmatisms as pragmatists. According to the more optimistic Lovejoy, there are only thirteen kinds. Since classical pragmatism begins in Peirce, and all later pragmatists belong to a philosophical tendency he began, I think the best way to understand what pragmatists of all stripes have in common is to look briefly at the genesis of Peirce's position. Peirce is an anti-Cartesian, more precisely an anti-foundationalist, or post-foundationalist, or again an a-foundationalist, who reacts against Descartes in the formulation of his position. Cartesian epistemological foundationalism can be characterized through two central claims. On the one hand, it insists on an indefeasible foundation, known to be true beyond the possibility of the most radical doubt. On the other, it claims that all further true statements can be rigorously derived from the indefeasible foundation.

Peirce's well-known attack on foundationalism is formulated in a series of early articles criticizing Descartes. In part because it is known that Peirce's theories arise out of his critique of Descartes, the view that Peirce rejects Cartesian epistemological foundationalism in formulating his own position is well established in the discussion.[2] Peirce is concerned with the logic of scientific inquiry as it actually occurs, hence scientific practice, or the practice of scientific inquiry, as distinguished from religious, artistic, or political practice, but not practice in general, nor the analytic reconstruction of the scientific method which is now familiar in philosophy of science. Like Descartes, he has a method; but, unlike Descartes, his method is not conceived as a theory yielding absolute theoretical truth, but rather as a practical approach yielding no more and no less than the best results we can in practice arrive at by using a logic of scientific investigation. Unlike Descartes, who describes his method early on but later progressively abandons it, Peirce continues to hold to his method throughout his writings.

Although his basic position later underwent important changes, at least its main outline was already apparent in a series of early articles directed against Descartes.[3] It is even more clearly apparent in the constructive statement he drew up some ten years later of his own view of the logic of scientific investigation.[4] We can reconstruct Peirce's theory of knowledge as arising out of his concern to think through the process of knowledge as it actually occurs, as distinguished from an abstract analysis of its theoretical conditions. Peirce's critique of Descartes, which is crucial to the formulation of his own position, is intended to show the disparity between his French predecessor's enormously influential, but abstract theoretical approach to the problem of knowledge in general, and the utterly different problem of understanding knowledge as it in fact arises in experience, especially within modern science.

Peirce's rejection of fundamental aspects of the Cartesian position enables him to formulate his own rival view. To begin with, Peirce distinguishes, as Descartes does not, between real doubt and theoretical doubt, which at best afflicts only philosophers concerned with overcoming difficulties raised by other colleagues as opposed to real life. According to Peirce, we cannot doubt everything, since we are always already in the world, hence embedded in a web of belief. Belief is the state arrived at when doubt has provisionally (but not definitively, since nothing about knowledge is definitive) been left behind as the result of overcoming practical doubt as it really arises within the process of inquiry. Stable beliefs, which are sought in the process of inquiry, are or are not comparable to the laws of science. There is a distinction between knowing that something is true, for instance, in contemporary language, because one has grasped the mind-independent real world, or merely believing it is true. Peirce, who wisely settles for mere belief, gives up the Cartesian idea of unrevisable certainty, for instance through the supposed grasp of independent reality as it is, in favor of evaluating claims to know on the basis of their expected consequences. According to Peirce, ideas are not true because they tell us the way the world is; rather beliefs are accepted because there is in practice no practical as opposed to theoretical reason (such as the hyperbolic doubts Descartes raises against himself in the *Second Meditation*) to doubt them. In that respect, Peirce's pragmatism can be understood as a theory of meaning, or what the words mean, as opposed to a theory of truth, since he denies truth in the sense that "truth" means the direct or even the indirect grasp of independent reality.

Peirce's position begins pragmatism which it further provides with a rough outline to which all later pragmatists continue to react. Pragmatism, which cannot be reduced to Peirce's position, also cannot be separated from it. Pragmatism in Peirce's formulation and in later formulations has, I take it, a set of features already found in Peirce, which in most, perhaps all, cases, can be determined by negating the relevant features in Descartes. These include a rejection of Cartesianism, more precisely an effort to stake out a meaningful view of knowledge after foundationalism; a concern with the practice as distinguished from the theory of knowledge; a disdain for absolute claims, such as apodicticity; a stress on future results, or consequences; a concern with a collaborative approach to knowledge, hence the abandonment of the monological approach to the cognitive subject; and an understanding of the subject as real, finite human beings.

Some main types of epistemological pragmatism

These six elements, centering on the rejection of Cartesian foundationalism while continuing to believe in the possibility of knowledge, provide a loose conceptual framework with enough room to include nearly anyone who falls under the pragmatist rubric while excluding nearly anyone else who does not. In my view, the pragmatic effort to continue the epistemological discussion after foundationalism gives up the idea that we can or must know anything as grand as mind-independent reality in favor of, as Peirce famously says, the effects of our conceptions, since "our conception of these effects is the whole of our conception of the object."[5] In view of the continued interest in realism, it is important to note that Peirce does not say that we know mind-independent reality as it is, but only that it is a limit to which we approach in the long run.[6]

In this sense, pragmatism is a second-best approach to knowledge understood as practical in virtue of the belief that theoretical approaches which, in the modern discussion, focus on making good on some form of epistemological foundationalism, have always and will always fall short of the mark. Since pragmatists contend that claims to know in some absolute sense cannot be made out, they do not give up the quest for knowledge in a weaker, more sustainable form, hence decline any form of skepticism deriving from the inability to make out the stronger, more traditional claims to know. Peirce is interested in what would now be called philosophy of science; James is interested in truth and many other themes; and Dewey is more interested in the link between theory and practice than in knowledge as such; but all three are concerned with knowledge under practical conditions, understood as a real alternative to the traditional but unrealistic approach to knowledge under theoretical conditions. It is less clear that this distinction is respected in more recent pragmatism, which has more often than not been analytic in tone if not always in content.

The pragmatic landscape can be described from many different perspectives. Migotti, who differentiates reformists and revolutionaries,[7] includes as pragmatists some writers I would like to exclude from the fold. Partially following Migotti, Haack distinguishes between pragmatists, neo-pragmatists, and sympathizers.[8] This approach suggests, incorrectly I think, that the only real pragmatists, the only ones worthy of the name, are the members of the first generation, while further leaving open what "pragmatism" means.

In the present context, where "pragmatism" refers to the concern with knowledge after foundationalism, no fewer than six kinds of pragmatism can be distinguished. These include the classical (American) pragmatists of the first generation (Peirce, James, Dewey, but also Schiller). Then there is a large, nondescript collection of scholars of pragmatism, including too many names to mention. Next come a small class of mainstream analytic pragmatists, including Quine, Putnam and, according to Rorty, Davidson, who share a commitment to the problem of knowledge from an analytic perspective after the analytic critique of classical English empiricism. Then there is a form of pragmatism with a strongly Sellarsian tinge in Brandom and perhaps McDowell. There is further a form of pragmatism stated in more or less analytic language by a group of writers who have at best loose ties to the analytic tradition, including Margolis, Rescher, Bernstein and Haack. Finally, there is an epistemologically very radical type of pragmatism in Rorty, Apel and Habermas, on which I will be concentrating here.

As I view them, the radical pragmatists share the name but not necessarily the doctrines of the others alluded to above. Unlike the others, all of whom are defined by their rejection of Cartesianism, hence their effort to consider the real possibilities for knowledge after foundationalism, radical pragmatists like Apel, Habermas and Rorty are all foundationalists, or at least crypto-foundationalists. Each is committed to an approach to, and a claim for, knowledge which is closer, in fact on occasion so very close, to Descartes that the very sense of staking out a second-best approach to knowledge, central to pragmatism, is difficult, perhaps not possible, to discern.

Apel's foundationalist pragmatism

With the possible exception of Chisholm, no one has done more recently to make the case for foundationalism than Karl-Otto Apel, who proposes a transcendental form of ethical foundation with Kantian and other overtones. In invoking ethical foundationalism, Apel suggests a link, specifically deriving from his reading of Peirce, between claims for truth and knowledge, intrinsic to discussion of any kind, and social utility.

Apel, who proposes to transform transcendental philosophy[9] by substituting a plural subject for the traditionally monological subject,[10] is concerned with two main themes: a reflexive, transcendental–pragmatic foundationalism, or the rational justification of ethics; and the difference between real and merely ideal conditions of communicative ethics, also called discourse ethics. With respect to the first theme, Apel contends, in responding to criticism – Hans Albert has objected that foundational efforts lead to an infinite regress,[11] or a so-called Munchausen's trilemma[12] – that in that case there can be no rationality. With respect to the second theme, Apel maintains that the difficulty is not the application of general rules to concrete situations through judgment, such as Kantian *Urteilskraft* or Gadamerian *phronesis*, but rather the more general difficulty of the possibility of a universalistic communicative ethics. Like Kant, Apel maintains that each person should act as if he were a member of an ideal speech community. Like Aristotle, Apel argues that to reject this claim is to become involved in a so-called performative contradiction.

Apel calls his approach "transcendental pragmatics" (*Tranzendental-pragmatik*) to indicate that it combines transcendental reflection in the Kantian sense as well as a pragmatic relation to the real world. He employs the term "transcendental hermeneutics" (*Transzendentalhermeneutik*) to refer to the Heideggerian idea of reflection as grounding reason through a hermeneutical circle. According to Habermas, Apel's breakthrough to this theory occurred in 1969 in an article on "Scientism or transcendental hermeneutics? (*Szientismus oder transzendentale Hermeneutik?*)". His later article, "The a priori of the communication society (*Das Apriori der Kommunikationsgemeinschaft*)", marked the beginning point for a theory of discourse ethics, which Habermas has also taken up.[13] Apel has elaborated his view of foundationalism over the years in a large number of papers. I will take as representative the long article in which this view first appeared in 1973, which is the basis for his later discussion: "The a priori of the communication society and the foundations of ethics: concerning the problem of a rational foundation of ethics in the scientific period."[14] I will further consider a later restatement which amplifies the original theory.

Apel's general theme, which is stated in the subtitle of the article, is that in reflecting on the relation of science and ethics we realize the need to justify a general ethical theory. He claims that the very idea of an intersubjective justification is apparently precluded by the prevalence in our scientific age of the scientistic idea of normative neutrality, or value-free "objectivity."[15]

His reasoning is based on two points: ethical claims must be universal, not local, and moral judgments must possess objective validity which has been abandoned in the philosophical retreat from ultimate norms.[16] According to Apel, Marxism dogmatically asserts we cannot rationally justify ethical norms, as do moral arguments which tend to be decided on strictly pragmatic grounds, often by appealing to experts who apply various kinds of rules.[17] Analytic philosophy typically opposes the justification of ethical norms on three grounds. First, following Hume, it denies that normative, or prescriptive, claims can be derived from merely descriptive statements. Second, it contends, since science depends on descriptive statements, that a scientific justification of norms is not possible. Third, it maintains, since only science provides objective knowledge, that an intersubjective justification of ethics is not possible.[18]

In response, Apel contends that the objectivity of value-neutral science cannot even be understood without presupposing the intersubjective validity of moral norms in order to demonstrate the possibility of a rational justification of ethics.[19] Agreement in ordinary language is a final limit; it represents not the attainment, hence not a limit reached in practice, but rather the anticipation of the realization of a normative ideal.[20] Even the possibility of philosophy requires a distancing of thought from the world through the presupposition of a transcendental language game linked to the analytical critique of moral norms.[21] Not only science but all problems of whatever kind that utilize rational argumentation necessarily presuppose the validity of universal ethical norms.[22]

The objection that every justification presupposes logic points to a circular relation between logic and ethics leading to an infinite regress discussed in Popper and especially Hans Albert.[23] Apel contends that this type of objection is only valid against a deductive form of foundationalism, whereas his view is linked to a transcendental–pragmatic subject described in Charles Morris's three-dimensional semiotics.[24] Yet it is difficult to see that, he has identified the universal presuppositions of real discussion, since whatever norms we happen to appeal to depend on what we happen to accept in a given historical moment. Peirce never directly claims that the development of consensus over time among scientific investigators[25] demonstrates anything more than agreement acceptable as knowledge, which is very different from claims to truth. Apel's further claims that all argument of whatever kind presupposes a rational community both really and ideally,[26] and that rational agreement is the basis of democratic society[27] do not establish the reality of universal norms.

In the restatement of his view, Apel specifically links his view with Cartesian foundationalism that it is said to realize[28] in appealing to Peirce. The result is to blur the basic distinction, basic as well to the formulation of Peirce's anti-Cartesian position, between Cartesian foundationalism and Peirce's anti-Cartesian rejection of foundationalism. Apel, who contends that the problem of rational justification of any kind whatsoever requires foundationalism as its condition, claims that Peirce shows an unbreakable link between the objective, scientific–technological investigation of nature and the intersubjective possibility of consensus[29] underlying everything that we do. For Apel, this link is presupposed by the typical modern interest in human self-emancipation. Its use lies in formulating regulative principles of practical and postulated scientific progress.[30]

Like all foundationalism, Apel's ethical foundationalism turns on its claim for truth and knowledge. Most of his references are to recent philosophers, but his general problem is very old. The tacit Socratic assumption that truth and knowledge will result from unconstrained agreement is restated in Apel's ethical foundationalism as a claim for potential agreement that limits all rational discussion. Like Socrates, Apel holds that even potential consensus represents truth, more precisely ethical truth relevant to social concerns.

This claim is indefensible, since consensus, or agreement, and truth are obviously independent of each other. Consensus, potential or real, is not in principle a reliable indicator of truth understood, say, as the grasp of mind-independent reality. It would only be a reliable indicator if there were a decision procedure in place to exclude false agreement. The truth claims of mathematics and the natural sciences rest on the application of a decision procedure, unavailable to adjudicate ethical claims or general discussion. No one would consider consensus around a political program, as there was around Nazism in Germany in the early 1930s, as indicating anything as grand as truth.

Apel, who relies on Peirce for his conception of an acceptable truth claim, reads the latter against the grain. According to Apel, truth understood as the postulate of consensus in the logic of the sciences cannot be reached by finite individuals.[31] Yet consensus is only reached in discussion among finite individuals. In fact, this is "bad" Peirce, since it refers to something beyond experience to understand it, whereas Peirce very clearly restricts attention to what is found in experience.[32]

In his early critique of Descartes, Peirce rejects foundationalism in favor of a pragmatic approach to truth. His position combines fallibilism (roughly the denial that we can ever claim perfect certitude or exactitude, which is clearly inimical to foundationalism as usually understood),[33] and the view of the long run (roughly that what we mean by "true" is the opinion we will arrive at in the long run of what we take to be the real).[34] Yet since we can never go beyond the representation of the object to the subject, we can never claim that what we take to be knowledge in fact coincides with independent reality.

Apel's theory reflects a persistent confusion between justification (*Begründung*) and foundationalism (*Letztbegründung*), between knowledge and truth. In ethical matters, where there is no decision procedure, the opinion around which consensus forms must emerge from unconstrained discussion. Yet consensus is wrongly interpreted as indicating anything more than the articulation of an opinion generally held in a particular group at a particular time. Consensus is wrongly construed as providing an epistemological foundation.

Habermas on truth and pragmatism

It is not surprising, – since Habermas is strongly influenced by Apel, including Apel's reading of Peirce – that Habermas's own position reflects similar confusions about pragmatism about which he makes even stronger claims. His well-known effort to provide critical theory with a respectable epistemological basis supposedly lacking in Marxism already results in *Knowledge and Human Interests* in what, much like in Apel, resembles transcendental pragmatism. Like the early members of the Frankfurt School, especially Horkheimer and Adorno, Habermas stresses a view which does not reduce rationality to instrumental reason.[35] There are a great many themes in Habermas, including the study of Marx and Marxism, the renewal of critical theory, study of social theory in all its many forms, efforts, like Heidegger, to engage in dialogue with leading contemporary thinkers, and so on. But Habermas's main theme seems to be the "switch" from the theory of consciousness in classical German idealism, which, after an early effort to reconstruct historical materialism,[36] he came to believe is exhausted, without further possibilities for development, to a theory of intersubjective communication. This interest, or set of interests, has led him to develop, in various phases of his writings, a critique of Marx and Marxism,[37] a *Theory of Communicative Action*,[38] a theory of discourse ethics,[39] and most recently a theory of law and of the democratic state.[40]

Habermas began to refer to pragmatism, especially Peirce, but more recently to Mead as well, more than a quarter of a century ago, after his slow withdrawal from Marx and Marxism, but before the emergence of his own theory of communicative action. In a discussion of what he calls communicative reason in *The Philosophical Discourse of Modernity*, he suggests that the theory of communicative action, namely his own position, builds on the pragmatic tradition. According to Habermas, Peirce and Mead for the first time raise the religious motivation of solidarity to philosophical status in the context of a consensus theory of truth and a communicative theory of society.[41] This passage is important in indicating that Habermas believes his own views of truth and society carry further impulses in Peirce's and Mead's consensus theories of truth and communicative theories of society.

Habermas's consensus theory of truth is, as its name suggests, truth based on unconstrained consensus very similar to Apel's own conception. Habermas's theory of communicative action, which is outlined in an immensely long, complex book, comes down to his concern to work out the normative basis of a critical social theory through an alternative to a no longer defensible philosophy of history within which the problem of the model of capitalist modernization can again be taken up.[42] To the best of my knowledge, the fullest treatment of Peirce occurs in *Knowledge and Human Interests*.[43] The most detailed treatment of Mead occurs in a study of his view of subjectivity in a recent collection of essays.[44]

The theory of communicative action and the reading of Mead are both peripheral to the present concern with Habermas's relation to pragmatism. At present, I will concentrate on his views of Peirce and of truth, since his interpretation of the former is the basis of his view of the latter. In *Knowledge and Human Interests*, where he devotes a chapter to Peirce in the context of a post-positivist discussion of knowledge, Habermas's grasp of the history of philosophy fails him repeatedly. According to Habermas, positivism, which inclines toward scientism, replaces theory of knowledge with philosophy of science; it further gives rise to what he calls "self-reflection of the sciences" in Peirce and again in Dilthey, both of whom remain under the spell of objectivism.[45]

In Habermas's account, Peirce is able to avoid the objectivism of early positivism because of his knowledge of Berkeley, Kant and medieval scholasticism, but above all in virtue of his reflection on positivism.[46] Yet although Peirce certainly knew Kant very well, and claimed to know large portions of the first *Critique* by heart, the main factor in the genesis of Peirce's position was certainly his critique of Descartes. Habermas regards Peirce as the first to see that knowledge relies on uncompelled and permanent consensus in the form of an ultimate answer to every scientific question.[47] He is correct about the idea of consensus, but incorrect that it is uncompelled, that it is permanent, or that every scientific question can receive a definitive answer. Peirce contends that consensus is compelled by experience, that it is always open to change, and that answers to scientific questions are only definitive in the long run, hence never within our lifetime. Peirce, in Habermas's reading, distinguishes between the concept of reality and the concept of truth in contending that reality is what we can correctly state about it. Yet this overlooks the fact that for Peirce reality is a limiting concept, which is very different from the claim, already mentioned, that the meaning of a concept is its consequences. Habermas simply conflates Peirce's views of reality and meaning.

The problem of truth looms large in the writings of Peirce and James. Habermas's account of Peirce is intended to call attention to his relation to Habermas's own version of the consensus theory of truth. This view occurs in several places in Habermas's writings. These include the inaugural lecture, "Knowledge and human interests,"[48] where it is adumbrated; the study of the *Legitimation Crisis;*[49] and an article where he considers the theory of truth in some detail in suggesting that truth just means warranted assertability.[50] In the lecture, following Husserl, he criticizes the objectivism of the sciences,[51] which takes the world as merely given, in favor of the idea that meaning, or connections, hence knowledge, is constituted by the subject.[52] This suggests an anti-Platonic, quasi-Kantian idealist claim according to which independent reality is not grasped as it is but is in some sense "constructed" by the knower as a condition of knowledge. He goes on to argue that interpretation is based on consensus within the framework of tradition.[53]

Habermas, who wisely denies the very idea that we in some way grasp mind-independent reality as it is, intends his claim as a revised form of the Socratic assumption, which functions normatively in the entire philosophical tradition, of dialogue as a source of truth. In his account of theories of truth, he restates this Socratic view in claiming that in principle all discussion intrinsically aims at universal agreement as the result of unconstrained dialogue. Habermas's innovation is to insist that the failure to realize that the necessary conditions for such dialogue do not always exist is to transform theory into ideology. Accordingly, he maintains that the truth of statements is based on the anticipation of the good life. But Habermas goes beyond Socrates' hypothesis of the utility of dialogue in his even more controversial claim that under the proper conditions discussion does produce truth.[54]

I agree that since we cannot know that we ever grasp mind-independent reality, cognitive claims are based on agreement between observers, in a word on consensus. That is only controversial if one thinks, as Platonists used to think and metaphysical realists still think, that we can know the real.[55] Many people, for instance Michael Devitt, believe that there is no reason to settle for, say, a constructive empiricism which looks for, as Van Fraassen suggests, mere empirical adequacy in a theoretical model[56] since to know means to know the way the world is.[57] This view is very popular among scientists. Stephen Weinberg, the quantum physicist, holds that science would turn out to be irrational were this not the case.[58]

In the present context it will suffice to point out two difficulties with Habermas's version of this view. On the one hand, there is a deep confusion between knowledge and truth. To say that we accept cognitive claims on the basis of agreement, that they exhibit what Dewey calls warranted assert-ibility, or again that they represent what we mean by "knowledge," does not mean that they are true. Since truth and consensus are independent concepts, one cannot infer from consensus, even unrestrained consensus, to truth. On the other hand, the very idea that we can go beyond consensus – yielding what Peirce calls belief, which through the process of scientific inquiry takes the place of doubt – places Habermas beyond anything prag-matism can accept. The difference between Habermas and pragmatism can be stated simply as follows. Both hold that we cannot directly know mind-independent reality. The former claims that we can, however, know it indirectly through unconstrained consensus, hence attain truth as described in theories of truth. The latter maintains that we have knowledge based on intersubjective agreement, but not truth.

Rorty's skepticism and pragmatism

Rorty's position has changed greatly over the years from his early, enthusi-astic support of the general analytic project to his later epistemological skepticism. Rorty's philosophical itinerary can be conveniently sketched in terms of the two main phases in the position of Ludwig Wittgenstein, one of his main philosophical heroes. Initially Rorty believed that analytic philos-ophy might differ from all other prior movements in that it in fact realized the main philosophical concerns through the turn to language. In this phase, he was close to the early Wittgenstein's belief that through language we can know the way the world is. This attitude presupposes a form of epistemolog-ical foundationalism in which a one-to-one correspondence can be established between what Wittgenstein called atomic facts and atomic sentences. Russell reworks classical empiricism in his logical empiricism, which is generalized in the early Wittgenstein's contention that meaningful sentences possess a logical structure picturing the world. His picture theory of meaning depends on the idea that meaningful sentences are analyzable into simple sentences, consisting of simple, or atomic, sentences with the same logical structure as the atomic facts they depict. On this view through the proper use of language we can correctly represent the independent world, since, as Wittgenstein famously claims, a picture depicts reality through its pictorial form.[59]

Rorty was initially committed to the general analytic view that the proper approach to philosophy necessarily runs through theory of language, what he famously called "the linguistic turn". In his long preface to a collection bearing that name,[60] he cautiously suggests that the philosophical tradition had come to a high point and to an end through the linguistic turn. At this point, he understood the linguistic turn in a thoroughly Wittgensteinian manner to mean that philosophical problems could either be solved or dissolved by, in his words, reforming language or learning more about it.[61]

Unlike most of his analytic colleagues, who are mainly uninterested and even uninformed about the history of philosophy, Rorty has always possessed a lively interest in both. Even when he was most attracted to analytic philosophy, he was aware that the turn to language might not suffice to somehow bring the tradition to a close by forever solving or resolving its main concerns. Wittgenstein later came to believe that this idea of philosophy was systematically misleading and that the problems of philosophy were pseudo-problems to be exorcised, or dissolved, rather than solved or resolved, by examining our use of language. Rorty later developed a similar view that the proper attitude toward philosophy is therapeutic, not constructive, which has continued to guide his more recent work.[62]

In *Philosophy and the Mirror of Nature*, the book which marked the transition from his earlier to his later position, which will probably be the central item in his bibliography and which has guided all his later work, Rorty argues that philosophy comes to a peak and to an end in analytic philosophy. In his version of this tale, philosophy centers on the theory of knowledge which, to make good on its claims, appeals to the analytic variant of epistemological foundationalism, which he conflates with the foundations of knowledge. This book is a long attack on the very idea of a philosophical theory of knowledge. Rorty, who initially believed that analytic philosophy either had or eventually would come up with an acceptable view of knowledge, later came to the conclusion, which he defends in this book, that there is nothing interesting to say about knowledge, hence no good reason to continue the epistemological debate.

According to Rorty, philosophy aims to be a foundational discipline with respect to the other cognitive disciplines. Wittgenstein, Heidegger, and Dewey, the three philosophers he most admires, all believed early on that philosophy needed to realize the old Platonic view of philosophy as foundational which Rorty simply attributes to Kant.[63] According to Rorty, we would be better off aiming at a post-Kantian culture in which there is and can be no all-encompassing theory founding the cognitive claims of the other disciplines.[64] This could mean that Rorty was content to adopt a democratic approach in which each discipline was self-justifying. His view is, however, more radical. On the one hand, he simply denies that other cognitive disciplines are grounded in philosophy. On the other, he affirms that, since we cannot know the way the world is, in effect we do not know at all.

One might hold, as pragmatists have always held, that since, as Rorty points out, there is no such thing as a Kantian overarching permanent neutral framework,[65] knowledge is limited to belief which assuages doubt. Rorty's more radical view, a kind of post-epistemological skepticism, can be paraphrased as the claim that theory of knowledge peaks in analytic foundationalism, which fails, so epistemology fails. Rorty, who holds that philosophy aims to be a general theory of representation,[66] denies that knowledge can ever demonstrate correspondence to reality.[67] He disagrees with Sellar's view of science as the measure of all things. As Rorty tells it, justification is social but not representational.[68] Knowledge claims depend on social justification, which should not be confused with accurate representation, which expresses what society lets us say.[69] It would be a mistake to continue the epistemological quest by other means, for instance, through hermeneutics.[70] Unfettered conversation leads only to mere edification as the goal of knowledge, in a word more conversation, but nothing more, certainly not truth.[71]

In succeeding works, Rorty has continually identified with pragmatism in general. When he discusses pragmatism, Rorty is apt to talk less about Peirce, more about James, but especially about Dewey.[72] Yet it is hard to fathom what Rorty means by "pragmatism." His view seems clearly muddled. It apparently includes those who favor realism and those who reject it, those who favor traditional claims to know the way the world is, and those who reject them, those who uphold a correspondence theory of truth and those who deny it. An instance is his effort to convince us that Davidson is a pragmatist,[73] whereas the realist Davidson, who eschews conceptual frameworks, categorial schemes, perspectives, or points of view, defends the very correspondence theory of truth the anti-realist self-described pragmatist Rorty rejects.[74] Other than in a kind of conceptual nostalgia, it is hard to see why Rorty still bothers to invoke pragmatism at all in view of his fixation on the failure of epistemological foundationalism. Pragmatists generally, above all Peirce, are concerned with knowledge if we give up trying to find a way to perfect foundationalism. In turning away from Descartes and his heirs, Peirce and James, but less Dewey, offer theories of knowledge after we give up our foundationalist hang-ups. Rorty spends his time decrying the whole enterprise of knowledge, which he assimilates to a meaningless enterprise. In giving up foundationalism and giving up truth, he also gives up an interest in knowledge, which is central to pragmatism.

Conclusion: the epistemological promise of pragmatism

This chapter has examined the difference between American pragmatism and radical pragmatism in Apel, Habermas and Rorty. I have argued that pragmatism can be described as a concern with knowledge after foundationalism, but that the radical pragmatists are all concerned with the very foundationalism that pragmatism gives up.

We need to separate the promise of pragmatism[75] from what can be called its epistemological promise. Pragmatism has long been overshadowed by analytic philosophy, which originated at about the same time, and which is now losing any vestige of its original shape, in part because of the clear failure of its main projects. These include the effort to specify the conditions of knowledge through a theory of reference stemming from Frege, the concern to produce a viable theory of language, the project of a unified science (or at least physicalism or extensionalism in the naturalizing movement stemming from Quine), and so on.

Plato, Descartes and Kant tell us we should be concerned with truth and knowledge, where knowledge requires knowing the truth about the way the mind-independent world is. In the wake of the failure of foundationalism, a basic distinction has appeared between knowledge and truth. After the failure of foundationalism we should not become epistemological skeptics, although we do need to give up truth as ordinarily defined. The truth is that there is only knowledge but no truth understood as a reliable grasp of the mind-independent world. The radical pragmatists are all committed to a traditional idea of truth, in Apel and Habermas who seek it, and in Rorty who, failing to distinguish between knowledge and truth, rejects them both.

I think the promise of pragmatism lies in its continued concern with knowledge after the philosophical demise of truth. Pragmatism is precisely interesting in that it does not give up the debate, but continues it in a different way in acknowledging that after foundationalism we can nonetheless have interesting views of knowledge. The difference between the pragmatists and the radical pragmatists is the neglect of that simple but absolutely crucial point by the latter, hence their basic misunderstanding of the epistemological promise of the pragmatist debate.

Notes

1 See "Thirteen pragmatisms," in A.O. Lovejoy, *Thirteen Pragmatisms and Other Essays*, Baltimore, Johns Hopkins University Press, 1963, pp. 1–29.

2 See e.g. Richard J. Bernstein, *Praxis and Action: Contemporary Philosophers of Human Activity*, Philadelphia, University of Pennsylvania Press, 1971, p. 175, n. 13. Bernstein draws attention to the link between the rejection of foundationalism in Peirce, and its subsequent rejection in Quine, Popper, Sellars and Feyerabend.

3 For his critique of Descartes in a series of papers written in 1868, see "Questions concerning certain faculties claimed for man," "Some consequences of four incapacities," and "Grounds of validity of the laws of logic: further consequences of

four incapacities," reprinted in *The Essential Peirce: Selected Philosophical Writings*, edited by Nathan Houser and Christian Kloesel, Indianapolis, Indiana University Press, 1990, I.

4 For early statements of his view of the logic of scientific inquiry as moving from doubt to belief, see "How to make our ideas clear," and "The fixation of belief," reprinted in *The Essential Peirce*, I.

5 "How to make our ideas clear," in *The Essential Peirce*, I, p. 132.

6 See "How to make our ideas clear, in *The Essential Peirce*, I, pp. 137–41.

7 See M. Migotti, "Recent work in pragmatism: revolution or reform in the theory of knowledge?" in *Philosophical Books*, 29, 1988, pp. 65–73.

8 See "Pragmatism," in *A Companion to Epistemology*, edited by Jonathan Dancy and Ernest Sosa, Cambridge, Blackwell, 1993, pp. 351–7.

9 See his "Einleitung" to *Transformation der Philosophie*, I, pp. 9–76, especially pp. 9–22.

10 This move is more familiar in Habermas's recent writings. According to Vogel, for instance, this is the main insight in Habermas's theory of communicative action. See Steven Vogel, *Against Nature: The Concept of Nature in Critical Theory*, Albany, SUNY Press, 1996, p. 145.

11 See Hans Albert, *Traktat über kritische Vernunft*, Tübingen, J.C.B. Mohr (Paul Siebeck), 1991, pp. 9–34.

12 See Albert, *Traktat über kritische Vernunft*, "Münchhausen" comes from Nietzsche's *Beyond Good and Evil*. See Friedrich Nietzsche, *Beyond Good and Evil*, translated by Walter Kaufmann, New York, Random House, 1966, § 21, pp. 28–30.

13 Habermas, who is critical of Apel's ethical foundationalism, denies it provides either an ultimate justification or a response to an ethical skeptic. See "Discourse ethics: notes on a program of philosophical justification," in Jürgen Habermas, *Moral Consciousness and Communicative Action*, translated by Christian Lenhardt and Shierry Weber Nicholsen, Cambridge, MIT Press, 1993, p. 43. This passage, which seems to indicate that Habermas renounces foundationalism, is contradicted by another passage in the same book, where he notes that claims for validity are unconditional. See Habermas, *ibid.*, pp. 19–20. For critical discussion of Habermas's foundationalism, see Barbara Herrnstein Smith, *Belief and Resistance*, Cambridge, Harvard University Press, chapter 7, pp. 105–25.

14 "Das Apriori der Kommunikationsgesellschaft und die Grundlagen der Ethik. Zum Problem einer rationalen Begründung der Ethik im Zeitalter der Wissenschaft," in K.-O. Apel, *Transformation der Philosophie*, Frankfurt a.M., Suhrkamp, 1973, II, pp. 357–435.

15 See Apel, *Transformation der Philosophie*, II, p. 359.

16 See Apel, *Transformation der Philosophie*, II, p. 362.

17 See Apel, *Transformation der Philosophie*, II, p. 370.

18 See Apel, *Transformation der Philosophie*, II, p. 378.

19 All theory of any kind presupposes "the a priori of the ordinary language understanding in the context of the life world as that which cannot be gone behind" (Apel, *Transformation der Philosophie*, II, p. 389).

20 See Apel, *Transformation der Philosophie*, II, p. 390.

21 Transcendental reflection on meaning shows that "the presupposition of the validity of moral norms in general is a 'paradigmatic' condition of the possibility of the justification of norms belonging to the language game" (Apel, *Transformation der Philosophie*, II, p. 394).

22 See Apel, *Transformation der Philosophie*, II, p. 397.

23 See Hans Albert, *Traktat über kritische Vernunft*, Tübingen, J.C.B. Mohr (Paul Siebeck), 1991.

24 See Charles Morris, "Foundations of the theory of signs," in *Encyclopedia of the Unified Sciences*, Chicago, University of Chicago Press, 1938, 1969, I, no. 2, and "Szientismus oder Transzendentalhermeneutik? Zur Frage nach dem Subjekt der Zeicheninterpretation in der Semiotik des Pragmatismus," in Apel, *Transformation der Philosophie*, II, pp. 178–219.

25 See C.S. Peirce, *Collected Papers*, V, § 354; see also II, § 654. For Apel's view of Peirce, see his article, "Von Kant zu Peirce. Die semiotische Transformation der transcendentalen Logik," in Apel, *Transformation der Philosophie*, II, pp. 157–77 See also C.S. Peirce *Schriften*, edited by K.-O. Apel, Frankfurt a.M., Suhrkamp, 1967.

26 See Apel, *Transformation der Philosophie*, II, pp. 424–5. See also *ibid.* p. 428, where this point is made even more clearly.

27 "It seems to me that here the basic principle of an ethics of communication is suggested that also provides the initially missing basis of an ethics of democratic agreement through consensus. The indicated basic norm takes its obligatory character not through some factual recognition of those who reach consensus, say, in a contract model, but rather it obligates all those who have attained 'communicative competence' through the socialization process to strive for consensus with respect to a form of voluntary solidarity in all situations, which concern the interests, that is, the potential claims, of others; and only this basic norm (together with the norms that contracts are fulfilled) – and not something like the fact of limited agreement – secures moral necessity for the individual normative agreements" (Apel, *Transformation der Philosophie*, II, p. 426).

28 "In this way, in my view, through transcendental reflection on the conditions of possibility and validity of understanding we have reached a Cartesian foundationalist point [Letztbegründung]" (Apel, *Transformation der Philosophie*, I, p. 62).

29 See Apel, *Transformation der Philosophie*, I, p. 68.

30 See Apel, *Transformation der Philosophie*, I, p.72.

31 See Apel, *Transformation der Philosophie*, II, p. 404.

32 See "Consequences of common-sensism," in *Collected Papers of Charles Sanders Peirce*, edited by Charles Harteshorne and Paul Weiss, Cambridge, Harvard University Press, 1934, V, 5.525, pp. 367–8; see also "Issues of pragmatism," in *ibid.* 5.452, p. 305.

33 See "The scientific attitude and fallibilism," in *Philosophical Writings of Peirce*, edited by Justus Buchler, New York, Dover, 1955, p. 58.

34 "How to make our ideas clear," in Peirce, *Philosophical Writings of Peirce*, p. 38.

35 For a representative sample, see Max Horkheimer, *Eclipse of Reason*, New York, Seabury, 1974.

36 See Jürgen Habermas, *Rekonstruktion des historischen Materialismus*, Frankfurt a.M., Suhrkamp, 1976.

37 For discussion, see Tom Rockmore, *Habermas on Historical Materialism*, Bloomington, Indiana University Press, 1989.

38 See Jürgen Habermas, *Theorie des kommunikativen Handelns*, Frankfurt a.M., Suhrkamp, 1981, 2 vols.

39 See Jürgen Habermas, *Justification and Application: Remarks on Discourse Ethics*, translated by Ciaran P. Cronin, Cambridge, MIT Press, 1993.

40 See Jürgen Habermas, *Faktizität und Geltung. Beiträge zur Diskurstheorie des Rechts und des demokratischen Rechtsstaats*, Frankfurt a.M., Suhrkamp, 1992, 1994.

41 See Jürgen Habermas, *Der philosophische Diskurs der Moderne*, Frankfurt a.M., Suhrkamp, 1985, p. 378.

42 See Habermas, *Theorie des kommunikativen Handelns*, II, p. 583.
43 See Habermas, *Knowledge and Human Interests*, chapter 5: "Peirce's logic of inquiry: the dilemma of scholastic realism restored by the logic of language," pp. 91–112.
44 See "Individuierung durch Vergesellschaftung. Zu G.H. Meads Theorie der Subjecktivität," in Jürgen Habermas, *Nachmetaphysisches Denken*, Frankfurt a.M., Suhrkamp, 1988, pp. 187–241.
45 See Habermas, *Knowledge and Human Interests*, p. 69.
46 See Habermas, *Knowledge and Human Interests*, p. 91.
47 See Habermas, *Knowledge and Human Interests*, pp. 92–3.
48 See Habermas, *Knowledge and Human Interests*, pp. 300–17.
49 Habermas here sees unconstrained consensus as realizing Rousseau's concept of the rational will. See Jürgen Habermas, *Legitimation Crisis*, translated by Thomas McCarthy, Boston, Beacon Press, 1975, p. 108.
50 See Jürgen Habermas, "Wahrheitstheorien," in *Wirklichkeit und Reflexion*, edited by Helmut Fahrenbach, Pfullingen, Neske, 1973, pp. 239–40.
51 See Edmund Husserl, *The Crisis of European Sciences and Transcendental Phenomenology*, translated by David Carr, Evanston, Northwestern University Press, 1970, § 14, pp. 68–70.
52 See Habermas, *Knowledge and Human Interests*, p. 304.
53 See Habermas, *Knowledge and Human Interests*, p. 310.
54 For discussion, see Rockmore, *Habermas on Historical Materialism*, pp. 43–4.
55 Putnam defines metaphysical realism as follows: "On this perspective, the world consists of some totality of mind-independent objects" (Hilary Putnam, *Reason, Truth and History*, New York, Cambridge University Press, 1981, p. 49).
56 See Bas C. Van Fraassen, *The Scientific Image*, Oxford, Clarendon Press, 1980.
57 See Michael Devitt, *Realism and Truth*, Princeton, Princeton University Press, 1991.
58 See Steven Weinberg, "The revolution that didn't happen," in *The New York Review of Books*, 8 October 1998, XLV, 15, pp. 48–52.
59 See Ludwig Wittgenstein, *Tractatus Logico-Philosophicus*, London, Routledge and Kegan Paul, 1961, 2.17.
60 See *The Linguistic Turn: Essays in Philosophical Method*, edited by Richard M. Rorty, Chicago, University of Chicago Press, 1967, 1992.
61 See Rorty, *The Linguistic Turn*, p. 3.
62 See Richard M. Rorty, *Philosophy and the Mirror of Nature*, Princeton, Princeton University Press, 1979, p. 7.
63 See Rorty, *Philosophy and the Mirror of Nature*, pp. 5–6.
64 See Rorty, *Philosophy and the Mirror of Nature*, p. 7.
65 See Rorty, *Philosophy and the Mirror of Nature*, p. 266.
66 See Rorty, *Philosophy and the Mirror of Nature*, p. 3.
67 See Rorty, *Philosophy and the Mirror of Nature*, p. 333.
68 See Rorty, *Philosophy and the Mirror of Nature*, p. 170.
69 See Rorty, *Philosophy and the Mirror of Nature*, p. 174.
70 This is the theme of the last chapter in the book. See Rorty, *Philosophy and the Mirror of Nature*, pp. 357–94.
71 See Rorty, *Philosophy and the Mirror of Nature*, p. 390.
72 See Richard M. Rorty, *Consequences of Pragmatism*, Minneapolis, University of Minnesota Press, 1982.
73 See "Pragmatism, Davidson and truth," in Richard Rorty, *Objectivity, Relativism and Truth, Philosophical Papers*, New York, Cambridge University Press, 1991, I, pp. 126–50.

74 See Donald Davidson, "A coherence theory of truth and knowledge," in *Truth and Interpretation: Perspectives on the Philosophy of Donald Davidson*, edited by Ernest LePore, Oxford, Basil Blackwell, 1986.
75 See John Patrick Diggins, *The Promise of Pragmatism: Modernism and the Crisis of Knowledge and Authority*, Chicago, University of Chicago Press, 1994.

4

FORMING COMPETENCE

Habermas on reconstructing worlds and context-transcendent reason

Myra Bookman

Pragmatism, for Habermas, is a heroic teacher. Yet for all its lessons on the limits of philosophy, he often wonders if taken to its limits, pragmatism, not unlike hermeneutics and poststructuralism, indiscriminately relinquishes philosophy's honor as the keeper of rationality. How do explanations of everyday practices cross paths with the philosophical inclination toward reason and universalism without whirling into a Kantian mire? Habermas wants to police this crossroad by invoking "empirical theories with strong universalist claims."[1] By continually revealing his implicit draw toward formal constraints on outcomes, converging the "true" and the rationally "justified," he differentiates himself from important currents of the pragmatist tradition. His refusal to eliminate the constitutive significance of an intersubjective lifeworld reflects his affinities to it.

To accomplish his mediating goal, Habermas turns to a theorist outside the philosophical fold, Jean Piaget, for the insertion of ideas, "genuinely philosophical," to "detonate" the conversation into motion.[2] He looks also to language philosophers who move beyond the limitations of traditional approaches. This chapter will show how these alliances serve Habermas to demonstrate the dialectic between experience and reflection – a dialectic that results in a trajectory toward propositionalizing the formal elements hidden in content. First, he relies on Piaget's "developmental" approach to knowledge in both individuals and societies, which is driven by modified assumptions of formal causality.[3] Second, he recognizes an early German "linguistic turn" against Kant dating from Hamann, Herder, and Humboldt and utilizes their impulses to push Austin and Searle's speech-act theory in a formal direction.[4] Habermas moves brilliantly among these discourses to vindicate a "postmetaphysical" reason, which "detranscendentalizes" as it retains the "idealizing force of context-transcending" forms.[5] I will (1) explicate precisely how Habermas uses Piaget's "developmental logic" to effect a truce that protects reason's increasing role in the reconstruction of experience; (2) show how he applies this "logic" to communicative competence as he propels speech-act theory beyond context-dependence; and (3) describe how all of this requires a move from "universal" to "formal," which

Habermas understands in a "tolerant sense,"[6] and requires "the strong apriorism of Kantian philosophy to give way to a weaker version."[7] I will begin with the last, since it serves as a scaffold for the entire argument.

From universal to formal using the reconstructive sciences

Habermas takes two important theoretical steps in order to reveal how individuals become competent rational subjects through a process of reconstructing everyday experiences. First, he suggests a weaker interpretation of "transcendental" than is traditionally proposed.

> From now on, transcendental investigation must rely on the competence of knowing subjects who judge which experiences may be called coherent experiences in order then to analyze this material with a view to finding general and necessary presuppositions. Every reconstruction of a basic conceptual system of possible experience has to be regarded as a hypothetical proposal that can be tested against new experiences. As long as the assertion of its necessity and universality has not been refuted, we term "transcendental" the conceptual structure recurring in all coherent experiences. *In this weaker version, the claim that this structure can be demonstrated a priori is dropped.* [emphasis added][8]

Since Habermas recognizes that this move echoes Piaget's Kantianism, it becomes entirely consistent for him to invite Piagetian theory to explicate the ontogenic mechanisms that support the journey toward increasingly sophisticated conceptual structures. I will show how Habermas systematically invokes Piaget in the next section. Here I want to continue with the implications of Habermas's changed transcendentalism. With a little help from Piaget's "developmental logic," the transformation to a weaker version of transcendentalism bolsters the theory of communicative rationality. It enables Habermas to move beyond Austin and others' context-bound empirical pragmatics to show how particularized communicative experiences, like other everyday experiences, ultimately can become understood through generalized conceptual structures.

Habermas's renunciation of strong transcendentalism is a preliminary step on the path which leads him to eventually reject the term "universal" in favor of a completely different term to account for notions of necessity. He discusses the problem of nomenclature in an early essay, "What is universal pragmatics?"[9] In the essay's first publication in 1976, Habermas explains his hesitation to use Apel's terminology for the combining of everyday language with unavoidable presuppositions. Apel chooses "transcendental hermeneutics" or "transcendental pragmatics." Although Habermas understands that

Apel accepts a weak transcendentalism similar to his own, he worries that the term will foster misunderstanding. Such terminology might conceal (1) the important "break with apriorism" that they both make; (2) their mutual rejection of Kant's sharp separation between empirical and transcendental analysis; and (3) their determination to blur the distinction between *a priori* knowledge and *a posteriori* knowledge.[10] For this early publication, "universal pragmatics" prevails as the term Habermas chooses for his program. But its reign was short. In a new translation in 1979, he prefers "formal pragmatics," which he explains in a footnote.

> Hitherto the term "pragmatics" has referred to the analysis of particular contexts of language use and not to reconstruction of universal features of using language. To mark this contrast, I introduced a distinction between "empirical" and "universal" pragmatics. I am no longer happy with this terminology; the term "formal pragmatics" – as an extension of formal semantics – would serve better.[11]

Habermas understands "formal" in a "tolerant sense ... as a methodological attitude we adopt in the rational reconstruction of concepts, criteria, rules, and schemata."[12] He argues there are generalized sorts of pre-theoretical knowledge, which are context-transcendent. In the domain of language, individual interlocutors and philosophers alike can reconstruct such intuitions and empirical observations into rules of communicative competence. These reconstructions, grounds for *validity* claims within a context of communication, are analogous to *truth* claims in semantics that are derived through formal logical and linguistic analysis. This new attitude denies the representational elements of language their singular place as rational aspects of language. No longer confined to content, or to assertions or propositions, formal pragmatics affirms that the elements of effective *communicative force* or *action* – aspects of utterances that seek mutual understanding – inhere at an abstract level across languages and can be subjected to rational formal analysis. Habermas, of course, distinguishes *communicative action* from *strategic action*, wherein the former works toward normative agreement typically based on conventional social–moral knowledge but holds the possibility of developing into a communicative competence that draws upon a more context-independent postconventional knowledge. *Communicative action* therefore potentially becomes subject to conscious rational formalization that can be used toward understanding and agreement. It is important to tease *communicative action* out of all possible communicative activities so it can be juxtaposed against *strategic action*, which is oriented toward interest positions and success and can embody deception, distortions, and manipulation. Habermas's project is to show that there is a kind of interactional communicative act that is not strictly instrumental, is subject to rational reconstruction, has the potential to develop toward postconventionality, and can be separated from both latent and manifest strategic communication. Therefore, contrary to many of the philosophies of language that Habermas draws upon, he does not construe the *communicative force* of an utterance as a necessarily irrational component of language – a view typically presupposed by earlier work, traditions that separate language and speech, pit locutions against illocutions, distinguish competence from performance, and reduce language to localized games of convention.[13]

With all of the aforementioned theoretical scaffolding, Habermas sets out to explain necessity without resorting to innatism or apriorism. He invokes Piaget to illuminate the cognitive mechanisms that enable movement toward context-transcendent conceptual structures, which Habermas applies to communicative competence and later to the moral universalism entailed in discourse ethics. Key always are the everyday events that figure as the medium.

The "germ" of reason carried in experience – Piaget, Kohlberg, and the roots of American Pragmatism

The "aporia" of salvaging "truth … in the spirit of the Enlightenment," a truth rescued from religion and metaphysics, that "haunted Greek philosophy like a shadow from the moment of its encounter with the Jewish and Christian tradition onward,"[14] continue to haunt Habermas. In a recent reflection he reveals his long road toward resolution as he sketches a common sensibility in Kohlberg's refinement of Piaget's moral development work and in the roots of American Pragmatism. In this rare autobiographical musing, Habermas reflects on a fond memory of his "American friend, Larry Kohlberg." He recalls Kohlberg's affinity for Walt Whitman's poetry, William James's "intuitions," and the tradition that stretches across Peirce, Royce, Morris, Mead, and Dewey. Habermas's reminiscences disclose the train of his own thoughts regarding justificatory discourses as universal procedures for adjudicating conflict in the public sphere. He ponders the relationship of genesis and validity. If this tradition, which affirms the necessary interaction of individual and community, and the "universalistic, egalitarian values of the radical democratic tradition," is so deeply American, does it nevertheless result in a profoundly valid "conviction" regardless of its genesis? Conceding that he "will defend a thesis that will not sit well with the spirit of the times" he tells us that any person with a reasonably normal social environment "cannot fail" to acquire moral intuitions of the Jamesian kind.

> The maxim asserts the reciprocal dependence of socialization and individuation, the interrelation between personal autonomy and social solidarity, that is part of the implicit knowledge of *all*

communicatively acting subjects; it does not merely express a more or less subjective opinion concerning what some person believes is the good life. That proposition articulates an intuition we acquire in various different contexts on the condition we grow up in surroundings that are not completely undermined by systematically distorted communication. [original emphasis][15]

To explicate the mechanisms that support the gradual transformation of these "intuitions" into explicitly known propositions, Habermas invokes the "reconstructive sciences," that is, the developmental studies of Piaget and Kohlberg. Admittedly such empirical studies are only indirect tests of philosophical theories but they are useful in pushing modifications in those theories. Habermas continually lauds thinkers who demonstrate the interdependence of science and philosophy and demonstrates how empirical investigations confirm or challenge long-standing philosophical theories. Among examples of Einstein's challenge to Kant's ideas of natural science and Kohlberg's to Kant's moral metaphysics, Habermas adds that a number of psychological developmental investigations into cognition, perspective-taking, and moral consciousness cohere with the Aristotelian insight that we acquire moral intuitions implicitly through socialization. But such lessons occur for Aristotle in the domain of practical reason and Habermas refuses to accept Aristotle's detaching of practical reason from theoretical reason. So Habermas puts these socialization processes in a medium of communicative action where presuppositions can be rationally reconstructed and "already carry within them the germ of morality."[16]

Now, positing the "germ" of necessity in everyday events is a curious statement for a theorist like Habermas who, while he struggles with the "aporia" of truth, succumbs neither to innatism nor apriorism, nor to religious or metaphysical teleologies. Since Habermas seems intuitively drawn to Piaget (and his theoretical progeny, Kohlberg), perhaps it would be instructive to look at the structure and assumptions of Piaget's model, in addition to simply thinking of his work as providing empirical evidence. Piaget, like Habermas, seeks a way to retain the notion of "necessary knowledge," which is constitutive of rationality and independent of time and place, but is nevertheless constituted in time. "I consider myself to be profoundly Kantian, but of a Kantianism that is not static, that is, the categories are not there at the outset; it is rather a Kantianism that is dynamic," says Piaget in a discussion in which he refutes Chomsky's innatism but denies empiricism's "empty bucket."[17] He elaborates when he locates himself

> close to the spirit of Kantianism ... like many of those who accept the dialectical method ... and consider the a priori as dissociable from the notions of chronological priority or of level. The necessity

characteristic of the synthesis becomes then a terminus *ad quem* and ceases to be as in the case above [Kant] a terminus *a quo* which still remains too close to the pre-established harmony.[18]

For Piaget, Leibnizian "pre-established harmony" reflects an entirely too "static and non-evolutionary concept" of the human structuring subject, reminiscent of Kant and Aristotle.[19] Note Habermas's very similar "dynamic Kantianism" when he critiques traditional philosophies of consciousness. He explains that

> naturalism has cast doubt on whether it is at all possible to approach consciousness as a foundation, as something uncondi- tioned and original: Kant had to be brought into accord with Darwin. Later, the theories of Freud, Piaget, and Saussure offered third categories that avoided the basic conceptual dualism of the philosophy of consciousness.[20]

In his further attempt to "deflate the extra-ordinary" and to keep everyday interactions in the mix, Habermas credits pragmatists from Peirce to Quine with uncovering internal connections between genesis and validity – that is, locating the origins of cognition in dealings with persons and things.[21] While both Piaget and the pragmatists successfully undermine the traditional notion of theory over practice in Habermas's view, he, like Piaget, is interested in the fact that validity emerges nevertheless. With time and practice, we seem to discover the reason that inheres in everyday activities and communication. Reason's definition and salient characteristics, ever elusive and contentious throughout the history of thought, overlap for Piaget and Habermas. Both see reason intimately entwined with successful problem-solving. Piaget observes that "functional invariants" in everyday life ultimately accord with the "categories of reason," which can be recog- nized, symbolized, and manipulated.[22] The "entire rationality complex" is described similarly by Habermas as one that "needs a lifeworld background whose *substance* is articulated in the medium of language: a lifeworld back- ground that forms more or less suitable contexts, and provides resources, for attempts to reach understanding and to solve problems." And remarkably, Habermas continues in the same passage to contend that reason requires communication communities to retain "a universalist anticipation of a 'muted transcendence from within' that does justice to the irrefutably unconditional character of what is held-to-be true and what ought-to-be- true."[23] Can the "germ" of reason that hides in the content of life's encounters be explained by a modification of "formal causality?"[24]

Piaget's enormous corpus of empirical data on children's mastery of neces- sary knowledge constantly compels him to ask why the process of "constructing" the structures of intelligence yields rationally necessary outcomes. How does necessary knowledge result from contingent or non-necessary events? Without positing predetermined fixity – either in the mind or in the world – Piaget seems to support a dynamic "formal causality" instead. While he rejects the classical Aristotelian theory of "forms," formal causal principles play a key role in the development of Piaget's cognitive structures; that is, his "constructivist" approach views outcomes as "inevitable" rather than "innate."[25] Why inevitable? In an influential book on the development of symbolic behavior, Bates offers a modern interpretation that construes Aristotle's forms as possible solutions to sets of constraints given in real-world problems.[26] These solutions can obey physical laws, logico-mathematical laws, or rules, procedures, or capacities underlying linguistic systems. When relevant to human cognitive structures, solutions are internalized so that a set of similar tasks group into a similar solution or principle, and thus that the entire construction process need not be engaged over and over for particular exemplars of that set of tasks. However, when a problem arises that presents new constraints and challenges to already internalized solutions, a process toward new, more rational, solutions may be realized. In the context of a non-oppressive inter-subjective setting, a dynamic "pull" toward new, more sophisticated formal solutions is set in motion. Since "form" at one stage becomes the "content" of the next higher stage, any formalization can always give way to a more inclusive solution.[27] At every stage developmental solutions obey certain formal constraints (hence the invariant sequence of stages) and therefore are not random, an idea I will pursue below. But first note a physical example that demonstrates how formal constraints operate. Drawing on the 1917 classic *On Growth and Form*, by D'Arcy Thompson, Bates explains that

> In formal causal terms, the reason why soap bubbles are round is that roundness is the only possible solution to achieving maximum volume with minimum surface. Hence, the "explanation" for round-ness is task determined, a formally constrained solution to a problem.[28]

Bates makes parallel arguments, which she bolsters with empirical data, regarding the development of grammar in children, cognitive structures as Piaget theorizes them, and finally the acquisition of rules, procedures, and capacities in all aspects of language development.[29]

While individual and collective cognitive adaptation drives the push toward more and more sophisticated forms, which serve as solutions or formal ways of organizing classes of problems, it needs to be clear that these forms are not chance or random attempts – the best of which are retained. This is not a trial and error process. The germ of the solution inheres *in the relationship* of the current operating stage of the individual or the group *and* the problem. The formal synthesis *emerges* and is neither innate nor "pregnant" in the problem's appearance or perceptual presentation.[30] As Habermas recognizes, the process of "adaptation" here is only loosely analogous to currently accepted processes of biological evolution, which are based on mutation processes. There is a "functional equivalence" at best, because "mutation produces chance variations, whereas the ontogenesis of structures of consciousness is a highly selective and directional process."[31] Piaget, too, rejects trial and error – which he calls "groping" – as explanatory in the progressive development of intelligence.

> [T]here are two ways of interpreting groping. Either one asserts that groping activity is directed from the outset, by a comprehension related to the external situation and then groping is never pure, the role of chance becomes secondary, and the solution is identified with that of assimilation ... or else one states there exists a pure groping, that is to say, taking place by chance and with selection, after the event, of favorable steps. Now, *it is in this second sense that groping was first interpreted and it is this second interpretation that we are unable to accept.* [emphasis added][32]

Therefore, formal constraints drive more and more adequate ways of reconstructing and reorganizing content – and the way in which each step follows its predecessor is rarely random. Errors can occur but attempts are rationally driven and modified intersubjectively.

My intention in this section was to demonstrate how a "tolerant" sense of formalism provides the assumptive thread that weaves together Habermas's "formal pragmatics" (discussed in the next section), Piaget's "genetic epistemology," specified and refined in the domain of morality by Kohlberg, and the classical roots of American Pragmatism. In short, the commonality that inheres in all three is that given reasonably "undistorted" interactions with people and objects, an asymptotic movement toward more and more adequate, read "rational," solutions to problems will emerge. Adequacy, in all three cases, refers to the competence to engage in rationally grounded thought processes and actions when appropriate. But because, in his later work, Piaget's conclusions become increasingly biological and "functional," Habermas glimpses the danger of the "naturalistic fallacy."[33] Kohlberg, in Habermas's view, avoids the "is"/"ought" problem that places Piaget's theory in jeopardy because Kohlberg unambiguously states the "claim that a psychologically more advanced stage of moral judgment is more morally adequate, by moral philosophic criteria."[34] For this reason, Habermas is increasingly drawn to Kohlberg as his source for the moral aspects of his own work on communicative action and discourse ethics, although his reliance on Kohlberg is by no means unequivocal. Habermas not only questions the "naturalness" of the final stage of "postconventional morality," but also questions some aspects of the substantive portions of the theory.[35] Yet, after detailing these issues throughout the 1980s and suggesting the ways in which his own discourse ethics can counter some of the anomalies and problems, Habermas continues to invoke central themes of Kohlberg's reconstructive model in his later writings.[36]

Habermas ends the chapter that begins with fond memories of Kohlberg by tying him firmly to the tradition from which he drew "nourishment" – the American Pragmatist tradition. Habermas concludes with a tribute to that tradition which "developed the ideas of an unlimited communication community and a universal discourse ... transcend[ing] all existing states of affairs while retaining the character of a *public* court of appeal."[37] These ideals frame "formal pragmatics," which explain how communication can contain the germs of both rationality and morality.

Formal pragmatics – the lifeworld begets truth and rightness

Habermas's expansion of pragmatism and the pragmatics of language owes a great debt to the "developmental logic" of Piaget, which provides the mechanism of cognitive "decentration" as the process that enables increased formalization. Piaget's ideas, coupled with Weber's concept of "disenchanting" or "denaturalizing of worlds," help Habermas theorize a communicative competence that moves toward "rationalization." Piaget's theory of a child's continual "decentering" from her own egoism to a more and more inclusive and rational organization of everyday events describes a restructuring that occurs not only through "reciprocal actions between subject and object ... but [through] reciprocal action between individual subjects."[38]

> Thus for Piaget there is cognitive development in a wider sense, which is not understood solely as a construction of an external universe but also as a construction of a reference system for the *simultaneous* demarcation of the objective and social worlds from the subjective world. Cognitive development signifies in general *the decentration of an egocentric understanding of the world*. Only to the extent that the formal reference system of the three worlds is differentiated can we form a reflective concept of "world" and open up access to the world through the medium of common interpretive efforts, in the sense of a cooperative negotiation of situation definitions ... The function of the formal-world concepts ... is to prevent the stock of what is common from dissolving in the stream of subjectivities repeatedly reflected in one another. They make it possible to adopt in common the perspective of a third person or nonparticipant. [original emphasis][39]

Through a gradual process of reconstructing a "lifeworld ... formed of more or less diffuse, always unproblematic, background convictions ... which also stores the interpretive work of preceding generations," we develop "world-concepts" (corresponding to the lifeworld, as well as to the objective, subjective, and social worlds) and commensurate validity claims, which provide "formal scaffolding."[40] For Habermas, this process relies deeply on communication, language, and interpretation. This reliance is paired with the notion that there is more than *one* world – more than the objective world. Each of these worlds, the "lifeworld," and the objective, subjective, and social worlds, is scaffolded by its own rationality. Hence the need to show how context-transcendent pragmatic presuppositions, whose validity claims correspond to the rational underpinnings of each world, can be expressed formally, and are analogous to but are not the same as semantic truth. Habermas accomplishes this by expanding traditional speech-act theory beyond its empirical limits to include the universal structural properties of reaching understanding.

Since "reaching understanding is the inherent telos of human speech," we should be able to determine the formal presuppositions that participants accept as valid and to distinguish them from merely de facto accord.[41] Habermas lays out this territory quite elaborately throughout his writings since his inauguration of "formal" in exchange for "universal" in 1979, with the most detailed descriptions in the 1980s in his two volumes of *The Theory of Communicative Action*. I won't recapitulate those arguments or details here. Rather, I want to conclude with a sketch of how he most recently summarizes his own trajectory toward a cognitivist, formalist, universalist theory that locates the germ of rationality in the intersubjective aspects of communication.

Describing a general "turn toward pragmatics" in language theory, Habermas reveals the key idea that distinguishes "formal–pragmatic analysis" of speech acts and its corollary "validity claims" from the "empirical pragmatic" formulations of Austin and Searle.[42] Habermas hopes to supersede Austin who erroneously construed the illocutionary force of an utterance – the communicative aspect that seeks understanding using social knowledge – as the irrational component. Habermas contends that this component of language, like representational components, can be subjected to rational formalization. Searle, like Austin, remained too tied to truth-semantic conceptualizations of meaning and validity. This proved to be a serious limitation for both. Their attempts at a systematic pragmatic analysis of language, in the end, theorized little beyond descriptions of communicative acts bound to particular cultural contexts.[43] Habermas wants to escape the tie to particularized contexts and show how certain presuppositions contained in effective communication cut across social and cultural contexts and can be abstracted, formalized, and utilized toward understanding regardless of setting, assuming a certain level of competence among interlocutors.

To be sure, Habermas understands that the representational function of an utterance as measured against truth conditions is an important part of validity and he certainly doesn't want to dispense with it in his linguistic analysis – but for him it is only *one* aspect of validity. He wants to expand validity claims so that the "fulfillment of the expressive and the interactive functions is also measured against conditions that are analogous to truth" and in this way "subjective truthfulness and normative rightness" become "truth-analogous concepts for the validity of speech acts."[44] In other words, we cognitively thematize the interactive aspects of language just as we do the substantive content. Each ability develops along a different but analogous pathway and each has the potential to flee the limitations of context-dependence.

Habermas's intellectual journey toward formal pragmatics has been intricate. From Peirce, Mead, and other pragmatists, Habermas draws out the significance of intersubjectivity in the communicative process. He owes to Piaget the explication of how necessary knowledge results from contingent events. Kohlberg helps him to avoid the naturalistic fallacy by retaining philosophical moral criteria while still appealing to the "reconstructive sciences." Habermas details his journey further in a recent recollection that describes his location in a generation of philosophers writing after World War II, who were influenced both by the hermeneutic approach and by the analytical tradition.[45] He sees the complementarity of these traditions as enabling both Apel's "transcendental pragmatics" and his own "formal pragmatics" to come out of the "linguistic turn" that was evolving in philosophy during those years. Apel, like Habermas, responded to the tensions of particularism and universalism. He tells us that many in his generation were unwilling to relinquish the cognitive (semantic) aspects of language to the "*a priori* of meaning," as Heidegger and Wittgenstein did. So Habermas identifies with Apel's attempt to "recover the universalist tendencies from Humboldt's philosophy of language" while, at the same time, summoning a "pragmatically transformed Kant."[46] Both Apel and Habermas pay homage to the Hamann–Herder–Humboldt tradition in the German linguistic turn, which anticipates a "pragmatic turn" in which the communicative function of language holds within itself a route to context-transcendent knowledge.[47]

Habermas, like Apel, wants to rescue language from its hermeneutical and conventionalist direction (Heidegger, Wittgenstein, Gadamer), while retaining the importance of interpretation, forms of life, and intersubjectivity. A pragmatic approach will tease out the universal for both Apel and Habermas. A contemporary "current" that includes Putnam and Dummett as well as Apel pleases Habermas. They take the linguistic turn seriously, without paying the price of mistaking "being true" for "taking for true."[48] But Apel lacks a "meaning theory" in the sense of the analytic tradition, according to Habermas. Here is where his own "formal pragmatics" rises to the occasion. Habermas's model argues for two separable kinds of validity claims that arise in communication: (1) *truth* with respect to things and events; and (2) *rightness* with respect to social–moral learning. Each can be criticized in its own right and each is backed by different kinds of reasons. Habermas's treatment of .he third traditional domain of validity claims, that of the aesthetic, occurs relatively infrequently in his writing since he typically confines his comments to the "linguistic turn." But in a series of "Questions and counterquestions" that arose in 1985, Habermas responds succinctly to criticism that he "under-illuminates" the aesthetic. He maintains that there is a certain independence to the "logic" of an "aesthetic–practical rationality;" hence there is "unmistakable indication for a validity claim" as well as a kind of "learning process" that occurs as a result of works of art. In fact, he conjectures that it resembles a developmental "learning process" but he remains "skeptical" whether Piaget's analysis is as appropriate here as it is for the analysis of stages of postconventional conceptions of law and morality.[49] While he does not offer another reconstructive analysis in this regard, Habermas posits that the relevant experience of the aesthetic is a "transformation of the *form* ... in the direction of the decentering and unbounding of subjectivity."[50] And to bring it all back to Habermas's self-declared pragmatism, this decentering that occurs through the aesthetic opens up a sensitivity to what is as yet unassimilated and uninterpreted in the everyday world. While these remarks provide a rough idea of where Habermas stands on questions of the aesthetic, in general Habermas's discussions of the aesthetic remain somewhat tentative and typically arise in response to critics or as critiques geared toward theorists who conflate the aesthetic with other questions.

His critical theory legacy notwithstanding, Habermas's own work on aesthetics' ameliorative role within the context of modernity remains backgrounded to his continuing systematic honing of communicative competence in the domains of *truth* and *rightness*. Recent writings focus on semantic truth and social–moral rightness and their respective validity claims and specify how they each have an independent cognitive function. Each progresses along its own pathway of learning and achieves increasingly more inclusive understanding. An ever-increasing adequacy of cognitive organization results from these learning processes. These transformations emerge within a dialectical relationship of already existing worldviews and new challenges not adequately handled by those existing worldviews – all in the course of communication. All of this assures movement toward rationality within everyday situations as well as in political and legal spheres given the absence of "systematically distorted communication."[51] So, in the end, theorizing the role of truth and rightness trumps the aesthetic for the amelioration of the problems of modernity, Habermas's central mission. He proceeds by digging deeply into the tradition of Peirce, Royce, Dewey, and

Mead to excavate the consensus-making power of reason – an intersubjective outcome that emerges from problems detected in concrete situations. Since the success of his mission requires an analysis of patterns of communication that meets his universalist ideals by moving beyond context-bound descriptions of social conventions and yet doesn't entail a strong apriorism, he follows the lead of an early "pragmatic turn" in German philosophy. He reconstructs Austin's and Searle's key "empirical pragmatic" insights into a context-independent "formal pragmatic" analysis. Finally, since philosophy must understand its limits while it safeguards rationality, it will need the help of the empirical sciences. For Habermas, Piaget and Kohlberg with their view toward universality have been particularly useful in this regard. Kohlberg's gloss on Piaget refines a description of development as increasingly inclusive context-transcending *forms* and *formalizations* of cognitive organization – forms that reconfigure content not only in the objective world of semantic representation but also in the social world of moral rightness.[52]

Notes

1   Jürgen Habermas, *Moral Consciousness and Communicative Action (MCCA)*, trans. Christian Lenhardt and Shierry Weber Nicholsen, Cambridge: MIT Press, 1983/1990, p. 15.
2   *Ibid.* p. 15
3   Piaget credits Aristotle with the founding of both biology and logic by locating the "forms" in the subject's discourse in the case of logic and in the structure of the organism in biology. In this way, Aristotle differentiates himself from Plato's realism. But, according to Piaget, Aristotle neglects the transformations possible in the activities of the epistemological or operational subject and, in the end, remains mired in "the systematic and static realism" of the rest of Greek thought. Had he "some intuition of evolution" or transformations, "he would without a doubt have produced a theory of the progressive construction of logical forms starting from organic forms." Throughout his work Piaget respectfully refers to Aristotle's "famous doctrine" of forms and laments that "instead of being directed toward a dialectical constructivism ended ... in a static hierarchy ... and whose built-in finality ... excluded any epistemology of the subject's activity" (J. Piaget, *Insights and Illusions of Philosophy (IIP)*, New York: Routledge, 1965/1997, pp. 48–9). E. Bates suggests that a modified "formal causality" defined as "the principles or laws that govern the range of possible outcomes in a given situation ... i.e., the forms that are possible solutions to classes of constraints" best describes the driving force of Piaget's model (*The Emergence of Symbols*, New York: Academic Press, 1979, p.16).
4   J. Habermas, 'Hermeneutic and analytic philosophy: two complementary versions of the linguistic turn?', paper presented at the Society for Phenomenology and Existential Philosophy Conference (SPEP), Denver, CO, October 1998; C. Lafont, *The Linguistic Turn in Hermeneutic Philosophy*, trans. Jose Medina, Cambridge: MIT Press, 1993/1999.
5   J. Habermas, *Between Facts and Norms (BFN)*, trans. William Rehg, Cambridge: MIT Press, 1992/1996, ch. 1, 'Introduction'.
6   J. Habermas, *On the Pragmatics of Communication (OPC)*, edited by M. Cook, Cambridge: MIT Press, 1998, p. 29.

7 *Ibid.* p. 42.
8 *Ibid.* p.42.
9 Published 1976, reprinted in *OPC*.
10 *Ibid.* pp. 44–5.
11 *Ibid.* p. 92, n. 1.
12 *Ibid.* p. 29.
13 See J. Habermas, *Postmetaphysical Thinking* (*PT*), trans. William Hohengarten, Cambridge: MIT Press, 1988/1992; see also *MCCA* and *OPC*.
14 J. Habermas, *Justification and Application* (*JA*), trans. Ciaran Cronin, Cambridge: MIT Press, 1993, pp. 133–4.
15 *Ibid.* pp. 113–14.
16 *Ibid.* p. 132.
17 J. Piaget, "The psychogenesis of knowledge and its epistemological significance", in M. Piattelli-Palmerini (ed.) *Language and Learning*, London: Routledge & Kegan Paul, 1979–80, p. 150.
18 J. Piaget, *IIP*, p. 57.
19 *Ibid.* p. 51.
20 J. Habermas, *PT*, p. 47.
21 *Ibid.* p. 49. Habermas goes on to attribute contributions in this regard to Dilthey, Gadamer, Sheler, Husserl, Merleau-Ponty, Apel, and Kuhn, while rejecting Rorty's conventionalism.
22 J. Piaget, *The Origins of Intelligence* (*OI*), New York: International Universities Press, 1952, pp. 8–9.
23 J. Habermas, *OPC*, pp. 336–8.
24 See Note 3 above.
25 E. Bates, pp. 18–19.
26 *Ibid.*
27 J. Piaget, *Structuralism*, New York: Harper Colophon Books, 1968/1970, p. 35.
28 E. Bates, p. 17.
29 *Ibid.* p.19.
30 See *IIP* and *Structuralism* for Piaget's adamant contrasts between his "constructivist" approach and the "Gestaltists."
31 J. Habermas, *Communication and the Evolution of Society*, trans. Thomas McCarthy, Boston: Beacon Press, 1979, pp. 171–2.
32 J. Piaget, *OI*, p. 397.
33 J. Habermas, *MCCA*, p. 34; see also *JA*.
34 L. Kohlberg, cited in *MCCA*, p. 35. For some theorists, however, such traditional philosophic criteria themselves constrain thinking regarding ethical possibilities. See C. Gilligan, *In a Different Voice*, Cambridge: Harvard University Press, 1982/1993 and E. Levinas, *Otherwise than Being*, Pittsburgh: Duquesne University Press, 1974/1981.
35 Habermas raises

>   questions such as whether Kohlberg's description of postconventional stages of moral consciousness needs to be improved, whether the formalistic approach to ethics in particular unduly ignores contextual and interpersonal aspects, whether the notion of a logic of development … is too strong, and finally, whether Kohlberg's assumptions about the relationship between moral judgment and moral action neglect psychodynamic aspects.
>
>   (*MCCA*, p. 41)

See also J. Habermas, "Justice and solidarity: on the discussion concerning Stage 6," *The Philosophical Forum*, 21, 1–2 (Fall–Winter 1989–90), pp. 32–52.
36 See *JA* and *BFN*.
37 *JA*, p. 130.

38 J. Piaget, cited in Habermas, *Theory of Communicative Action*, vol. I, trans. Thomas McCarthy, Boston: Beacon Press, 1981/1984, p. 69.
39 J. Habermas, *ibid.* p. 69.
40 *Ibid.* p. 70.
41 *Ibid.* p. 287.
42 J. Habermas, *PT*.
43 While Habermas is "indebted to Searle for the version of speech-act theory that has been most precisely explicated up to now," Searle's work is nevertheless limited in that "he admits only one clear-cut universal validity claim that had already been privileged by truth semantics" (J. Habermas, *PT*, p. 71). In other words, Searle remains too bound to propositional truth, i.e. how words represent the world, which he considers "primordial," and therefore runs the risk of assuming that "p" represents a "state of affairs" in the world instead of representing something that reflects the propositional structure or the validity claims of that particular language. "In language, the dimensions of meaning and validity are internally connected" (J. Habermas, *OPC*, p. 270).
44 J. Habermas, *PT.* p. 75.
45 SPEP paper, Note 4 above, will be used in this section unless otherwise noted. Direct quotes only will be cited by page number.
46 *Ibid.* p. 2.
47 See Lafont, *The Linguistic Turn in Hermeneutic Philosophy*.
48 SPEP paper, p. 12.
49 J. Habermas, *OPC*, pp. 410–15.
50 *Ibid.* p. 413 (emphasis added).
51 SPEP paper, p. 19.
52 Thanks to Mitchell Aboulafia for useful feedback generously offered on earlier drafts of this chapter.

Part II

LAW AND DEMOCRACY

5

THE SIRENS OF PRAGMATISM VERSUS THE PRIESTS OF PROCEDURALISM

Habermas and American Legal Realism

David Ingram

> Myth-making and fatherly commands must be abandoned –
> the Santa Claus story of complete legal certainty; the fairy tale
> of a pot of golden law which is already in existence and which
> the good lawyer can find, if only he is sufficiently diligent; the
> phantasy of an aesthetically satisfactory system and harmony,
> consistent and uniform, which will spring up when we find
> the magic wand of a rationalizing principle. We must stop
> telling stork-fibs about how law is born and cease even
> hinting that perhaps there is still some truth in Peter Pan
> legends of a happy juristic hunting ground in a land of legal
> absolutes.
>
> (Jerome Frank)[1]

"From the outset I viewed American pragmatism ... as the radical-democratic branch of Young Hegelianism."[2] With this encomium, Habermas expressed his debt to that other pragmatist tradition – not the linguistic tradition of Karl Bühler, Ludwig Wittgenstein, John Searle, and J.L. Austin that enabled him to link meaning with action, but the epistemological tradition that led him to link truth with universal emancipation.[3] More precisely, he had in mind the idea, first articulated by Peirce and later taken up by Mead and Dewey, that "communities ... have an internal impact on scientific research and on social conditions generally."[4] In sum, what pragmatism taught Habermas was that knowledge is something acquired by persons in *reasoning together*. The lesson he drew from this reverberates throughout his subsequent philosophy: not bureaucratic hierarchy but *participatory democracy* is the best organization for problem-solving.

The democratic idea that enlivens classical pragmatism also informs an important tradition of American legal pragmatism, often referred to as Legal Realism.[5] Unfortunately, Habermas's objections to Legal Realism show that he has not sufficiently appreciated this fact. While some American Realists might have been cold cynics without an ounce of idealism coursing through their veins – believing that court decisions could be explained entirely (as Habermas puts it) "on the basis of the judge's interest position and social background, her political attitudes and personality structures, or through ideological traditions, power constellations, and economic pressures inside and outside the legal system" – others clearly did not.[6] For Progressive Realists, democratic procedural justice constituted an indispensable idea guiding all legal reform. They, too, shared Habermas's worry about judicial tyranny. Like him, they recognized that the use of law for advancing social policy makes it all the more imperative that law be legitimated by fair democratic procedures rather than by traditional precedents or abstract principles. But they also recognized that social law is more open-ended and flexible in its determinations than other types of law, thereby requiring at least some administrative and judicial interpretation in its application.

The subservience of law to the personal discretion of administrators and judges is a major concern of Habermas's. He does not dispute the Realists' view that the modern corporate-welfare state has rendered older forms of jurisprudence otiose. Nor does he dispute the inevitability of administrative and judicial interpretation in applying law. What he objects to is their alleged willingness to abandon democratic ideals in deference to bureaucratic social planning.

Most of us are familiar with the fact that the corporate welfare state replaced older legal forms with new bureaucratic legal instruments. The older, formalist jurisprudence associated with classical liberalism could not adequately absorb the revolutionary social transformation wrought by the overthrow of laissez-faire capitalism; its futile effort to secure property, contract, and tort law on a purely rational basis – without regard to social facts – paralleled its equally futile reduction of economic freedom to individual consent. The New Deal replaced this individual-centered conception of freedom with a more community- and corporate-centered variety.[7] Responding to this change, Realists regarded economic rights as outcomes of democratic decision rather than as conclusions to be deduced from the inherent nature of law. At the same time, their concern over the absence of a stable democratic consensus supporting reform led them to entrust reform-friendly administrators and judges with extensive lawmaking powers. In Habermas's opinion, Realists ultimately sided with the social engineering agenda of public interest adjudication. Doing so, however, meant more than just abandoning democratic populism. It meant abandoning the rule of law as a system premised on predictable and fair procedures in favor of ad hoc decision-making. "From the standpoint of Legal Realism ... one can no longer clearly distinguish law and politics ... because judges, like future-oriented politicians, make their decisions on the basis of value orientations they consider reasonable ... [or] justified on utilitarian or welfare-economic grounds"(*BFN*, p. 201).

Habermas's depiction of Realist jurisprudence raises two issues that are of interest to me. The first concerns the accuracy of his description of Legal Realism. In my opinion, parts of this description more aptly apply to skeptical positions mapped out by certain strands within the Critical Legal Studies (CLS) Movement or conservative positions staked out by the Law and Economics Movement than it does to the Progressive strand of American Legal Realism, which remained loyal to Pragmatism's democratic ideals.

The second concerns his response to the role personal discretion plays in administrative and judicial applications of law. This response hinges on Habermas's appeal to certain procedural ideals that ostensibly inform everyday common sense. Contrary to Richard Rorty, Habermas insists that ideals of truth and justice are not inimical to pragmatism, but actually inform any orientation toward problem solving. Problems manifest themselves whenever reality is questioned, which happens whenever our beliefs about reality lose their certainty. But questioning itself is conducted in the name of truth, justice, happiness and other ideals. Owing to their open-ended perfectibility (universality and indeterminateness), ideals can never be fully realized in any particular instance. Reforming knowledge and reality thus becomes an indefinite task. Yet each successful "solution" to a problem approximately fulfills the ideal, so idealism is not an invitation to revolutionary anarchy but (as Hegel and his left-wing followers argued) a revolutionary call to establish reality on a genuinely rational – lawful and legitimate – basis.[8]

Laws limit action in predictable ways that enhance the rational pursuit of individual aims. Predictability is also ensured by procedures governing law's creation, interpretation and implementation. But predictability is at best relative. Procedures embody ideals of justice. Because the task of interpreting and realizing these ideals can never be terminated, law retains some residue of indeterminacy. Such uncertainty affects not only legislative *outcomes* (which are subject to diverse political influences) and judicial and administrative *decisions* (which are subject to personal discretion in hard cases), but also the *interpretation* of constitutional principles and procedures (which are subject in somewhat lesser degree to both politics and personal discretion).

What, then, saves the rule of law from anarchic indeterminacy? For the most radical postmodernists within the CLS Movement, nothing. They hold that law is hardly more than a conflict of warring paradigms, value orientations, and context-relative perspectives whose ultimate outcome must be decided on the arbitrary whims of judges and administrators. Social criticism finds as little theoretical support here as do ideals of truth and justice. Things appear vastly different from the standpoint of Progressive Realism.[9] Although Progressive Realists also doubted the coherence of a capitalist legal system, they steadfastly retained ideals whose internal coherence stood in marked contrast to that system. These ideals included the constitutional entrenchment of basic rights and the democratization of judicial and administrative decision-making. In what follows, we will see how these same aims are theoretically articulated in Habermas's own legal pragmatism.

Habermas's theory of judicial decision-making

Habermas explains the genesis and operation of law from pragmatic (realistic) and philosophical (idealistic) perspectives. Like earlier sociologists of law, he notes that modern law emerged in the seventeenth century as a useful instrument for resolving religious conflict and securing property rights associated with a capitalist economy. Like them, he also holds that its effectiveness in stabilizing social conflict depended on its perceived fairness and impartiality (*BFN*, p. 78).

In Habermas's opinion, Legal Realism underestimates the importance of this moral idealism. Realists properly reject formalist conceptions of moral idealism that ground legal reasons in the *a priori* intuitions of perfectly rational individuals; and they properly reject communitarian conceptions of moral idealism that ground such reasons in the anonymous authority of shared historical traditions. For no conformity to any prior authority explains why reasonable people voluntarily comply with statutes that are made in response to new social problems. The reasons for such compliance must rather be found in social reality itself, as defined by the scientifically informed judge. Yet, like the good pragmatist that he is, Habermas reminds us that the social reality that judges confront is also not given prior to the multiple perspectives of legal subjects. Hence, if judges are to obtain access to this reality objectively, they will have to balance these perspectives fairly, by bringing them into communication with one another in the form of a transformed community of interpretation.

Habermas's discourse-ethical theory of law thus aims at combining both formal liberal and communitarian ideals in a way that is sensitive to the pragmatic requirements of statutory legislation. It grounds the legitimacy of social policies in democratic procedures that have a purchase in moral reason, or justice, broadly construed. Moral reason, in turn, informs expectations that any person engaged in the impartial resolution of disagreements must have, such as an orientation toward reaching agreement compelled solely by the better argument. What distinguishes the better argument from the most persuasive rhetoric are additional idealizations concerning the equal opportunities and capacities of the interlocutors, their freedom from external pressures and internal prejudices, and their willingness to accept reasons solely on the basis of their merits.

The best way to appreciate the advantages of Habermas's discourse-ethical theory of law is to compare it to the overly formalist procedural theory elaborated by Kant. Habermas understands his theory to be a "radical" – and in a highly qualified sense, communitarian – revision of Kant's liberalism. As such, it derives its inspiration from Kant's (and Rousseau's) concept of legitimacy: legitimate are laws that are backed by impartial reason; despotic are laws that are backed only by partisan interests (*BFN*, 100). However, for our purposes it is important to note how much of Kant's Platonism Habermas rejects. Habermas rejects the deductive model of legal reasoning deployed by Kant. Principles of pure practical reason are too abstract and indeterminate to enable a legislator to infer determinate statutes. Legal reasoning must therefore assume a different form: determinate statutes must be conceived as the outcome of a democratic process of deliberation which interprets and applies rational principles. Consensus achieved by impartial procedure demonstrates the validity of a statute, not its deduction from pure reason (*BFN*, pp. 103–6).

Habermas's defense of a democratic paradigm of legal reasoning (see below) is not merely philosophical, however. Kant's model is also rejected on pragmatic, sociological grounds. A deductive (or individual-centered) model of legal reasoning is limited in the kinds of laws it might legitimate. Morally enlightened persons might individually reason that, everyone being of equal and supreme worth, no one ought to harm another or obstruct her freedom. Basic categories of criminal and civil law might be inferred this way (as direct consequences of moral reason when applied to outward behavior) but not the categories of political or social law (*BFN*, pp. 108, 110).

However, as Habermas notes, Kant's insistence that laws express a general will seems to imply political and social rights as well. Civil and due process rights guaranteeing personal freedom from arbitrary interference on the part of others (including the state) cannot be consistently maintained in the form of autocratic decrees. Public autonomy, or democratic self-determination, must therefore complement private autonomy; and social equality must complement democratic equality (*BFN*, p. 120).

Habermas's conceptual argument in support of political rights depends upon combining the concept of legal form (universal and consistent application of law) with the principle of discourse ethics, which asserts that "just those norms are valid to which all possibly affected persons could agree as participants in rational discourse" (*BFN*, p. 107). In this way Habermas both injects Kantian universalizability into the formal requirements of the rule of law and redefines universalizability to imply rational consensus on general interests (or fair compromise between particular interests) achieved in fully inclusive democratic deliberation (*BFN*, p. 108).

Despite its deductive (or conceptual) nature, Habermas's defense of rights is thoroughly pragmatic. For what are deduced are not particular legal rights but the universal pragmatic forms ("unsaturated" principles and categories of abstract right) with which any legitimate legal system must comply (*BFN*, p. 125). Because different legal systems pragmatically reflect the concrete historical circumstances of the particular polities they regulate, they should permit the citizens of such polities to determine for themselves the specific scope and meaning of general rights. In order for the *public* to determine freely and fairly the scope of *private* freedom, citizens must be guaranteed substantial material equality in education, opportunity and motivation. So construed, it is "only at the pragmatic level" that Kantian ideals of freedom and equality acquire reality. Only fully inclusive forms of participatory democracy presuppose and realize equality and autonomy (*BFN*, p. 130).

Public fora, parliamentary bodies, courts, and administrative proceedings all incorporate democratic ideals in their deliberations, albeit with greater or lesser success (Habermas advocates making government proceedings more public and participatory than they currently are). Such ideals assume a different form depending on legal context. In order to avoid usurping democratically authorized lawmaking powers, judges must restrict their role to applying laws. However, applying laws in hard cases that touch on the specific scope and meaning of constitutional rights involves more than mechanically subsuming the case in question under a definite, preselected, rule. It also involves interpreting the case as well as the law in terms of a whole body of statutory precedents, legal principles, and moral, ethical, and pragmatic considerations (*BFN*, pp. 207–13).

Here, the discourse-ethical principle of universalizability finds an analogue in the principle of impartial application, which requires that a single (technical) rule or (abstract) principle be applied that most completely and accurately captures the complex meaning of disputed circumstances. In rendering her interpretation of these circumstances, the judge is obligated to integrate *impartially* the perspectives of all the involved parties with the perspectives of uninvolved members of the community. So construed, judicial interpretation is not (*pace* Ronald Dworkin) guided by standards of coherence (fitness *vis-à-vis* extant law) and integrity (fitness *vis-à-vis* moral ideals enjoining equal respect and concern for all) that a *single* person (the judge) applies on her own.[10] Rather,

> interpretations of the individual case, which are formed in light of a coherent system of norms, depend on the communicative form of a discourse whose socio-ontological constitution allows the perspectives of the participants and the perspectives of uninvolved members of the *community* (represented by an *impartial* judge) to be *transformed* into one another ... [thereby explaining] why the concept of coherence employed in constructive interpretation refers to the *pragmatic* presuppositions of the argumentative process.
>
> (*BFN*, p. 229 – my emphasis)

If the meaning of law is constituted by acts of judicial interpretation that ultimately extend beyond a narrow reading of the legal system (principles, rules, and precedents) to encompass a dynamic and indeterminately transformative mediation of indefinitely multiple, contextually situated perspectives, how can citizens rely on the law as a predictable sanction that has some certain and definite connection to a democratically authorized statute? Habermas's answer is not entirely reassuring: citizens can rely on the procedures for interpreting law, whose substantive meaning – though hardly fixed – is less certain than the substantive meaning of statutes and cases. Instead of guaranteeing a predictable "single right decision," procedural rights

> guarantee each legal person the claim to a fair procedure that in turn guarantees not certainty of outcome but a discursive clarification of the pertinent facts and legal questions ... [in which] affected parties can be confident that ... only relevant reasons will be decisive, and not arbitrary ones.
>
> (*BFN*, p. 220)

For Habermas, legal certainty thus boils down to the fair mediation of conflicting partisan perspectives and legal paradigms. As we shall see, nothing more nor less than this intuitive balancing was assumed by Realists. Still, they held that the ideal expectation of a single right decision is met, and legal crisis and uncertainty avoided, only if the body of statutory law is itself sufficiently coherent.[11] Habermas agrees. In his opinion,

> this counterfactual assumption [of coherence] has a heuristic value only as long as a certain amount of "existing reason" in the universe of existing law meets it halfway. According to this presupposition, then, reason must already be at work – in however fragmentary a manner – in the political legislation of constitutional democracies.
>
> (*BFN*, p. 232)

As we shall see, given the compromised nature of political life and legal relations under post-liberal capitalism, such rational coherence may not obtain. Aside from reflecting the contradictions of capitalism, law's complexity alone supports Habermas's contention that such systems are far from coherent. Although judges are normally relieved of the burden of justifying laws – that is the legislator's responsibility – the very prevalence of "norm collisions" means that "judges cannot avoid a reconstructive assessment of the norms given as valid" (*BFN*, p. 232).

The convergence of Habermas and the Realists regarding the compromised nature of law in capitalist society is especially evident in his discussion of conflicting liberal and social-welfare paradigms – a topic that had also been dealt with extensively by his Frankfurt School predecessors, Otto Kirchheimer and Franz Neumann.[12] As Habermas remarks, liberal and

welfare paradigms help reduce the indeterminacy that affects judicial decision-making. With some exceptions, liberal conceptions of formal equality
(sameness of treatment) find greater application in criminal law, while
welfare conceptions of substantive equality (differential treatment) find
greater application in social law (*BFN*, pp. 220, 394). Paradigms like these
rank legal norms in transitive order by pairing them with generalized
descriptions of specific situations to which they apply. For example, situations described in terms of free economic exchange pair well with a liberal
paradigm, which in contract law favors a principle of *caveat emptor*, in the law
of torts a principle of deterministic causation linked to individual liability,
and so on (*BFN*, p. 221). By contrast, situations described in terms of
unavoidable social costs – such as market disallocations caused by rising
interest rates – pair well with a welfare paradigm, which in contract law
favors a principle of minimum wages and benefits, in the law of torts, indeterminate (overdetermined) causation (or proof of negligence without
causation) linked to shared liability, etc.[13]

Unfortunately, paradigms succeed in reducing indeterminacy only to the
extent that they become ossified into closed ideologies that exclude alternative interpretations of situations and rights. Conflicts between liberal and
welfare paradigms in the same area of law, involving competing descriptions
of the same situation, thus reintroduce indeterminacy at a higher level. This
fact, Habermas notes, reinforces Realist skepticism that "coherent case interpretations inside a *fixed* legal paradigm remain fundamentally
underdetermined, for they compete with equally coherent interpretations of
the same case in alternative paradigms" (*BFN*, pp. 221–2).

Habermas, as we have seen, is not as optimistic as Dworkin that conflicts
between paradigms can be resolved, given the contradictions and complexi-
ties of modern capitalist society.[14] Because advocates of competing
paradigms contest the same legal terrain, the outcomes of specific court
decisions in settling hard cases is still often uncertain (as CLS scholars rightfully observe). Thus, there is considerable disagreement among members of
the Supreme Court today concerning whether the Voting Rights Act guarantees only the individual right to cast an equally weighted ballot (as
formalists maintain) or a group right to elect members of one's (racial,
ethnic, etc.) group in some rough proportion to their numbers (as non-
formalists maintain). Nonetheless, in Habermas's opinion the absence of
coherence in the legal system does not render totally futile the execution of
justice. Judges must allow a dialogue to emerge between advocates of
competing paradigms, so these paradigms themselves become "reflexive," or
self-critical. Reflexive paradigms incorporate elements from one another: a
reflexive welfare paradigm incorporates and reinterprets the liberal paradigm
of individual rights; it empowers clients (communities and individuals)
democratically by allowing them to define their own needs as active citizens
with claims to entitlement rather than as anonymous pathological cases

dependent on begrudging charity. Conversely, a reflexive liberal paradigm incorporates and reinterprets the welfare paradigm of social equality; it empowers clients democratically by allowing them to view their freedom as socially conditioned by the satisfaction of basic needs (the "dialectic of legal and factual equality") (*BFN*, p. 391). By mediating liberal and welfare paradigms, judges have a better chance at applying the one principle, paradigm, or rule among the several competing alternatives that most fairly applies to the case at hand. This is why Habermas thinks that the extreme politicization and personalization of law described in Realist and CLS literature is overwrought (*BFN*, p. 217).

The only way to resolve contradictions between liberal and welfare paradigms, then, is through recourse to a more general legal paradigm, which Habermas variously refers to as "reflexive," "democratic," or "procedural." The reflexive paradigm requires that the choice and interpretation of the other paradigms be open to democratic discussion. It means that before legislators and judges make decisions about how people should be treated similarly or differently and what concrete rights they should have, they should first consult them (*BFN*, p. 421ff.). For instance, a decision about racial redistricting should be made only after African Americans living in a specific community have had an opportunity to discuss their politically representable commonalities and differences in public fora and to decide for themselves whether their interests, taken individually and collectively, will be better advanced by this policy rather than another policy.

In sum, Habermas's discourse-ethical theory of law represents a novel attempt to combine the advantages of deontologism with the advantages of pragmatism. Both deontologism and pragmatism resist the temptation to reduce rights to traditional precedents or positive commands. However, in the former's insistence on unconditional adherence to ideal procedure and in the latter's insistence on conditional adherence to social need, there arises the appearance of a contradiction. The appearance is dispelled once we see that unconditional adherence to democratic procedure is itself essential to any conditional acceptance of social policies. In the discourse-ethical theory of law, policies oriented toward consequences do not trump rights, they realize them; for rights do not descend from *a priori* moral axioms, but from democratic deliberation.

Does this constitute a significant qualification of Habermas's deontologism? Certainly; for the precise meaning and force of democratic procedure itself must be resolved democratically. Does it constitute a circle of mutual qualification and justification? Certainly; but not in a vicious or question-begging sense. For as Habermas points out, the process of interpreting and amending constitutional procedure is itself regulated by procedures that serve to check despotic tendencies. Discourse ethics explains these checks in terms of a separation of powers (or fora of deliberation and decision) that nonetheless communicate with one another and with the broader public.

But doesn't this conception of "reflexive law" reduce constitutional proce-dure to a revolutionary project of uncertain outcome? Of course it does, because the outcome of democratic deliberation is always uncertain; but it doesn't absolutely, because it guarantees that every stage in this project will be determined by some *relatively* certain procedure.

The pragmatism of American Legal Realism

Pragmatically minded Realists wrongly charge Habermas with seeking too much ideal certainty in rational procedures when he should be embracing the less ideal uncertainty of democratic politics. Habermas reverses the charge by accusing Realists of seeking too little procedural certainty in deference to arbitrary judicial discretion. Is he right about this?

The question is difficult to answer. Legal Realism connotes an attitude, not a unified movement or methodology. It questions the possibility of transforming law into an exact science in which concrete decisions can be deduced from abstract principles without regard to extra-legal considera-tions. This attitude is hardly unique to it. Progressives writing at the turn of the century were skeptical of legal science in this sense. Today, so are propo-nents of two otherwise radically opposed movements: the conservative Law and Economics Movement and the radical CLS Movement. Most impor-tantly for our purposes, so is Habermas.

Fact is, Realists were neither methodologically nor ideologically homoge-neous. Some saw their pragmatism as a relatively neutral method of exposing hidden political biases in what were ostensibly scientifically neutral legal deductions.[15] Others saw it in just the opposite light, as an attempt to base legislation and adjudication on one set of political values (associated with democratic Progressivism) instead of another, more conser-vative set of values (associated with laissez-faire capitalism).[16] Again, there was little agreement among Realists about what sorts of extra-legal consid-erations should guide legal thought. Some held that higher moral principles or ethical values of a more parochial (national) nature ought to guide jurists; others held that value-free social science alone should be authoritative.

Without trying to defend an authentic version of Legal Realism, I will accept Morton Horwitz's judgment that the most significant and lasting contribution of American Legal Realism was its cognitive relativism. Cognitive relativism here means questioning "the traditional foundations of thought and structures of understanding," challenging "the claimed objec-tivity of deductive and analogical reasoning," and accepting "the socially constructed character of frames of reference, categories of thought, and legit-imating concepts."[17] Most important for our purposes is Horwitz's claim that this "interpretative or hermeneutic understanding of reality" represents a middle course between a conservative sociological (and legal) positivism, on one hand, and a radical moral relativism, on the other – *uncritical* extremes that undoubtedly characterized some Realist positions.

Assuming that Horwitz is right, the enduring contribution of Realist thought would be a *critical* theory of jurisprudence that acknowledges the need to balance or integrate competing legal paradigms and interpretative perspectives in a manner that does justice to the discursive ideal of impartiality, as Habermas himself understands it. This view differs from the neo-pragmatism and postmodernism informing CLS, which typically stresses the radical incommensurability of paradigms and perspectives and therewith the impossibility of rendering them equal justice.

In what follows, I will show that the problem of competing paradigms (formalist versus substantivist, liberal versus corporate-welfare) emerged in American jurisprudence in roughly the same way it emerged in German jurisprudence. I will then argue that Realists responded to this crisis in two radically different ways. The first wave of Realists did so by affirming a connection between law and morality; Progressive Realists held that judges had a duty to reconcile competing paradigms and points of view in a way that fairly represented a full range of popular beliefs and sentiments. The second wave of Realists, by contrast, denied any connection between law and morality. Having gained ascendancy during the New Deal, they encouraged wide judicial and administrative discretion in interpreting and applying laws in light of value-free science.

The crisis of Legal Formalism

During the latter half of the nineteenth century, Anglo-American jurists like Christopher C. Langdell used arguments similar to those found in Kant and Hegel to make property, contract, and tort law more predictable and transparent by immunizing it against the dual uncertainties of common law litigation and democratic politics.[18] Their aim was to transform law into a neutral, deductive science on par with natural science.

In step with this academic form of legal formalism was another, less politically neutral, variety. Indelibly etched into American jurisprudence by the likes of A.V. Dicey, the Vinerian Professor of Law at Oxford, this view held that "the rule of law" (an expression first coined by Dicey), depends upon securing the "rational" and "impartial" justice of laissez-faire capitalism against political incursions by administrators acting in the name of democratic majorities.[19] To American jurists schooled in the Madisonian precept, expounded in *The Federalist Papers* (no. 10), that "the most common and durable source of factions has been the various and unequal distributions of property," Dicey's admonition recalled a familiar theme: the need to preserve the "natural" sanctity of private property against tyrannical attempts to redistribute wealth for the sake of the social good.

Theoretically, scientific and economic formalism are distinct; in practice, however, they were closely linked. Scientific formalism sought to immunize the rule of law against changes emanating from the external pressures of a dynamic social reality; its resistance to pragmatic, consequentialist forms of reasoning was of a piece with its conservativism. Formal legal reasoning relied upon tight categorical distinctions between different areas of law and different legal concepts. For instance, the rules and principles of contract law were reduced to "will"; those of tort law to "negligence"; etc. Most important, principles of private law were regarded as "natural," "rational," and "unchanging," as distinct from the fluctuating political imperatives informing public law. The net effect of categorical reasoning was to eliminate conflicts between different principles and rules of law, thereby circumventing any need for balancing "differences of degree" by appeal to consequences.

Categorical reasoning also involved distinguishing between formal procedures and substantive outcomes, processes and consequences, rights and remedies, proximate causes and remote causes, etc. In contract law, for example, formalism required that all agreements entered into voluntarily (as objectively evidenced by signed oaths demonstrating a "meeting of minds") be upheld as valid, regardless of any substantive impact on third parties. Following this procedural model, substantive inequalities in bargaining strength between wealthy employers and their employees were as irrelevant in determining the voluntariness of agreements as were considerations of moral unconscionability in determining their justice.[20]

Besides categorical thinking, formal jurisprudence relied upon generalization; purifying legal categories of anomalies and other extrinsic elements went hand in hand with reducing diverse technical rules to unifying general principles. Ironically, the desire to reduce different rules of law to more unitary principles exposed a fundamental contradiction within formalist reasoning: by analogically stretching the conceptual boundaries of rules and categories held to be conceptually distinct, it weakened the coherence of the system and paved the way for extra-legal criticism of a pragmatic nature. For example, with the emergence of the stock market, the need to "analogically" extend "physicalist" conceptions of property to include market values and future expectations of income became increasingly urgent; however, it also led to the notion that any government regulation of a business that decreased its profitability amounted to a "taking" that required "compensation." Not only was government prevented from taxing income, it could not even regulate the very monopolies whose conduct threatened the freedom and income of smaller competitors and consumers.

Legal Realists had little difficulty exposing the absurdities of formalist reasoning on issues like regulation and taxation. Their general strategy, however, involved attacking formalist reasoning on philosophical as well as pragmatic grounds. Arguing philosophically, they denied that uniquely determined decisions could be derived from indeterminate propositions of a general nature. In the famous words of Justice Oliver Wendell Holmes Jr., whom they frequently cited, "General propositions do not decide cases."[21] A similar philosophical objection was leveled against common law analogical reasoning. Recall that formalist jurisprudence was constrained to extend "physicalist" conceptions of property to include such non-physical things as "market value." This extension was made possible by use of analogy. Appealing to Lockean conceptions of natural law, formalists held that anything that someone had invested with value was private property; by analogy, anything that others were willing to pay for had (market) value; therefore, anything created by a private party that anyone was willing to pay for was private property. Using this analogy, formalists could argue that any government regulation that impeded the unhampered ability of businesses to increase their future market value – whether it be the imposition of occupational safety codes, minimum wages standards, anti-trust laws, or even income taxes – amounted to a kind of "taking," or divestiture of private property that required equal compensation by the government. Realists countered that such abstract analogizing was but a fallacious subterfuge for masking partisan, pro-business sentiments behind the facade of rational neutrality.[22]

Realists also objected to formalist jurisprudence on pragmatic grounds. To begin with, the complexity of new corporate capitalism generated new conceptions of corporate property and ownership that effected profound changes in contract and tort law. On the old model, stockholders were business partners who shared equal liability and equal powers of decision-making; on the new model they were investors whose liability and decision-making powers were limited. On the old model, employees were "agents" or "servants" assumed to carry out the will of their "masters"; on the new model, they were masses of factory workers, whose connection with management was often impersonal and indirect. On the old model, the terms and effects of simple, face-to-face transactions between local proprietors of small, family-owned farms and businesses were relatively transparent and determinate; on the new model, the terms and effects of complex, impersonal transactions – involving multiple parties (stockholders, managers, financiers, middlemen, subcontractors, employees, etc.) operating gigantic enterprises with offices, markets, and suppliers spanning the globe – were anything but transparent and determinate.

The growing complexity of corporate capitalism thus meant that the transparency of the terms and the determinacy of the effects of legal agreements that had been naively presupposed by classical formalists were becoming even less representative of social reality than they had once been. The emergence of trusts and monopolies threatened to constrain the freedom of consumers and business proprietors in ways that had never been imagined; the capacity of large businesses to employ at will and for whatever wage (and under whatever condition of employment) masses of desperate workers (many of them newly arrived immigrants) threatened to constrain the freedom of workers to enter into mutually advantageous contracts. Finally, the enormous wealth generated by corporate capital created new inequalities between rich and poor, powerful and powerless, that threatened to explode the liberal-democratic basis underlying the legitimacy of law generally.

What formalists denied – and what Realists affirmed – was the emergence of a new legal paradigm that now competed with the old. With its individualistic, natural law assumptions, the older, liberal paradigm was being superseded – at least in part – by a newer, corporate-welfare paradigm. The classical liberal invocation of a hard distinction between private and public law was abandoned along with the view that private law rested on reasons that were *privately intuitable or monologically deducible*. Once legal reasoning was regarded like any other rational inquiry or deliberative process, it made more sense to think of it as *social* activity open to public, democratic participation. But public reason did not obviously favor any legal paradigm. The problem of competing rules and standards that had always challenged the formalist pretense of mechanically deducing the *one* rule that necessarily applied in any given hard case was now being exponentially magnified by the emergence of new rules and standards. Resolving on which paradigm, standard, or rule best applied to a given case would be a matter for public, not private, reasoning.

It would be presumptuous to infer from their critique of the elitist, intuitionist nature of formalist legal reasoning that all Realists embraced a dialogic, Habermasian solution to the problem of judicial decision. Because most of them believed that classical liberal and corporate-welfare paradigms competed with if not contradicted one another, they held that in any given hard case, the two would likely be equally relevant, if not equally compelling given the circumstances of the case. In cases where neither was more compelling than the other – a situation that at least some Realists countenanced – the choice would be left entirely to the judge's discretion, based upon "hunches." However, the deliberative process leading to this determination would have involved, Realists maintained, a consideration of many factors – legal precedents, social values, moral standards, sociological facts, statutory aims, etc. – in an effort to find the rule or standard that best fit the case.

The question arises whether and to what extent Realists understood pragmatic jurisprudence to be principled, or guided by "predictable" standards of impartiality. Horwitz remarks that Realists adopted a "particularistic" jurisprudence that led their detractors to accuse them of being unprincipled nominalists and casuists. Defending Realists against this charge, he notes that particularistic jurisprudence involved not rejecting but grounding general legal concepts in real social practices that in turn lent these concepts contextually diverse significations and applications.[23] Of course, excessive dependence on customary practices and standards can degenerate into an unprincipled contextualism and relativism – traces of which can certainly be found in Realist literature. However, a cursory examination of some of that literature will show, I believe, that many Realists understood the process of judicial reasoning to be guided by principles of impartiality in a manner not so different from Habermas.

To begin with, Progressive Realists differed from contemporary neo-pragmatists and postmodernists in embracing relatively robust conceptions of truth, reason, and moral justice. For many, Dewey's pragmatic "logic of inquiry" provided the proper antidote to sterile, deductive conceptions of reasoning.[24] In "Logical method and law" (1924), Dewey accepted Holmes's rejection of formalist reasoning, but took partial exception to his view that "the life of the law has not been logic: it has been experience."[25] In Dewey's opinion, legal deliberation possesses a pragmatic logic, or procedure, that distinguishes it from the formal logic of legal exposition. Whereas the latter involves rationalizing conclusions already obtained, the former involves reasoning to conclusions not yet obtained, conclusions that function as responses to problems embedded in indeterminate and uncertain situations. Legal certainty and stability, Dewey notes, is indeed a legitimate aim of pragmatic inquiry. But the logic of legal inquiry, which aims at "adjusting disputed issues in behalf of the public and enduring interest," is "a logic *relative to consequences rather than antecedents*," an "intellectual survey, analysis, and insight into the factors of the situation to be dealt with."[26]

For Dewey, the logic of inquiry designates a general procedure of reasoning common to all areas of practical conduct. In law, its "collectivistic character" is determined by the overall guiding aim of "social justice." Thus, one could say that justice and "collective intelligence" are as integral to reasoning on Dewey's account as on Habermas's. In Dewey's words, "Everything discovered belongs to the community of workers ... Every new idea and theory has to be submitted to this community for confirmation and test."[27]

Dewey concludes this meditation on rational inquiry by summarily observing that "scientific thought is experimental as well as intrinsically communicative." Progressive Realists were inclined to agree with him. Citing Dewey's insistence on experimentalism, Jerome Frank, one of the leading Realists of his day, insisted that a fearless devotion to truth was necessary for criticizing the belief in "infallible law." At the same time, he criticized as "anarchic" the refusal to acknowledge as conditionally "fixed and settled" some "rules" (or "temporary absolutes").[28]

Progressive Realists were emphatic that among these absolutes was a commitment to impartiality. Arguing that "a judge ... would err if he were to impose upon a community as a rule of life his own idiosyncrasies of conduct and belief," Benjamin Cardozo noted that

> One of the most fundamental social interests is that law shall be uniform and impartial ... There shall be symmetrical development, consistently with history or custom when history or custom has been the motivating force, or the chief one, in giving shape to existing rules, and with logic and philosophy when the motive power has been theirs ... The social interest served by symmetry or certainty must then be balanced against the social interest served by equity and fairness or other elements of social welfare.[29]

Cardozo's opinion that the judge's impartiality in balancing social interests stems "from life itself," *just as the legislator gets it*, anticipates Dewey's conviction that technical decision-making needs to be opened up to democratic participation. Other Realists were more explicit in drawing this conclusion. Commenting on the fact that "our social experience is limited to one class of people though we must govern all classes," Herman Oliphant warned judges against relying on their own experience and knowledge. "Socialized jurisprudence," as he understood it, would require a procedure of consultation, both with science and with all those affected by a decision.[30] Felix S. Cohen was even more explicit. Rejecting the "intuitionist" view that judges simply act on personal "hunches" in deciding hard cases, he observed that the "realistic judge"

> will frankly assess the conflicting human values that are opposed in every controversy, appraise the social importance of the precedents to which each claim appeals [and] open the courtroom to all evidence that will bring light to this delicate practical task of social adjustment ... It is more useful to analyze a judicial "hunch" in terms of the continued impact of a judge's study of precedents, his conversations with associates, his reading of newspapers, and his recollections of college courses, than in strictly physiological terms.[31]

The Realists' reconstruction of judicial reasoning as an impartial process of reconciling or balancing different perspectives, values, and interests through open and public "conversations" with scientific experts, affected parties, and the broader community was also reflected in their reconstruction of fundamental legal categories such as "rights." Critics like Ronald Dworkin often charge Realists with dispensing with rights, or subordinating rights to welfare-maximizing policies. This criticism is overreaching and reveals the inadequacy of Dworkin's own conception of legal coherence.[32] Realists replaced the older, *rationalist* or *natural law* theory of rights with a *relational* one. Following the lead of Oliver Wendell Holmes and Wesley Hohfeld, they regarded rights as essentially legally enforceable social duties, a view that Habermas himself accepts with minor qualification.[33]

What follows from this view is that rights are properly conceived as outcomes of democratic processes in which ethical and consequentialist reasons supplement moral ones. Admittedly, this means that any strong distinction between rights and welfare maximizing policies will be weakened. The same applies to the adjudication of conflicting rights, where resolution follows the weighing of many factors, among them the public's interest. This infusion of politics into law need not jeopardize the impartiality and integrity of de facto rights, so long as processes of legislation, adjudication, and execution abide by just procedures.

The consequences of pragmatism

I have argued that many Progressive Realists endorsed a model of impartial judicial reasoning that converges with the discourse-ethical proceduralist model defended by Habermas. But later Realists did not, and for two related reasons. The first reason has to do with their particularistic method of legal reasoning. Progressive Realists did not provide a systematic reconstruction of the procedural ideals underlying their theory and practice. Their hostility to Enlightenment rationalism and to over-generalizing formalism, both of which they perceived to be an ideological mask for libertarian individualism, partly explains this neglect. It may be, as Bruce Ackerman remarks, that the political instability surrounding the New Deal in the years leading up to and following its inception also made it less risky to simply reinterpret older common law categories pragmatically on a case-by-case basis – for instance, by simply extending the older doctrine of contractual consideration suitably qualified by new ideas of unconscionability and equality in bargaining power – than to synthesize that older tradition of liberal thought with newer regulatory and political forms of law associated with democratic-welfare paradigm.[34] However, absent any rational construction of a liberal social-democratic paradigm, their emphasis on impartially weighing different values, interests, and perspectives all too easily evolved into a kind of relativistic intuitionism that, somewhat paradoxically, worked to conserve a reactionary (common law-based) liberalism. Hostility to normative theorizing, in turn, provided a pretext for conceiving Realism as a non-moral sociology of law. Karl Llewellyn, who along with Jerome Frank first coined the expression "Legal Realism," accordingly conceived Realist jurisprudence as a value-free "technology" divorced from political ideals of any sort. Notably, some Realists – most prominently Lon Fuller – understood well the reactionary implications of this turn to social science, which, far from bracketing values, actually ended up letting "the Ought acquiesce in the Is, let[ting] law surrender to life."[35] Unfortunately, Fuller's Critical Realism would soon be forgotten. As Horwitz ruefully notes, because Llewellyn's famous list of Realists[36] tended to exclude Progressive Realists like Fuller who did not share his narrow, sociological positivism, subsequent commentators (including Habermas) have generally overlooked the idealism of early Realist thought.[37]

The second reason why later Realists did not endorse a participatory model of judicial reasoning is related to the first. The advent of the New Deal suddenly catapulted Realists from being outside critics to being inside administrators. The need to justify technical expertise and decision-making in the face of a recalcitrant court obviously favored the positivistic – not the critical – brand of Realism. Here again, the positivistic assumption of value relativism combined with scientific hubris fed the appetite of uncritical interest aggregation and public welfare maximization that would later become the hallmark of the conservative Law and Economics Movement.[38]

The new breed of Realism, exemplified in James Landis's *The Administrative Process* (1938), sought to justify administrative social engineering by questioning the classical separation of powers doctrine. The older, "delegation" model assumed that administrators simply discover the most efficient means for implementing clearly defined legislative ends. The model accurately described the functioning of the Interstate Commerce Commission (1887), which had in fact been delegated very specific powers. But it did not apply to the Federal Trade Commission (1914), which was given broad power to eliminate unfair competition; and it did not apply to the Securities and Exchange Commission (1933).

Landis's desire to mold American government along the lines of European bureaucracy presumed the general vagueness of social and regulatory mandates as well as the indeterminacy of democratic outcomes. However, in all fairness to Landis, its elevation of administrators to supreme legislators could not have succeeded had the art of administration not been portrayed in democratic rather than decisionistic terms. For confirmation of this fact, we need look no further than President Franklin Roosevelt's own wry comment that "many [in the legal profession] prefer the stately ritual of the courts, in which lawyers play all speaking parts, to the simple procedure of administrative hearings which a client can understand and participate in."[39]

Roosevelt's remark was made on the eve of Realism's decline. By the end of the Second World War, naive faith in the democratic accountability of government administration had fallen into disrepute. The same could also be said of administrative pretensions to scientific impartiality. By the 1960s, claims of professional expertise to truth rang hollow; and even Realists observed with dismay that the experts on regulatory commissions tended to come from or reflect the orientation of the industries being regulated.[40] Such skepticism regarding the competence of scientific expertise in all areas of law would culminate decades later in Foucault's withering critique of the arbitrary normalizing power of social scientific management over all aspects of life.[41] This "juridification" of everyday life (as Habermas and Kirchheimer put it) involves more than the "institutionalization of class conflict through collective bargaining law and labor law, and in general the juristic containment of social conflicts and political struggles."[42]It also involves a "patho-logical" expansion of bureaucratic regulation in areas of everyday life – education, family, health, and welfare – that had formerly been the responsi-bility of free citizens acting in concert with one another.[43]

The positivistic strand of sociological Realism might have withstood this assault on its normative, legal authority had it not been for its relativistic conception of morality. In the aftermath of the Holocaust, older natural law theories seemed to provide a more practical support for rights than conse-quentialist ones. Habermas's procedural account of law, I believe, can be situated within this tradition as well, along with the procedural interpreta-tion of natural law advanced by Lon Fuller, who, as noted above, started out his career as a Realist.[44]

Proceduralism is often seen as providing a less metaphysical and less reductive alternative to natural law theory. However, it is important to note that its capacity to delimit the range of moral relativity is itself rather limited. Take, for instance, the legal process school of law associated with Henry Hart and Albert Sachs. This school conceded relativism in "substan-tive understandings" while affirming moral consensus at the level of institutional procedure.[45] Political theorists from Joseph Schumpeter to Robert Dahl also sought to defend democracy as a system of impartial rules whose process alone bestowed legitimacy on majoritarian outcomes that, in and of themselves, might not conform to substantive standards of justice.[46] Despite the initial promise of equating democracy with something as ideo-logically neutral as the rules of the game governing plural interest group competition, these theorists conceded that impartial procedures could be distorted by substantive bargaining inequalities emanating from civil society. Subsequently, as Horwitz notes, whatever egalitarian content process theories possessed came from incorporating substantive conceptions of justice and value-laden sociological descriptions of majoritarian outcomes that were not conceptually embedded in the procedures themselves.[47]

The normative emptiness of proceduralist theories of law brings to mind the indeterminacy of formalist approaches generally. As Realists noted early on, substantive values reflected in concrete paradigms, not vague normative generalities, are needed to resolve residual problems of indeterminacy, since only determinate, substantively well-defined norms provide meaningful direction and prescriptive force. Indeed, the history of post-war jurispru-dence shows that appeal to procedures (democratic or otherwise) has just as easily served conservative as well as progressive agendas. The debate over group rights, proportional representation, and racial redistricting is particu-larly illustrative of this indeterminacy, with both sides appealing to different paradigms in interpreting the same procedural principles of democratic fair-ness and "equal protection."

Habermas accepts this indeterminacy as the price any procedural theory of law must pay if it is to make good its claim to universal validity. The interesting question, then, is whether the bare idea of impartiality implicit in a procedural theory of law entails any determinate content and, if so, whether it entails it intrinsically (analytically and conceptually) or extrinsically, in conjunction with some value-laden sociology of law. Habermas and Progressive Realists agree that a proceduralist account of law minimally entails participatory demo_racy (extending, perhaps, to the workplace).[48] Are they right about this?

One answer to this question – a mixed one – is provided by John Rawls. In *The Law of Peoples* (1993, revised 1999) Rawls argues that there is nothing intrinsically liberal or democratic about either human rights or the rule of law.[49] Indeed, he seems to suggest that reasonable (or at least not *un*reasonable) peoples inhabiting what he calls "decent consultation hierarchies" might disagree with "us" about the superiority of liberal democracy over less free, less egalitarian forms of corporate polity based upon a "common good conception of justice." At the same time, Rawls is quite emphatic that social science might show that liberal democracies are in fact better at protecting human rights and the rule of law than other forms of polity.[50] And he adds that, from within the political culture of liberal democracies, the concept of human rights and the rule of law are scarcely to be disassociated from liberal democratic values and institutions. Notwithstanding the fact that reasonable citizens inhabiting liberal democracies will endorse liberal democratic values and principles as superior to other values and principles, they should, Rawls insists, tolerate and respect as equals nations governed by principles of basic decency. Not to do so would be unreasonable, because these nations also endorse basic human rights and the rule of law.

While a Progressive Realist might agree with Rawls that the connection between law and liberal democracy is primarily extrinsic and instrumental – at best a coincidence justifiable by appeal to value-laden sociology – Habermas would insist that it is internal, or conceptual. That does not mean that he thinks it impossible to conceive a non-democratic constitutional regime – far from it (*BFN*, p. 78). It does mean, however, that a non-democratic constitutional regime will fall short of the idea implicit in its respect for individual rights. For Habermas, this idea possesses substantive content: the normative ideal of individual self-determination (autonomy) expressed in legal rights could not be consistently respected if individuals did not also freely consent to these rights as products of their own discursive deliberation. In his words, "popular sovereignty and human rights go hand in hand" (*BFN*, p. 127).

Who is right here, Habermas or Rawls and the Realists? In answering this question, let me note that Habermas himself seems to rely more on value-laden sociology, and less on conceptual analysis *strictu sensu*, in making his case for the substantive idea of autonomy informing his defense of liberal democracy. But that idea is by no means universally accepted, even by political sociologists who consider themselves liberal democrats. For instance,

Habermas conceives of autonomy as implying a strong capacity to dissociate oneself from national identities – which, unlike Rawls, he finds to be not only endangered but utterly artificial and ideological divisive. Indeed, it may be argued that the kind of critical reflexivity he imputes to citizens inhabiting liberal democracies is none too congenial to maintaining the integrity of any "cultural life form," let alone a national one. Habermas, of course, would not concur in this radical assessment of his views. But consider his disagreement with Charles Taylor over Quebec's language laws. There he insisted that this particular case of legislating "group rights," designed ostensibly to protect an endangered cultural identity, amounted to infringing the rights of individuals to shape their own identities freely.[51] Even if (as later remarks suggest) this assertion was not intended to cast aspersions on all conceptions of group rights, it certainly rendered them suspect.[52] At the very least, it suggested that either defenders of group rights are deeply confused about their support of liberal democracy or Habermas's idea of autonomy represents a *non*-universalizable "comprehensive" philosophical doctrine, in Rawls's sense of the term.

I mention Habermas's tendency to over-extend (over-generalize) concepts because it mirrors in some respects the kind of over-generalization that Realists found so objectionable about formalism. Does the extension of a discourse-ethical, liberal-democratic conception of law to areas involving international law or judicial decision-making also threaten to dilute its meaning and expose internal tensions? Perhaps. Suppose the conception is extended to the international arena. Assuming that it makes individuals, rather than peoples (or nations), the primary beneficiaries of rights, it would seem to justify the use of at least some international sanctions in coercing nations into granting their citizens democratic rights. This might not seem very fair to decent consultation hierarchies accustomed to viewing themselves as near-equal partners in the international democracy known as the United Nations, but never mind. Suppose our newly created liberal democracies now decide to implement restrictive immigration policies in order to protect their way of life (their self-determination as a constitutional democracy). Such policies could contradict the egalitarian, discourse-ethical demand that capacities for discursive autonomy be fostered in individuals (refugees, economically destitute immigrants, etc.) no matter where they happen to be born.

Does the (over-)extension of a discourse-ethical model to jurisprudence also dilute its meaning and expose internal tensions? Habermas is well aware of the difficulties here. Unlike Socratic dialogue, judges and jurists cannot radically question core elements of law (especially when doing so implies usurping powers of a democratically elected legislature), and paradigm shifts involving radical re-interpretation of the constitutional tradition are hardly exercises in spontaneous deep reflection, generally taking years to work themselves out.[53] Habermas's model is even further weakened when applied to Anglo-American jurisprudence, with its heavy reliance on case law possessing customary rather than statutory (democratic) authority.[54] Again, the adversarial nature of legal proceeding that is especially marked in Anglo-American jurisprudence is no more exemplary of consensus-oriented dialogue than is the agonal discourse of democratic politics. Appearances notwithstanding, Habermas believes that adversarial contests can be effective instruments for revealing the truth and achieving justice so long as judges and counsel exercise vigilance in enforcing gag rules and other procedures designed to ensure impartiality (*BFN*, pp. 235–7). However, most ironically, in Habermas's discourse theory of adjudication, it is not Socratic dialogue or even procedure that ensures impartiality, but a single person (the judge) who is burdened with the lonely task of intuitively "transforming" the multiple perspectives of the various parties into an impartial legal description.

In summation, Habermas's attempt to mitigate the uncertainty of judicial decision-making by appeal to the certainty of discourse-ethical procedure might not succeed to the degree he would like it to; and it might have the unintended consequence of diluting and over-problematizing the procedure's normative-critical content. Habermas is on firmer ground with the Realists when he observes that pragmatic considerations and cultural values determine a particular polity's application and interpretation of basic normative procedures. But he fails to appreciate the extent to which these procedures themselves are a matter of social (and even individual) choice. We all know that the idea of impartiality informing liberal democracy can be represented by different procedural devices. For some, Habermas's discourse ethic captures the consensual, democratic sense of impartiality better than Rawls's various designs of an Original Position (both domestic and international). Others, however, would demur, arguing that these designs are superior to a discourse ethic in establishing the priority of basic rights over goods, including the priority of liberal tolerance over democracy. Which procedure is preferable cannot be answered apart from a pragmatic assessment of social realities. If concerns about international terrorism and peaceful cohabitation among peoples (some of whom not unreasonably prefer a political system incorporating a decent consultation hierarchy) are paramount, then the procedure deployed by Rawls in *The Law of Peoples*, which favors tolerance over democracy, might seem preferable. If the chief concerns are about the helplessness of cosmopolitan individuals in securing – in opposition to the indifference and hostility of their own and other governments – their basic rights to subsistence, freedom, and political self-determination, then the procedure deployed by Habermas (or by Rawls in *A Theory of Justice*) might seem preferable.[55]

This last example suggests that the absence of coherence in modern systems of law – due in part to the increasing complexity of social life at the *domestic* level – will only be exacerbated at the international level.

Confronting a new mass of global complications, interests, and conflicting perspectives, international law will be subject to much higher levels of uncertainty. Under conditions of procedural indeterminacy, international judges and jurists will have to strike a precarious compromise between their utopian principles and the political realities of a dynamic, multicultural globe. This is not a pragmatic argument against principle, but a principled argument for pragmatism. In the words of Horwitz,

> "result oriented" jurisprudence is regularly equated with oppor-
> tunism, and principled jurisprudence with sticking to one's
> principles regardless of consequences. Only pragmatism, with its
> dynamic understanding of the unfolding of principle over time and
> its experimental appreciation of the complex interrelationship
> between law and politics and theory and practice, has stood against
> the static fundamentalism of traditional American conceptions of
> principled jurisprudence ... Until we are able to transcend the
> American fixation with sharply separating law and politics, we will
> continue to fluctuate between the traditional polarities of American
> legal discourse, as each generation continues frantically to hide
> behind unhistorical and abstract universalisms in order to deny,
> even to itself, its own political and moral choice.[56]

Notes

1 From *Law and the Modern Mind* (1930), excerpted in *American Legal Realism*, edited by W.W. Fisher III, M. Horwitz and T.A. Reed, Oxford, Oxford University Press, 1993, pp. 206–7.

2 Jürgen Habermas, *Habermas: Autonomy and Solidarity: Interviews with Jürgen Habermas*, edited by Peter Dews, London, Verso, 1986, p. 151.

3 Following his exposure to Peirce's pragmatism in the early 1960s, Habermas concluded that
> only in an emancipated society, whose members' autonomy and responsi-
> bility had been realized, would communication have developed into the
> non-authoritarian and universally practiced dialogue from which both our
> model of reciprocally constituted ego identity and our idea of true
> consensus are always implicitly derived. To this extent the truth of state-
> ments is based on anticipating the realization of the good life.

(J. Habermas, *Knowledge and Human Interests*, Boston, Beacon Press, 1971, p. 314)

4 *Ibid.* p. 193.

5 Realism evinces a concern with the pragmatic and instrumentalist functions of law in a way that clearly distinguishes it from analytic, historical, and natural law approaches. It is instrumental in its view that legal theory ought to (1) view laws as tools for serving practical ends; (2) explain how laws can be made useful to administrators and public officials; (3) articulate the variety of uses to which law can be put, its legal machinery, etc. It is pragmatic in its reliance upon a distinctly American Pragmatist epistemological and moral tradition that privi-leges empiricism, experimentalism, and values associated with democracy. For further analysis of the uniqueness of Legal Realism *vis-à-vis* natural law, analytic, and historical approaches, see Robert Samuel Summers, *Instrumentalism and*

American Legal Theory, Ithaca, Cornell University Press, 1982, pp. 19–35, 268–81.

6   J. Habermas, *Between Facts and Norms: Contributions to a Discourse Theory of Law and Democracy*, trans. W. Rehg, Cambridge, MA, MIT Press, 1996 (hereafter *BFN*), pp. 200–1.

7   The centerpiece of the New Deal was the National Labor Relations Act of 1935 and far-reaching decisions rendered in such landmark cases as *Carolene Products Co.* (1938), which expressly subordinated market freedoms and property rights to civil liberties and political rights. The democratic vision underlying this sweeping paradigm shift in constitutional law – a vision that included workplace democracy as well as the full political and economic inclusion of racial minorities – is well documented by Karl Klare, "Judicial deradicalization of the Wagner Act and the origins of modern legal consciousness, 1937–41," in A. Hutchinson (ed.) *Critical Legal Studies*, Totowa, NJ, Rowman and Littlefield, 1989, pp. 229–55; and Bruce Ackerman, *We the People, Vol. 1, Foundations*, Cambridge, MA, Harvard University Press, 1991, p. 125. For a more detailed discussion of this paradigm shift, see David Ingram, *Reason, History, and Politics: The Communitarian Grounds of Legitimation in the Modern Age*, Albany, NY, State University of New York Press, 1995, pp. 40–5, 272–6.

8   J. Habermas, "Richard Rorty's pragmatic turn," *On the Pragmatics of Communication*, Cambridge, MA, MIT Press, 1998, pp. 343–82 (especially pp. 356, 359–60, 371–3).

9   Realists frequently commented on the conflicts between legal rules and on the gaps between rules and concrete decisions. These are sources of indeterminacy that CLS scholars would later develop. But while Realists were chiefly preoccupied with the referential vagueness of general statutes – a vagueness that could in principle be reduced by consulting the purposes of lawmakers – CLS scholars focus on the vagueness of more fundamental standards and principles. For example, a Realist would wonder whether a statute that allows capital punishment in cases involving the killing of witnesses applies to anyone killed by a convicted murderer (since anyone killed by a convicted murderer would have been a potential witness, had he or she not been killed). By contrast, a CLS scholar would wonder whether defining "witness" broadly (to include those murdered) or narrowly (to apply only to those already scheduled to testify in court) could be done in a way that was philosophically consistent.

    CLS scholars would also disagree with their Realist counterparts in holding that conflicts between competing rules within a single domain of law are often eliminated in favor of counterbalancing rules situated in two separate domains (thus harsh workfare statutes might be accompanied by lenient tax supplements for the working poor). And CLS scholars would argue that, within a single domain, a well-defined rule (allowing for the death penalty in cases involving aggravated homicide) might be offset by a vague standard (allowing for a reduced sentence in the presence of sufficiently mitigating circumstances). For a classic use of the rules/standards distinction in CLS criticism of tort law, see Duncan Kennedy, "Form and substance in private law litigation," in Hutchinson, pp. 36–55. Also see Habermas's discussion of this essay in *BFN*, p. 216; and my analysis of the same in *Reason, History, and Politics*, pp. 263–5. For a good summary of the differences between Realist and CLS schools of jurisprudence, see Mark Kelman, *A Guide to Critical Legal Studies*, Cambridge, MA, Harvard University Press, 1987, esp. pp. 11–13, 45–9.

10 Habermas presents his model of judicial interpretation as a more pragmatic alternative to that put forward by Dworkin. Dworkin believes that his theory of interpretation responds to Realist and CLS concerns about the indeterminacy of

law. In my opinion, Habermas's theory responds to these concerns more effectively, but only by pragmatically conceding that the indeterminacy postulated by Realist and CLS critics is partly unavoidable given social realities. To begin with, he doubts whether Dworkin's theory of interpretation adequately accounts for the certainty of legal judgments. On Dworkin's account, it seems that every new interpretation of a legal norm would alter the meaning of every other norm within the system. But Habermas also thinks that the kind of certainty and coherence sought by Dworkin may be impossible to achieve. In other words, he concedes that the Realists and CLS critics might be right; given the dynamic multiplicity of perspectives requiring dialogic mediation, the resolution of hard legal cases generally cannot be predicted on the basis of extant law. Cf. R. Dworkin, *Law's Empire*, Cambridge, MA, Harvard University Press, 1986. For a discussion of Habermas's critique of Dworkin in light of the CLS attack on coherence theories of law, see D. Ingram, *Reason, History, and Politics*, ch. 6. These problems with Dworkin's theory of coherence also undermine his critique of legal pragmatism. See Note 32 below.

11 Habermas argues that, due to the "binarily coded" nature of validity claims to rightness and appropriateness in judgment – validity claims that "do not admit of degrees of validity" – judges must assume that a "single appropriate" decision exists in any given case. However, in order for them to assume this they must also *counterfactually* assume (as Klaus Günther puts it) that "all valid norms ultimately constitute an ideal coherent system which gives for each case exactly one right [i.e. appropriate] answer." Cf. K. Günther, "A normative conception of coherence for a discursive theory of legal justification," *Ratio Juris* 2 (1989), p. 163.

12 Habermas's predecessors in the Frankfurt School, Otto Kirchheimer and Franz Neumann, grappled mightily with the contradictory mishmash of older and newer legal forms that characterized the new social state. In general, they sought to counter criticisms of social democracy that had been advanced earlier by Max Weber, who feared that using law for partisan social aims would destroy its formal impartiality. Like Habermas, they insisted that social policy aims could be harmonized with the democratic rule of law without (as Carl Schmitt had argued) requiring the undivided decision of a sovereign Führer as proxy for the unified legislative will of the *Volk*. Cf. Franz Neumann, *The Governance of the Rule of Law* (1936), republished under the title *The Rule of Law: Political Theory and the Legal System in Modern Society*, Leamington Spa, England, Berg, 1986; and Otto Kirchheimer and Franz Neumann, *Social Democracy and the Rule of Law*, edited by Keith Tribe, London, Allen and Unwin, 1987. Those seeking a comprehensive understanding of Neumann's and Kirchheimer's respective legal theories should consult William E. Scheuerman, *Between the Norm and the Exception: The Frankfurt School and the Rule of Law*, Cambridge, MA, MIT Press, 1994.

13 I would like to thank Jennifer Parks for bringing to my attention the degree to which proof of negligence alone, in the absence of any demonstration of causation, has been decisive in some recent tort litigation.

14 Habermas says that "confines of class," "social stratification" and "exploitation" are serious obstacles to realizing equal rights for all (*BFN*, p. 308). More strongly still, he insists that instead of simply continuing "the social welfare project" the "capitalist economic system" must be "restructured" socially and ecologically so as to bring "administrative power" under control (*BFN*, p. 410). For further discussion of Habermas's difficult attempt to reconcile market system and the rule of law, see D. Ingram, "Individual freedom and social equality: Habermas's democratic revolution in the social contractarian

justification of law," *Perspectives on Habermas*, edited by Lewis Hahn, Chicago, Open Court, 2000, pp. 289–307.

15 Karl Llewellyn's view of Realist jurisprudence as a value-free scientific "method" exemplifies this strand of Realist thought better than any other view. Such value-skepticism owes much to the youthful work of Oliver Wendell Holmes Jr, whose attack on the subjectivism and moralism in natural law approaches to tort law in *The Common Law* (1881) ushered in a new, economics- and statistics-based jurisprudence. See K. Llewellyn, "Some realism about realism," in K. Llewellyn, *Jurisprudence: Realism in Theory and Practice*, Chicago, University of Chicago Press, 1962, pp. 55, 72.

16 Progressive Realists like Benjamin Cardozo and John Dewey drew an explicit connection between law and democracy, thereby continuing along the Progressive path charted by Charles Beard and Wesley Hohfeld.

17 M. Horwitz, *The Transformation of American Law, 1870–1960*, Oxford, Oxford University Press, 1992, p. 182.

18 Continuing through the middle of the nineteenth century, American law still relied on the system of common law writs, or forms of action. This system appealed to remedies provided by the state, and so failed to provide a rational, prepolitical basis for individual property rights of the sort prescribed by Lockean social contract theory (*ibid.* p. 12).

19 A.V. Dicey, *Lectures Introductory to the Study of Law*, Macmillan, 1885.

20 In *Coppage v. Kansas* (1915) Justice Pitney ruled that "yellow dog" contracts prohibiting workers from joining unions were not coercive, since workers were formally free to refuse them. The fact that both parties to such a contract "are not equally unhampered by circumstances" was considered by him to be irrelevant.

21 *Lochner v. New York*, 198 US p. 45; 76 (1905) (Holmes, J., dissenting).

22 The clash between formalist and Realist views on the matter of analogical reasoning came before the Supreme Court in the case of *International News Service v. Associated Press* (1918), in which the Associated Press sought to enjoin a newly organized competitor from "stealing" news. Reasoning analogically for the majority, Justice Pitney (a proponent of classical formalism) upheld the injunction on the grounds that news was a *quasi*-property whose protected status pre-empted statutory limits. Dissenting, Justice Luis D. Brandeis argued that such analogical reasoning was both fallacious and politically obstructionist (in this case, curtailing "the free use of knowledge and ideas") when extended beyond very simple cases, *Int'l News Service v. Associated Press*, pp. 250, 262–3, 267 (Brandeis dissenting) US 215 (1918).

23 W.W. Fischer *et al.* (eds) *American Legal Realism*, Oxford, Oxford University Press, 1993, p. 166ff.

24 Dewey's other seminal writings on law include: "Austin's theory of sovereignty," *Political Science Quarterly*, 9 [1894], p. 31; and "My philosophy of law," in *My Philosophy of Law: Credos of Sixteen American Scholars*, edited by the Julius Rosenthal Foundation, Northwestern University, Boston, Boston Law Book Co., 1941.

25 Oliver Wendell Holmes, Jr, *The Common Law*, Cambridge, MA, Harvard University Press, 1963, p. 5.

26 J. Dewey, "Logical method and law," in *American Legal Realism*, edited by W.W. Fischer III, M.J. Horwitz, and T.A. Reed, Oxford, Oxford University Press, 1993, pp. 189, 193.

27 J. Dewey, *Individualism Old and New*, New York, Capricorn Books, 1962, pp. 154–5.

28 J. Frank, *Law and the Modern Mind*, excerpted in *American Legal Realism*, pp. 207, 211.

29 B. Cardozo, *The Nature of the Judicial Process*, excerpted in *American Legal Realism*, pp. 176–7.

30 H. Oliphant, "A return to *stare decisis*" (1928), excerpted in *American Legal Pragmatism*, pp. 200–1.

31 F.S. Cohen, "Transcendental nonsense and the functional approach" (1935), excerpted in *American Legal Realism*, pp. 222–3.

32 R. Dworkin, *Law's Empire*, Cambridge, MA, Harvard University Press, 1986, p. 152. Dworkin concedes that legal pragmatists might defer to rights and precedents in justifying their decisions, but not because rights and precedents have some "force and ground" independent of the future welfare of the community. In short, pragmatists would not value "consistency" and "coherence" for its own sake (p. 162). In response to Dworkin, it could be noted that pragmatists would likely find adherence to principles of consistency and coherence very valuable indeed, but not because these principles possessed justification independent of their instrumentality in increasing public welfare. Dworkin's defense of an unconditional adherence to consistency (integrity), however, is deeply problematic. If being consistent is compatible with rejecting legal precedents that contradict more fundamental moral principles (as Dworkin says it is), then we must ask what makes these principles valid – utility or some *a priori* concept of associative community (rooted perhaps, as Habermas would say, in the pragmatic universals of communication)? Pragmatists could embrace Habermas's pragmatic universals as instrumental for problem-solving (thereby advancing human welfare), which explains why many of them rejected precedents (upholding racial discrimination, unrestricted market freedom, etc.) that were inconsistent with the notion of inclusive participatory democracy. Dworkin's view, however, requires not only that decisions comport with the practice of democracy – of allowing all voices to be fairly expressed and perspectives to be fairly represented – but it requires that they comport with the substantive moral and legal traditions of the community, as well. These two conceptions of coherence do not always cohere; and as Habermas notes, the latter conception not only elevates tradition over democratic self-determination, but paradoxically entails that each new application (interpretation) of a legal norm alters the fundamental identity of the legal system as a whole (as by a "ripple effect"), thereby rendering the meaning of law radically volatile and indeterminate, even to the point of interrupting its continuity with past law (*BFN*, p. 219). For a discussion of the "ripple effect" paradox, see H.J. Kress, "Legal reasoning and coherence theories: Dworkin's rights thesis, retroactivity, and the linear order of decisions," *California Law Review* 72, pp. 369–402 (1984).

33 Habermas explicitly endorses a relational view of rights. He also notes that legally enforceable rights impose duties of forbearance. However, while moral rights explicitly imply reciprocal duties, legal rights do not. Instead, legal rights take the form of permissions, or social entitlements that do not obligate citizens to act in any way beyond desisting from rights violations. Cf. J. Habermas (1996), p. 425; *The Inclusion of the Other: Studies in Political Theory*, Cambridge, MA, MIT Press, 1998, p. 256.

34 B. Ackerman, *Reconstructing American Law*, Cambridge, MA, Harvard University Press, 1984, pp. 15–18.

35 L. Fuller, "American Legal Realism," 82 *University of Pennsylvania Law Review*, p. 461 (1934).

36 K. Llewellyn, "Some realism about realism" (1931) in *Jurisprudence*, pp. 41–76. Llewellyn's famous list of twenty Realists (including Jerome Frank, Arthur L.

Corbin, Hessel Yntema, Herman Oliphant, Walter Wheeler Cook, William O. Douglas, and Charles Clark) is perhaps more notable for its glaring omissions. These included post-formalist and Progressive legal scholars (Oliver Wendell Holmes, John Chapman Gray, Roscoe Pound, Louis D. Brandeis, Benjamin Cardozo, Wesley Hohfeld, Learned Hand, and Harlan Fiske Stone) and philosophers (John Dewey, Morris Cohen, and his son, Felix). See Horwitz (1992), pp. 182–3.

37 Habermas cites (*BFN*, p. 538, n. 11) Summers (*op. cit.*) as the main secondary source for his description of Legal Realism (aside from a few fleeting references to Dewey and Fuller, he does not cite any primary sources). Although Summers' assessment is balanced (like Horwitz, he emphasizes the connection between Realism and social-democratic Progressivism), he concludes – somewhat unfairly, in my opinion – that Realists neglected the normative character of law, insisted on separating law and morals, "and failed to see major differences between legal and machine technologies" (pp. 278–9). This over-emphasis on the positivistic and instrumentalist side of Realism may reflect Summer's heavy reliance on Llewellyn's doctrinal writings, which are hardly typical of the Realist tradition.

38 Some of the most familiar names associated with the Chicago School of Jurisprudence are Ronald Coase, Richard Posner, and Guido Calabresi. While the Law and Economics approach extends the model of the contract in dealing with torts and other legal problems (for instance, by hypothetically viewing a harm as the outcome of both parties' failure to negotiate the relative costs of pre-emptive action), the Realist approach limits and undermines it. I leave open the question whether cost–benefit legal analysis might function to support progressive legal intervention rather than reactive non-intervention.

39 Franklin D. Roosevelt, veto of Walter–Logan Bill (86 Cong. Rec. 13, pp. 942–3 [1940]). Cited by Horwitz (1992), p. 231.

40 Horwitz (1992), pp. 133–246. In a 1960 report commissioned by President-Elect John F. Kennedy, no less a spokesperson for administrative lawmaking than James Landis himself noted with dismay that regulative agencies had developed a tendency toward "industry orientation … frequently expressed in terms that the regulates have become the regulators" (J. Landis, *Report on Regulatory Agencies to the President-Elect* 70 [G.P.O. 1960]). Another example of a supporter of administrative lawmaking turned critic is Louis Jaffe, who by 1954 had concluded that "expertise" had trumped the "rule of law" and that scientific "rationalism" had served as a mask for advancing the "self-interest" of private industry against democratic customs and the "fragile bonds of society." See L. Jaffe, "The effective limits of the administrative process," 67 *Harvard Law Review*, 1113, pp. 1129–30; and "The judicial universe of Mr. Justice Frankfurter," 62 *Harvard Law Review*, pp. 410–11 (1949).

41 M. Foucault, *Discipline and Punish: The Birth of the Prison*, New York, Pantheon, 1979.

42 Kirchheimer and Neumann were as repulsed by the anarchic implications of Schmitt's "decisionism" as by its anti-liberal and anti-democratic tenor. However, it was with considerable irony that they conceded Schmitt's thesis that the corporate-welfare state contains its class conflicts by instituting a dictatorial "decisionism" all its own. Liberal democracies must call upon judges and executive officers to resolve legislative gridlock born of uncompromising class conflict. Indeed, masking partisan legislation behind the facade of vague and general statutes forces judges and executive officers to act as lawmakers. Kirchheimer and Neumann's diagnosis of the implicit dictatorial decisionism implicit in the corporate-welfare state undoubtedly influenced Habermas's earlier ground-breaking studies, *The Structural Transformation of the Public Sphere* (1962) and

Legitimation Crisis (1973). In these works Habermas held that the corporate welfare state was indeed pulled in opposite directions, diverting vast resources to maintaining economic growth *and* compensating the victims of such growth. Institutionalizing class compromise rather than simple capitalist hegemony, the corporate welfare state cannot afford the destabilizing and delegitimating effects of exposing its contradictions – which to opposing factions appear as injustices – to open political debate. It prefers instead to mask its social laws in the mantle of "public interest" compromises, which in truth are neither in the public interest nor in the spirit of genuine compromise. Circumventing the public debate in which truly public (generalizable) interests are discussed and (absent consensus on such interests) truly equitable compromises are reached, public interest litigation (for example, adjudicating labor disputes of public concern in private civil courts) increasingly becomes a matter of arbitrary judicial discretion rather than legitimate democratic resolution. For Habermas, public interest litigation is symptomatic of the "refeudalization" and "depoliticization" of the corporate-welfare state. By encouraging deference to techno-experts and other non-elected administrative authorities in solving political problems ("technology and science as ideology"), the corporate-welfare state politicizes and personalizes legal decision-making in a way that is both undemocratic and partisan. Cf. F. Neumann, *Behemoth: The Structure and Practice of National Socialism: 1933–1944*, London, Oxford University Press, 1944, pp. 10–11, 166–9, 397–8, 468–9, 522–3; O. Kirchheimer, "Changes in the structure of political compromise" (1941), reprinted in *The Essential Frankfurt School Reader*, edited by A. Arato and E. Gebhardt, New York, Continuum, 1982, pp. 49–70; J. Habermas, *The Structural Transformation of the Public Sphere: An Inquiry into a Category of Bourgeois Society*, Cambridge, MA, 1989, pp. 141–52; *Legitimation Crisis*, Boston, Beacon Press, 1975, especially pp. 63ff., 111ff.; and J. Habermas, "Technology and ideology as science," in *Critical Theory: The Essential Readings*, edited by D. Ingram and J. Simon, New York, Paragon House, 1991, pp. 117–45.

43 J. Habermas, *The Theory of Communicative Action: Vol. II. Lifeworld and System: A Critique of Functionalist Reason*, Boston, Beacon Press, 1987, p. 357; and *BFN*, pp. 410–18. Like Foucault, Habermas alludes to the way in which social scientific and legal discourses conspire to pre-define the needs, identities, and rights of specific classes of persons, such as women. For his discussion of feminist legal theory as a test-case for a discourse-ethical conception of law, see *BFN*, pp. 418–27.

44 Fuller's Realist proclivities are especially evident in his demonstration – regarded by Horwitz (1992, p. 184) as "the single most influential piece of Realist doctrinal work" – that contract remedies are determined by norms inscribed in market institutions and social-juridical policies and not by "rights," be these understood as flowing from the subjective "wills" of contractors or the objective nature of the contract. (L.L. Fuller and William R. Perdue, "The reliance interest in contract damages" [1936–7], excerpted in Fischer *et al.* (1993), pp. 88–97.) Fuller's "procedural" turn is reflected in his Realist belief that legal theory must concern itself with procedures that are both moral and efficacious. See L. Fuller, *The Morality of Law*, New Haven, Yale University Press, 1964, pp. 96–7.

45 H. Hart and A. Sachs, *The Legal Process*, Cambridge, MA, Harvard University Press, 1958.

46 J. Schumpeter, *Capitalism, Socialism, and Democracy*, New York, Harper, 1942; and Robert Dahl, *A Preface to Democratic Theory*, Chicago, University of Chicago Press, 1956.

47 Horwitz (1992), pp. 253–8.

48 Among Realists, Dewey was the most eloquent defender of workplace democracy, as were the principal authors of the National Labor Relations Board Act of
1935. In contrast to some of his earlier dismissive comments about workplace
democracy, Habermas now concedes that models of market socialism "pick up
the correct idea of retaining a market economy's effective steering effects and
impulses without at the same time accepting the negative consequences of a
systemically reproduced unequal distribution of 'bads' and 'goods'" (J.
Habermas, "A conversation about questions of political theory," in *A Berlin
Republic. Writings on Germany*, trans. S. Randall, Lincoln, NB, University of
Nebraska Press, 1997, pp. 141–2). Cf. Karl E. Klare (*op. cit.*), pp. 229–55; and
David Ingram, "Individual freedom and social equality: Habermas's democratic
revolution in the social contractarian justification of law," in *Perspectives on
Habermas (op. cit.)*.

49 J. Rawls, *The Law of Peoples*, Cambridge, MA, Harvard University Press, 1999,
p. 78ff.

50 *Ibid* p. 75, n. 16.

51 J. Habermas, "Struggles for recognition in the democratic constitutional state,"
in J. Habermas, *The Inclusion of the Other: Studies in Political Theory*, Cambridge,
MA, MIT Press, 1998, p. 222.

52 Among the "difference sensitive" strategies he finds appropriate for including
cultural minorities and other subgroups within liberal democratic governance,
Habermas mentions a "federalist delegation of powers, a functionally specified
transfer or decentralization of state competencies, above all guarantees of cultural
autonomy, group-specific rights, compensatory policies, and other arrangements
for effectively protecting minorities" (Habermas, 1998, pp. 145–6). However,
his seemingly inconsistent endorsement of group rights for purposes of
protecting cultural autonomy should not mislead us into thinking that he still
believes in the strong integrity of what Will Kymlicka calls "societal cultures" or
that he privileges group-specific rights over individual rights; for, in the final
analysis, he affirms Kymlicka's own liberal view that the individual, not the
group, "remains the bearer of 'rights of cultural membership'" (p. 221).

53 Cf. B. Ackerman (1991); and D. Ingram (1995), pp. 40–1, 272–6.

54 Cf. Catherine Kemp, "Habermas among the Americans: some reflections on the
common law," 76 *University of Denver Law Review*, pp. 961–75 (1999).

55 Habermas would doubtless find Rawls's elevation of "peoples" as the primary
subjects of international law both mistaken (for Habermas, only individuals
possess rights) and *unrealistic*. In his opinion, Rawls's focus on peoples fails to
appreciate the extent to which global exchanges (migrations of capital and
labor) have undermined the sovereignty and cultural integrity of nation states,
while rendering *individuals* all the more vulnerable to depredations by multina-
tional corporations. Governments slash social expenditures and downsize
bureaucracies in order to meet the draconian conditions set by financial clearing
houses like the World Bank and the International Monetary Fund. If there is
any solution to the ecological damage, social unrest and violence unleashed by
the resulting inequality, it must begin, Habermas avers, not with the enforce-
ment of a weakly qualified principle of toleration, but with the establishment of
a cosmopolitan federation of democratic republics. For further discussion of how
the disagreement between Rawls and Habermas over immigration rights,
economic redistribution, etc., reflects differing conceptions of reasonableness, cf.
David Ingram, "Rawls and Habermas on the law of peoples," in *Nationalism,
Nation States, and Supranational Organizations*, edited by Michel Seymour,
Montreal, McGill University Press, forthcoming.

56 Horwitz (1992), pp. 271–2.

6

THE PROBLEM OF CONSTITUTIONAL INTERPRETIVE DISAGREEMENT

Can "discourses of application" help?

Frank I. Michelman

Introduction

In contemporary constitutional democracies, disagreements arise over applications of constitutional principles and guarantees. I mean *interpretive* disagreements, over the meanings (or senses) disclosed in constitutional-legal norms – or is it acquired by them? – as and when the norms are brought to bear on major classes of actions or events; for example, the norm of equality of citizenship being brought to bear on a government's use of "affirmative action." I mean, moreover, deep-seated disagreements, which no one expects really to abate in the face of rulings by official bodies such as constitutional courts.

Such disagreements can be reasonable on all sides. We have to face the fact that, in modern constitutional democracies, "reasonable pluralism" encompasses disagreement not only over comprehensive ethical and metaphysical views,[1] but further, and relatedly, over major questions of constitutional interpretation and application. Few, I believe, would deny the existence of this further general fact of reasonable constitutional-interpretive disagreement, a consequence of what John Rawls calls "burdens of judgment."[2]

Now, this fact would appear to threaten havoc for a certain mode of contemporary thought about the justification of the state's coercive power in a constitutional democracy. I call this mode of thought "constitutional contractarian," and among its notable expositors I include Jürgen Habermas, Charles Larmore, and John Rawls.[3] Constitutional contractarians cannot easily deal with the idea that the most basic constitutional norms *themselves* go up for grabs in disputes over their applications to cases or major classes of cases. For reasons I canvass below, we feel a need to say, along with Habermas, that disagreements over application are only about the best interpretations of "*the same* constitutional rights and principles."[4] This sense of need, I will suggest, springs from the seeming inability of basic constitutional principles, basic principles "of justice," to do the work assigned to them by constitutional contractarian thought, unless those principles are conceived as constant and fixed on their own level, safe above the fray of eruptive disagreement on the subordinate level of interpretation, of application.

The trouble is that it's not clear how a social norm can be known, identified, or discriminated, completely prior to and independent of its applications. In what I think we may fairly call a pragmatist view, social norms – no doubt, as we'll see, including positive-legal norms – are always under (re)construction. Participants in a public normative practice, such as law is, interminably reshape and reconfigure the schemes of norms they work with.[5] Moreover they do so precisely in and by their daily courses of decisions about what is here and now to be done, rendered in the specific, action-demanding settings of what we call norm-application. Pragmatism thus attacks our grip on the idea of the priority of norms to decisions – on the idea, that is, that prior agreement on the contents of the applicable norms is what grounds or determines whatever agreements we may find we have about the resolutions of particular social disputes or classes of disputes. As opposed, I mean, to the idea that the roots of such action agreements lie in shared tacit knowledge emergent from a shared form of life. Pragmatism leaves it unclear what the nominal norms – the nominal "principles of justice," for example – can possibly ever be or have been but traces of their applications to date and reflections, as such, of an infra-cognitive, historically contingent fund of cultural experience.

In the second and third parts of this chapter, using for illustration the political liberalism of John Rawls, I lay out in some detail the trouble caused for constitutional contractarian thought by the pragmatist claim of a constructive reciprocity between a normative principle's identity and its applications. Thereafter, I begin – assuredly I do not complete – the work of finding out whether and how this trouble may stalk a philosopher whom legal theorists readily identify with pragmatism, namely Jürgen Habermas.[6]

I get started with this in the fourth section, "Professor Günther's argument', where I take a laboriously close look at Klaus Günther's proposal to understand legal decision-making in a way that might be thought to avoid the trouble pragmatism makes for constitutional contractarianism. I make no claim that Professor Günther meant his proposal to avoid this particular trouble, and I conclude that it does not do so. But Günther here is a stand-in for Habermas, insomuch as Habermas expressly adopts and extensively incorporates Günther's argument in a way that could be read – although, again, it need not be – as offering the *Habermasian* response to the trouble pragmatism makes for constitutional contractarian thought.

Of course, there's no reason thus to construe Habermas's appropriation of

Günther, unless it's correct to associate Habermas with constitutional contractarianism. I have explained elsewhere why I do so.[7] In this space, I can only briefly – in the fifth section, "Habermas at last" – sketch my grounds for thinking that Habermas faces much the same sort of trouble as Rawls does from the pragmatist view of the rule/application relation. I find Habermas looking to Günther's proposal for some help with this trouble. I ask whether Habermas deviates from Günther in some way that improves the chances that help can be found there, and I answer that he does not. I do not attempt to say whether a cogent response to the troubles exists or may be found elsewhere in the work of Habermas.

Constitutional contractarian political justification

The basics

By "political justification," we may understand the justification of regimes and practices of positive legal ordering. As Habermas teaches, the question of political justification arises coevally with both the differentiation of abstract morality from ethical substance and the differentiation of enacted law from both. From the standpoint of political governors who presume to *enact* rules and principles of conduct *into* "positive" laws backed by threats of social force, the question is how it possibly may be right, among supposedly free and equal persons, to employ forcible means for ensuring average compliance with dictates laid down by nonconsensual, institutional acts and events. Speaking specifically of a democracy, the problem is to explain how "citizens [may] by their vote properly exercise ... coercive political power over one another."[8] From the reciprocal standpoint of those to whom the laws are directed, the question is that of how and on what conditions it may possibly be that any of us, alert as supposedly we are both to political equality and to ethical difference, could come freely to comply with institutionally enacted laws. The problem is to explain to ourselves how *other* people's exercises of *their* shares of political power may be rendered "justifiable to [*us*] as free and equal."[9]

John Rawls supplies an answer to these questions that he calls the liberal principle of legitimacy:

> Our ... political power is ... justifiable [to others as free and equal] ... when it is exercised in accordance with a constitution the essentials of which all citizens may be expected to endorse in the light of principles and ideals acceptable to them as reasonable and rational.[10]

In this claim about political justification, we can distinguish three key components of the sort of approach to this question that I call constitutional contractarian. They are as follows:

First key component: rational universalism   At the core of the constitutional contractarian approach to the justification of political coercion stands insistence on the normative primacy – that is, as objects of moral concern – of notionally free and equal individuals. Hence the demand that potentially coercive political acts be acceptable from the standpoints of *each* (not "all," in some collectivized sense of "all") of countless persons among whom rational conflicts of interest and vision abound. Constitutional contractarianism begins with the idea that exercises of political power are most surely justified when every affected, competently reasoning individual can approve them as in line with his or her own actual balance of reasons and interests.[11] The intersubjectivist inflection given that idea by Habermas – "a law," proposes Habermas, "is valid in the moral sense when it could be accepted by everybody from the perspective of each individual"[12]– only confirms the idea's insistent, radical, normative–individualist inspiration.

Second key component: civility   In order to have any practical bite, the rational-universalist test for the justification of laws must be one of hypothetical, not actual agreement, and so it is. It calls only for the consonance of the laws with reasons everyone *is considered* to have (by whoever applies the test). The test, as Habermas says, is one of "acceptability," not acceptance.[13] But of course it's still pie-in-the-sky to talk even about hypothetical-rational – much less actual – universal agreement to all of the laws of any contemporary constitutional democracy.

That fact doubtless helps explain why constitutional contractarians build counterfactual motivational suppositions into their justificational tests. Thus, in Rawls's formulation, political coercion is justified when its exercise accords with a constitutional regime that all may be expected to endorse in the light of principles and ideals acceptable to them not only "as rational" but also "as reasonable." "Reasonable," there, means imbued with the spirit of reciprocity, of recognition of others as free and equal – that they are free as you are, or are trying to be, your equals in having lives of their own to live and ideas of their own about how to live them.[14]

In an important way, the assumption of universal reasonableness loosens the rational-universalist test of political justification. A *reasonable* person stands ready to accept the laws as long as (a) she sees everyone else generally supporting and complying with them, and (b) she sees how the laws conform to a set of ideals and principles that merit mutual acceptance by a competently reasoning group of persons, all of whom desire, and suppose each other all to desire, to find and abide by fair terms of social cooperation in conditions of deep and enduring but reasonable disagreement over questions of the good.[15]

Third key component: constitutional essentialism   In modern societies, it seems beyond imagining that every discrete act of lawmaking could plausibly be portrayed as passing a universalization test, even where it is only a loosened test of hypothetical rational acceptability to the counterfactually reasonable. It seems that even such a loosened contractarian standard of political justification can only be meant for application to *constitutional* laws – the subset of laws that fundamentally shape, organize, and limit the country's lawmaking *system*, or what lawyers would call its proper-sense legal constitution.[16] Constitutional contractarian political justification rests upon the idea that the rational acceptability to you, as reasonable, of the constitutional system in force is tantamount to the rational acceptability to you, as reasonable, of the laws that issue from the system – including those particular laws with which you rationally and (but for the rational-reasonable acceptability to you of the lawmaking system) reasonably disagree.[17] That, after all, is the point of Rawls's claim that exercises of political coercion are justifiable insofar as they accord with "*a constitution*, the essentials of which all citizens may be expected to endorse." But what is Rawls doing with that phrase, "the essentials of which?"

Sufficient, legitimating constitutional agreements

As a first step towards an answer, let us introduce the idea of a *sufficient, legitimating constitutional agreement*. Four terms compose this idea, as follows:

First, what is supposed to be "legitimated" (in the sense of justified morally) by this agreement is *politics*, the coercive exercise of collective political power, through lawmaking, by and among citizens considered as individually free and equal.

Second, what is supposed to have the desired legitimating effect is *agreement* by each person affected. Not, however, actual agreement but counterfactual agreement – the "acceptability" of the political practice among persons affected by it, envisioning those persons not only as rational but also as reasonable.

Third, the legitimating counterfactual agreement is a *constitutional* agreement. We don't apply the universal-reasonable acceptability test to each and every specific law that crops up in a country's politics. We rather apply it to the country's system for lawmaking.

Lastly, then, "sufficiency." In order to meet the counterfactual test of rational acceptability to every reasonable person, a lawmaking system has to include a principle or guarantee affecting every topic for which a rational person, responding reasonably, would demand a guarantee as a condition of willing support for the system as a whole. For present purposes – and here I depart a little from Rawls's usage of the term – we may say that the set of "constitutional essentials" is equivalent to the set of minimally required principles and guarantees. The set must be extensive enough to compose a system for political decision-making about which every affected, reasonable person can rationally say: "A system measuring up to these principles and terms – all of them – is sufficiently regardful of my and everyone's interests and status as free and equal persons that I ought in all reason to support it and its legislative products, provided everyone else does."

It is of the utmost importance to our inquiry that the idea of constitutional essentials has a negative or limiting as well as a positive or demanding side. In a constitutional contractarian perspective, a constituted system can be over-full, in the sense that it can include some principle or mandate, the inclusion of which has the effect of *making* the system *not* reasonably acceptable to everyone. (As an appropriately controversial example, consider the inclusion in a constitution of a principle flatly prohibiting race-conscious government action, for any reason, under any circumstances, ever.)[18] When it comes to drawing up the list of constitutional essentials, false positives are no less fatal than false negatives to the project of constitutional contractarian political justification. A contractarian essential constitution, while it mustn't be too sparse, mustn't be too distended either.

The pragmatist challenge to constitutional contractarian thought

Of course, that doesn't yet mean that no supposed constitutional agreement can possibly pass contractarian muster. "Enough but not too much" is not, in the abstract, a logically unsatisfiable sort of demand. But let us add the two suppositions that (1) reasonable constitutional-interpretive pluralism is true, and (2) norms are not cleanly separable from their applications. It does then become hard to see how any set of essential constitutional provisions can satisfy the demand *in the way supposed to confer legitimacy on the politics conducted "under" that set of constitutional provisions.*

Constitutional principles and their applications

Cases arise – common and important cases – in which nominal constitutional *principles* that no one reasonably can reject seem to lack *applications* that no one reasonably can reject.[19] Here is an example. A constitutional system, presumably, is not rationally acceptable to everyone who is reasonable – the "agreement" is not a "sufficient" one – if it lacks a guarantee of full and equal freedom of conscience. The principle of full and equal freedom of conscience is, we may assume, one that everyone endorses as a constitutional essential. Unfortunately, members of society do have severe disagreements about the *application* of equal liberty of conscience to some common and undoubtedly major classes of situations. These include demands for taxpayer support of private religious schools (perhaps even if not of private schools generally) when there are state-funded secular schools open to everyone, and also demands for exemptions for religiously motivated acts from laws – such as health laws and zoning laws – that everyone can find burdensome but most people (it is widely believed) simply must be required to obey, for the general good of society.

To some members of society, it appears that equal liberty of conscience requires accommodations of both these kinds to religious needs. To others, it appears, to the contrary, that such special concessions to religion directly violate either equal freedom of conscience or some other, adjacent constitutional essential such as equal citizenship. It doesn't seem that either side is prepared to write off the other as insincere or obtuse. Yet their views are mutually incompatible. Both cannot prevail.

Imagine, now, that one or the other of these contradictory views is expressly written down in the constitution. Suppose it is the prohibitory, no-accommodation view. Is the constituted system now rationally and reasonably acceptable to everyone, in light of interests and concerns they may have as free and equal persons? Alternatively, suppose it is the mandatory, pro-accommodation view that gets specifically constitutionalized. Would we *then* still be sure the constituted system was rationally acceptable to every reasonable person?

What we're looking at is the possibility that *neither* a principle broadly requiring accommodation *nor* one broadly prohibiting accommodation can be a contractarian constitutional essential. Of course, this doesn't mean that *some* quite incisive principle of equal liberty of conscience can't still be a constitutional essential. Everyone may still agree that a universally reasonably acceptable constitution has to bar laws that expressly or intentionally punish, ban, or stigmatize people for religious confession as such, or that wantonly target religiously motivated activities for prohibition.

Such laws may fall within a universally agreed "central range of application," as John Rawls calls it, of equal liberty of conscience.[20] But the question of special accommodation for religion apparently does not. That question, it seems, may be one that a constitution cannot decide, either way, if it hopes to pass the universal-reasonable acceptability test.

How devastating is all this to the hope that *some* constitution might pass the test? To get started toward an answer, let us contemplate a constitutional system with no Bill of Rights guarantees beyond the truly uncontested cores of the liberal verities. Cores, I mean, so confined that they cannot be said to be violated either by state funding of religious schools *or* by refusal of such funding; by laws instituting affirmative action *or* by laws prohibiting it; by laws protecting a landlord's freedom to refuse to rent to unmarried or same-sex couples, or a downtown club's freedom to refuse membership to women, *or* by laws abolishing those freedoms. We're accustomed to think of all these laws as true grist for the constitutional-legal mill, as raising issues of validity that are already, in principle, decided by the law of the Constitution, waiting to be applied. But the issues raised by these laws all lie outside the uncontested central ranges of the basic liberties, and they would be left undecided by the "thin" constitution we are now envisioning.[21] Under that constitution, judges could not properly pretend to decide such issues as matters of constitutional law. Decision would be left, then, to ordinary legislative action – or, conceivably, to judicial action, but with everyone understanding that there is no right answer insomuch as diametrically opposite judicial judgments (or "applications") could both be constitutionally proper.

The question is whether a constitutional system with such a constricted set of Bill of Rights guarantees could possibly warrant every reasonable and rational person's agreement to abide by its legislative outcomes. To answer, we'd have to figure out whether some people have rationally cognizable interests of such import as to make it *not* reasonable to ask them to commit to a system that, for example, leaves all issues about accommodating religion to be resolved by future politics with no constitutional guarantees either way. So there is the question. Can a constitutional system professing no guarantees beyond the goes-without-saying central ranges of the core-liberal basic liberties be sufficient as a legitimating constitutional agreement?

A pragmatist construction of the problem

I want now to restate the same question as pragmatists might be inclined to see it. From the standpoint of constitutional contractarian political justification, there are always two alternative ways to describe debates over constitutional interpretation that arise in contexts of application. We can see them as debates over which of two or more competing "senses" are the ones really, already, "in" the items in a set of canonical normative propositions, where the set is already securely certified as a sufficient, legitimating constitutional agreement. Or we can see them as debates over *which* of the contesting, application-dependent senses *will render* this set of propositional items into a sufficient, legitimating constitutional agreement. An obvious problem with the first view is its puzzling implication – given the fact of reasonable interpretive pluralism[22] – that an ostensible, essential constitution's rational acceptability to the reasonable can somehow be known without knowledge of how major disagreements over the senses of its guarantees will be resolved in practice, when push comes to shove. And yet it seems that *only* by adopting the first view could anyone, at any given point in time, purport to judge that any given political regime is justified.[23] It seems, then, that the possibility of constitutional contractarian justification depends on citizens being able credibly to see debates over constitutional interpretation according to the first, counter-intuitive view, the one that allows a constitutional-essential item to be judged rationally acceptable to the reasonable *before* anyone knows what senses that item is going to acquire at the business end when brought to bear on major classes of cases of high ethical, political, or ideological salience.

Remember, now, how it is that constitutional essentialism becomes a key component in contractarian political justification. Seeing that we cannot hope to justify each discrete political act against a standard of universal reasonable-and-rational acceptability, we hope instead to justify by that standard a set of abstract, framing principles and ideals for a lawmaking system. But the difficulty, obnoxiously, seems to reappear at the point where the relatively abstract framing principles have to be applied to decide the legal validity of major policy choices. It is in those major-issue contexts that, in constitutional contractarian frame of mind, we become aware of the awkwardness of maintaining that a constitutional norm such as full and equal freedom of conscience remains invariant – remains one and the same norm – under reasonably contesting major applications of it (no accommodation versus required accommodation). It is an awareness that threatens disaster to the proposed constitutional contractarian justification of politics. For how can the justification succeed, if it turns out that the constitutional principles and ideals to which every rational and reasonable person could plausibly be said to owe agreement are just forms of words papering over unresolved and deeply divisive, but undeniably reasonable, political–moral *dis*agreements?

Are we seeing, here, why Habermas has to insist that constitutional-interpretive debates "are always about the best interpretation of the same constitutional rights and principles?"[24] Is Habermas so close to constitutional contractarian thought? Is his point that only on this perception of the persisting "sameness" of the constitutional essentials – their invariance under contesting major interpretations – that the constitutional essentials can play their pivotal role in constitutional contractarian political justification?

The pragmatist worry extended: public reason

Reasonable interpretive pluralism poses the following question to constitutional contractarian modes of political justification: *How can intelligent citizens possibly decide to approve, as rationally acceptable to all who are reasonable, an essential constitutional agreement so much of the actual content of which at the business end they cannot know, until after the Supreme Court or other powers that be will have finished ruling on a never-ending stream of major, contested, issues of constitutional interpretation?* Our assumption to this point has been that the question is unanswerable, but perhaps it is not.

Here is the form of a possible response. It may be true that no one can know, before the questions are decided either politically or judicially, whether or how the set of constitutional principles and guarantees will be applied to the matter of exempting churches from zoning restrictions, or to that of state-funded education vouchers redeemable at private religious schools. But what we *can* perhaps know beforehand is something about the spirit or terms in which such matters will be addressed, and *that* knowledge – it may be suggested – can thicken the constitutional system enough for it to merit universal reasonable acceptance. We can know, at least, that the right questions will be sincerely posed and pursued.[25] Nor should we forget about those central ranges of application of the basic liberties on which we *can* posit universal, reasonable-and-rational, substantive agreement. And the hope, then, is that the sum-total result is an essential constitution that a rational and reasonable person can still treat as a sufficient, legitimating constitutional agreement – or, in other words, can say about it something like this: a system for further lawmaking that I can see conforming, in practice, to the substance *and also the spirit* of this (sparse as the substance is), is a system that I can and in all reason ought to sign up with. The constraint of public reason – the guarantee that the right questions, at least, will be posed and sincerely debated – itself becomes one of the constitutional essentials.[26]

But the pragmatist insight is not yet at bay. The insight, it seems, leaves us no more securely able to know or say what questions practitioners are asking or debating without seeing what responses they are giving, than to know or say what principles practitioners are applying without seeing what applications they are making. If the principles are but traces of the applications made of them, then, by the same token, the questions are but traces of the responses forthcoming to them. The pragmatist critique would thus deprive constitutional contractarian thought of everything it meant to gain by introducing the idea of sincerely debatable, universally acceptable "right questions" (alias public reason) to supplement the idea of objectively applicable, universally acceptable directive principles (alias central rages of basic liberties).

Constitutional contractarians hope to fill out a sufficient and legitimating constitutional agreement with a guarantee that, for all lawmaking that raises issues affecting the basic structure of society but falling outside the obvious central ranges of the basic liberal guarantees, resolution will be sought only through sincere debate addressed to some universally acceptable right question or questions. According to John Rawls, for example, such a question will often be that of which resolution of the controverted lawmaking issue is the more conducive to the end of the adequate and full development and exercise by every person of the two moral powers of the reasonable and the rational.[27] It is in service to that same end, of course, that the universally rational and reasonable constitution must guarantee the central ranges of the basic liberties.[28] Exactly how are the two guarantees – the substantive central-ranges guarantee and the procedural public-reason guarantee – supposed to work together? The answer, it appears, lies in the relative tightness and looseness of the two guarantees. The "tight" central-ranges guarantee is relatively strong in *decisiveness* of application but correspondingly restricted in *scope* of application.[29] The "loose" public-reason guarantee extends to a much wider range of politically decidable matters, but at the cost of allowing in much more reasonable disagreement about what is to be done. The idea, surely, is to use the looser guarantee to supplement the tighter one, in hopes of combining them to produce, in sum, a sufficient, legitimating constitutional agreement.

It follows that, however loose a constraint we may suppose public reason's right questions to exert on public decision-making, we must suppose them to exert *some* constraint. The ideal of public reason cannot play its intended role in constitutional contractarian political justification, except on the supposition that citizens actually can see the constraint of public reason in force, in action. Citizens must be able actually to observe and verify the guiding effects on debate and resolution of lawmaking issues of everyone's posing the right questions.[30] Merely *nominally* guaranteed constraints on debate and decision can no more contribute toward establishing a constituted lawmaking order's rational acceptability to a reasonable person than can any other merely nominally guaranteed constitutional essential.

And now we face the question: how can any given constraint on debate and decision be observed to be really in effect unless that question is conceived (or "felt") to have its existence and content fixed prior to and independent of the debates and decisions in question? But this very possibility is the one thrown into doubt by pragmatism – which thus seems poised, again, to deny to the constitutional contractarian conception of the possibility of political justification what it seemingly cannot do without.

Professor Günther's argument

Klaus Günther's essay, "A normative conception of coherence for a discursive theory of legal justification,"[31] might be read as an offer to supply the constitutional contractarian conception with what it needs. Günther's undertaking is to explain how a set of "norms" (which could be a set of constitutional-legal guarantees) can both and simultaneously (1) be "valid in the sense of discourse theory"[32] (which looks close enough, for our purposes, to being rationally acceptable to every reasonable person, because it means such as all possibly affected persons could agree to in rational discourses[33]) and (2) "give one appropriate answer in every case"[34] (which looks close enough to being susceptible of publicly noticeable and verifiable application). Günther's claim is that legal practice has a way of bridging the apparent gap between the discourse-theoretic *validation* of norms, as correspondent to universal or generalizable interests, and the attribution of senses to those norms at the point of *application* to a contested case.

"Perfect norms"

To validate a norm discursively is to show that it would be found in a rational discourse to "represent a universal interest."[35] This is not hard to understand. Consider the norms enjoining promise-keeping and aiding neighbors in distress. They both evidently represent universal or generalizable interests, for it seems everyone has at every moment an interest both in the reliability of promises and in the availability of emergency aid. The problem for the objectivity and transparency of application of these abstract norms in an actual normative practice arises precisely because of the undoubted validity of them both, along with countless others equally abstract and all prone, by virtue of this very abstractness, to collide with each other in contexts of application.

Now *this* problem, proposes Günther, would vanish in a counterfactual world of perfect foresight and limitless time on everyone's part to join discourses on validation or "justification." In such a world, "each of the possible cases of application with all its features" could be made the topic of its own validating discourse.[36] As each of these exquisitely detailed cases came up in turn for consideration, any number of correspondingly detailed rules to govern it decisively – I'll call these "micro-rules" – might be passed in review, allowing each participant in the discourse to bring to mind "all the effects" on his and others' interests of having one or another of these candidate micro-rules in effect.[37] No candidate micro-rule could be adopted unless the discourse disclosed no possible situation in which observance of the micro-rule would violate a generalizable interest. Any candidate micro-rule that could pass such a discursive screening would be valid. It would become what Günther calls a "perfect norm." Note that Günther has *not* said that infinite time and foresight would disclose a perfect norm for every specifically detailed context of application – nor could he, without denying reasonable interpretive pluralism, a point I will soon develop. But perfect norms, wherever you *could* find them, would be extremely handy. Being a micro-rule, a perfect norm, Günther says, can perfectly "regulate its own application."[38] He means no case can arise to which the terms of a perfect norm extend at all that is not already, to all intents and purposes, decided by those terms.

Three worries

Günther's argument proceeds from there to suggest how legal practice can adequately mimic perfect-norm adoption. But before going on to see how he does that, I want to pause to ask whether, supposing that legal practice *could* replicate perfect-norm adoption, constitutional contractarians should find in this replication a promise of remedy to doubts cast on their justificatory project by pragmatist denial of the clean separability of norms from their applications. There are three worries.

The first is that no would-be prescription for action can be totally exempt from the pragmatist denial, no matter how exquisitely detailed, rule-like, and apparently formally realizable its content and form. If you take the denial to its limit, there is no possible access to the existence or content of any norm, even a "perfect" one, except by tacit-knowledge reconstruction of it from the experience of its applications. What pragmatists famously deny, after all, is that *any* rule can "regulate its own application."[39] Could Günther be repudiating that?[40]

Not likely. He is treating it, I think quite aptly, as a mere "analytic point about language,"[41] and one that is harmless to a practical project such as constitutional contractarian political justification. What a perfect norm is supposed to represent is the case of an immaterially small gap of thought between the validation of norm-terms and their application;[42] and surely the thought-gap sometimes can be made so small that shared, background culture safely can be relied upon to fill it.

The second worry (allowing for now that the first has been met) would be that Günther does not say – who could dare to say? – how *many* perfect norms could be discursively justified. To speak more finely to the point of constitutional contractarian concern, Günther does not say how *sufficient* would be the coverage of the notional agreement consisting of the total set of discursively validatable perfect norms. He says the number of cases *canvassed* would "coincide with the number of all possible cases of application."[43] He does not say an equivalent number of cases could successfully be *processed* in the sense that *some* discourse-ethically justified perfect norms would certainly be found for them. It seems he could not say so, without, in effect, abolishing the premise that makes our problem interesting, that of obdurate and reasonable constitutional-interpretive disagreement.

But now consider the alternative. The alternative is to leave the resulting total set of perfect norms full of holes at the point of application. It seems the size, shape, and location of the holes would more or less correspond to the size and shape of the society's current, actual cloud of obdurate, reasonable, norm-interpretive disagreement. The holes would be the shadows cast by that particular, empirical, historically contingent cloud. On the level of constitutional guarantees, the holes, it seems, would match the fields of normative dispute left unresolved by the set of uncontested central ranges of the basic liberties. Thus, the set of discursively justified, perfect constitutional norms would, by our prior analysis, leave us still lacking a sufficient, legitimating constitutional agreement.[44]

The third worry follows on the second and echoes the first, but is less easily cabined than the first is. If the set of discursively validatable, perfect constitutional norms leaves us lacking a sufficient, legitimating constitutional agreement, we stand in need of a supplementary public reason guarantee, entailing a set of constitutionally guaranteed right questions.[45] In the nature of the case, discursively justifiable right questions cannot be formed – cannot be "named" – at anything approaching the level of detail – of formal decisiveness – of a perfect norm. The whole point, we found, of falling back on "loose" or "procedural" guarantees – debate-constraining but not decision-determining – is to cover the holes; in other words, to cover those areas for which a sufficient, legitimating constitutional agreement has to give some kind of assurance, but for which no decision-determining guarantee is discursively justifiable. So it cannot be the case with debate-constraining, constitutionally guaranteed right questions, as we may imagine it being the case with decision-determining constitutional guarantees on the order of the central ranges of the basic liberties, that the gap of thought left between justification and application is negligibly small.

Of course, on some views,[46] the gap might not have to be *vanishingly* small, approaching zero as a limit, in order to block out plausible concerns about obdurate, reasonable, social disagreement at the point of application. On some views, how small a gap is required depends on an empirical contingency, namely, that of the depth and extent of the society's actually existent *sittlichkeit* – or, conversely, the depth of its obdurate, experienced-as-reasonable, constitutional-interpretive disagreement. In Habermasian terms, it is only in "post-metaphysical" social conditions that the gap has to be terribly small. *Given* such conditions, though – in other words, granting the fact of reasonable interpretive pluralism – the resulting challenge to constitutional contractarian thought seems clear and formidable. It is to explain how it may be possible for discursively justifiable right questions to be stated with sufficient concreteness to keep the gap small enough to block out the concern, without fudging or reneging on the ostensibly granted fact of reasonable interpretive pluralism.

With our three worries established, we may now proceed with our review of Günther's argument.

The division of labor between discourses on validity and discourses on application

Abstraction at the stage of validation

The point of the counterfactual idea of a perfect norm is to establish the conceptual possibility of norm-statements that are both (1) discourse-ethically validatable and (2) capable of decisive application to any and all cases to which their terms even arguably extend. Professor Günther suggests that legal practice can track this ideal by a certain division of discursive labor, designed to compensate for the hard fact that, at the stage of validation (recognition, adoption) of norms, we are forced by limitations on time and knowledge to deal only in what I will call (although Günther does not) "abstract" (as opposed to "perfect") norms.

Dealing in abstract norms is time- and knowledge-saving because the parties to discourses on validity need refer only to interests that would be infringed by any and all violations of whatever norm is in question, in order to see whether such interests are generalizable.[47] Thus, in considering a proposed abstract norm against promise-breaking, the parties need consider only their correspondingly abstract interests in security of reliance on promises (as distinguished, for example, from their more concrete interests in security of reliance on promises even at the sacrifice of security of reliance on emergency aid, when needed, from others on the scene). If the sheerly abstract interest in security of promises would be discursively found to be an interest that both is perfectly generalizable across persons and always commands *some* weight when a promise stands to be broken, the proposed abstract norm against promise-breaking would be valid.[48] (By contrast, the generalizability of any ranking of security-of-promises against security-of-aid would be much likelier to be a matter of obdurate, experienced-as-reasonable disagreement. Just for starters, different people will, for good reasons, be differentially sensitive to the risk of urgent need of aid from others.)

Obviously, though, the relative ease of reaching agreement on the discourse-ethical validity of abstract as opposed to perfect norms comes at a price, and the price is that no discourse-ethical validation of an abstract norm can certify that norm for controlling, decisive application to any, much less every, concrete case to which its terms extend. On the one hand, our sure foreknowledge of cases of "collision" between the abstractly stated obligations "to keep a promise" and "to help one's neighbor" must not be allowed to defeat recognition of both as valid abstract norms[49] – norms, then, that set incontrovertible, non-evadable premises for *arguments* yet to come over the "singular judgments" called for by concrete cases.[50] On the other hand, the discursive validation of no norm can be allowed to outrun its validating discourse. If cases of collision between proposed norm A and other valid, abstract norms have not yet been laid before the parties to any supposed validating discourse, then A can have as yet received no discourse-ethical validation as controlling for such cases.[51]

Were this the end of Günther's exposition, he'd have succeeded only in showing why, in circumstances of reasonable interpretive disagreement, a discourse-ethical standard of normative validity must result in normative "holes" of the very kind we have anticipated. Using Günther's illustration:

> We are not in any situation in which our neighbor needs our help obliged to keep a promise – and we are not in any situation where we are obliged to keep a promise required to help our neighbor.[52]

But, of course, it's not the end of his exposition. According to Günther, it is possible to close up the holes by persuasive argumentation, at the point of application, over which one or ones of the multiple, prima facie applicable, abstractly validated norms is "appropriately" applicable to the case, to the unavoidable suppression (as regards the case or class of cases in question) of all others with which it collides, but without impugning the validity of the situationally suppressed others.[53]

Appropriateness and coherence

How is legal practice supposed thus to judge the "appropriateness" of the application to a case or class of cases – and, correspondingly, the suppression in that case or class of cases – of particular abstract norms in a plurality of prima facie applicable, valid abstract norms? How can the author of any "singular judgment" in the case possibly respond to questions about why he chose (supposing he did) to decide the case as one under the control of "keep your promises" rather than as one under the control of "help your neighbor in distress," when both those abstract norms are valid and the terms of each extend to the case at hand?[54] Günther's answer is that the author "reach[es] the ideal of a perfect norm reconstructively."[55] The gist of it is this. Members of society labor under limitations of time and foresight. These limitations prevent them from expanding any single discourse on validity to include the anticipation and discussion of all the possible cases of "collision" among all the interests that are generalizable – hence all the norms that are discourse-ethically valid – when stated at the relatively high levels of abstraction that these limitations on time and foresight do permit. Such limitations of foresight and time do not apply to a judge faced with a concrete case that actually has come up. Such a judge, with the aid of precedents and extant professional doctrinal reconstructions,[56] can credibly determine *both* the roster of abstractly generalizable interests (valid abstract norms) at stake in the case *and* the prioritization of them that would have been implicit in the perfect norm – if any – that would have achieved discursive validation had it been possible for a discourse on validation to anticipate and process the case in all its particulars.

Conversely or reciprocally, the judge pronouncing the singular judgment launches both a precedent and a datum for future doctrine-construction. He thus contributes to the rolling production of a "coherent system of all valid norms," and, moreover, to a system that is both discourse-ethically justified and observably in force. (We speak here, of course, of a regulative idea.)[57] In that way, a judicial practice following Günther's model is geared to reaching "reconstructively" the ideal of just the right set and number of perfect norms.[58] It can, for example, expose in due time that "the [discursively justifiable] obligation to keep a promise *never meant* anything other than admitting the priority of the obligation to help one's friend" in distress.

Toward an appraisal

Appraisal of Günther's argument for our purposes must ask: (1) Does the argument take full account of the pragmatist claim of constructive reciprocity between norms and applications or may it fairly be so understood? (2) Insofar as it does or may, does the argument effectively address the apparent problem posed by the claim for constitutional contractarian thought? I am going suggest a "no" answer to the second, crucial question.

Günther calls "the coherent system of all valid norms" an unattainable ideal that we can hope only to approximate.[59] He is not merely noticing the Herculean immensity of the job, the extreme unlikelihood that mere 140-IQ mortals with eighty-year life expectancies could ever finish getting the stables cleaned and straightened. He is talking, too, of a deeper sort of unattainability. He is noticing the ideal's catch-your-shadow indeterminacy, once we've grasped the inevitable practical necessity (mere mortals that we be) to split off the business end of the discursive work from the stage of validation and postpone it to a stage of application. The whole point about the division and postponement of discursive labor is that it allows mere mortals to take up one (or maybe a few) at a time, which is the best we can do, the huge and indefinite number of contexts – "situations" – in which multiple valid abstract norms are prima facie applicable. That is the gain.

The price is Heisenbergian. Every fresh "application" of the system of norms – every fresh "singular judgment" of a situation not theretofore brought to mind – is an alteration of the always unfinished "full description" of the system. Every addition "changes the matrix of the colliding norms."[60] This is *not* Neurath's boat, which remains the same boat even after every last original timber has been replaced many times over. Günther could not be more explicit: "If every valid norm requires a coherent completion with all the other norms which can be applied prima facie to the situation, then the meaning of the norm is changing in every situation."[61]

"We face a situation we could not foresee," writes Günther, and it "forces us to change our interpretation of all the norms we accept as valid."[62] How much closer can you get to an exact distillation of the kind of trouble pragmatism makes for the constitutional contractarian justificatory idea of the sufficient and legitimating constitutional contract? Remember how we put it above? How, we asked, can intelligent citizens possibly decide to approve, as rationally acceptable to all who are reasonable, an essential constitutional contract so much of the actual content of which at the business end they cannot know, until after the Supreme Court or other powers that be will have finished ruling on a never-ending stream of major, contested, issues of constitutional interpretation?[63]

But Günther seems to draw back from the brink. "We are anticipating the end of history," he writes, "with the ideal of a coherent system of all valid norms which allows only one appropriate answer to each situation."[64] My reading: imagine a society's legal officers conducting their affairs in accordance with Günther's model. At whatever point in time we discover them, these officers are fresh from their most recent redoing of the matrix in response to the latest situation to come up. There is, then, no moment at which they cannot face the country and say: "We have in hand, right now, a unified system of norms that provides a unique answer to every last one of the known cases to which its terms extend. You can learn the system by learning the law. What more could you want? *Carpe diem.* The future is not yet." There is, to repeat, no point in time at which the society's legal officers cannot say it – over, and over, and over again.

Is constitutional contractarian thought now off the pragmatist hook? Not that I can see. I don't see how this "end of history" way of looking at things responds to the second or, therefore, to the third of the worries I listed above.[65] The second worry is that a coherent system of all *discourse-ethically validatable* norms cannot amount to a sufficient, legitimating constitutional agreement, if reasonable interpretive pluralism is true. It doesn't help, either, if every norm in the system has the virtue of decisive applicability to each and every situation *to which its terms extend* (i.e. the norms in the system either are "perfect" *ab initio* or are reconstructively re-perfected every day). The problem lies in the limited coverage of the terms of these perfect/perfected, discursively validatable norms. The worry is that there aren't enough of these norms – and can't be, if reasonable interpretive pluralism is true – to cover all the normative space a complete and legitimating constitutional contract has to cover. Günther's "coherent system of all valid norms" seems guaranteed by reasonable interpretive pluralism to leave holes in coverage that render it fatally incomplete for constitutional contractarian purposes.

I can't repeat too often that Professor Günther does not claim otherwise, nor is it incumbent on him to do so. Why, after all, should rock-bottom political justification be any concern of his? Professional legal practice has other important work to do. It is called upon to stabilize expectations and enable social coordination, by trains of decision-making that are foreseeable and, at least to that extent, internally justifiable.[66] These purposes, too, require legal practice somehow to cover the gaps that it seems discourse-ethical validation of norms and norm-complexes must leave uncovered, and Günther offers explanation of how it manages to do so.

Legal practice responds to functional requirements of stabilizing expectations and enabling coordination, Günther writes, by "bring[ing] valid norms into a transitive order where typical cases of collision are interpreted in advance."[67] Unlike ethics, which demands for every case-judgment a full, fresh, on-the-spot reconsideration of the bearing on the case of all valid norms, law extrudes "doctrine," meaning professionally certified, "advance" packagings of "different kinds of argument for the justification of an interpretation." Doctrine, cast in terms of "typical" patterns of collision among valid abstract norms, provides advance decision of cases manifesting such patterns.[68] A legal judgment is professionally correct if it "coincides" with all arguably applicable legal material, including not only statutes but doctrine.[69]

On the scale of formal decisiveness, doctrine stands midway between abstract and perfect norms. If we can call a doctrinal statement a modified perfect norm, we can no less aptly call it a modified abstract norm. It bears, accordingly, its measure of the original vice – lack of decisiveness – that dogs the entire race of abstract norms. "Since," as Günther writes, "we are unable to foresee each case of collision even within a legal system," the law repeatedly confronts situations "where a coherent interpretation of all prima facie applicable norms is possible only by reference to moral principles."[70] In other words, if every day's legal work anticipates history's end, it also repeats history's beginning. For every doctrine, there was a day on which its content had to be "decided" by someone's fresh, direct, original exercise of moral judgment. There is no doctrine that was not itself, on its birthday, the product of an act of interpretation that could have been a matter of obdurate and reasonable social disagreement. Günther knows this. Doctrines – or what he also calls "paradigms" of "transitively ordered and valid norms," geared to typical patterns of collision – "are determined," he says, "by a commonly shared life-form."[71]

So there we have it. In the last analysis, legal practice falls back on shared ethical substance, or at any rate shared ethical pre-understanding, to plug those "gaps of thought," as I called them, that inevitably stand between validations of norm-terms and their applications. Now that could be, in fact, all the law needs for securing its *instrumental* ends of stabilizing expectations and enabling social coordination. It is true, of course, that some inhabitants of any post-metaphysical society will be outsiders to whatever ethical pre-understanding it may be that has infiltrated and integrated that society's legal doctrine. However, these "others" may be few or paltry enough not to upset the apple-cart of legal foreseeability and legally girded stability.[72] Such, indeed, is the law's instrumentalist gamble, as depicted by Günther, and there is nothing in the premise of reasonable interpretive pluralism to rule it out.

The message for us should by now be clear: However instrumentally prudent or safe it may be for the law, no such exclusions of the other are admissible to the discourse of political justification. (Why else is a sufficient, legitimating constitutional agreement the elusive ideal that it is?) Postmetaphysical political justification cannot be even a little bit *sittlich*. On that point, no one has been more insistent than Jürgen Habermas. And the question, then, is how he can be a pragmatist too.

Habermas at last

Habermas as constitutional contractarian

I cannot in this space defend a view of Habermas as constitutional contractarian thinker. I can only summarize, as follows, the views I attribute to him that would render him so:[73]

A regime of positive legal ordering is not morally legitimate unless all of those subject to it may with good reason regard themselves as authors of at least the regime's most basic, framing constitutional principles of individual liberty, equality and civic association, and procedural regularity.[74] Given that the regime *is* one of positive legal ordering, there is only one way in which this may be possible. Those subject to the regime must, at all times, *be able to see already in force* a set of legally established, institutional arrangements that they, as participants in rational discourses, could find apt to the end of ensuring (insofar as institutional arrangements can ensure it) that the essential constitution is at all times subject to democratic-discursive checks for discourse-ethical validity.[75] In other words, the essential legal constitution must be such as to ensure its own exposure to democratic-discursive checks, and these must be, recursively, checks for the property of constituting a set of legal arrangements for the democratic-discursive making and checking of legal arrangements, starting with itself. Such a guarantee must extend beyond laws governing formal political processes. It must extend beyond the standard liberal guarantees of basic private and political liberties. It must cover, as well, the so-called private law that basically structures daily life in civil society.

What results, I think it fairly easily can be seen, is a demand for the equivalent of a sufficient, legitimating constitutional contract, including a constraint of public reason or "constitutional patriotism."[76] If so, then Habermas no less than Rawls needs a response to the pragmatist denial of the priority of norms to their applications. In this chapter, to repeat, I do not ask whether he has one. I ask only whether his appropriation of the argument of Professor Günther supplies the one he needs. We have seen that the argument as presented by Günther himself does not answer to that purpose, whatever other important purposes it may answer to.

Habermas and Günther

Whatever may have been Günther's intention, it seems that Habermas wants to direct the latter's "elegant proposal"[77] to a problem of political justification perceived in terms similar to our own:

> Within [the] sphere of adjudication, the immanent tension in law
> between facticity and validity manifests itself as a tension between

the principle of legal certainty and the claim to a legitimate application of law, i.e., to render correct or right decisions.[78]

Both ... certainty and legitimacy must be ... redeemed ... [in order] to fulfill the socially integrative function of the legal order.[79]

[T]he claim to legitimacy requires decisions that are not only consistent with ... the existing legal system. They are also supposed to be rationally grounded in the matter at issue so that all participants can accept them as rational decisions. Judges decide actual cases within the horizon of a present future, and their opinions claim validity in the light of rules and principles that are here and now accepted as legitimate. To this extent, the justifications must be emancipated from the contingencies of their historical genesis.[80]

If there is (to this point in our reflection) any difference between Habermas and Günther, it is only that Habermas expressly, repeatedly, and roundly rejects any semblance of a *sittlich* foundation for what is after all supposed to be the *universal* and *rational* acceptability of the law.[81] *Reason*, as Habermas says, "must already be at work" in the construction of semi-perfect legal norms such as Günther's "paradigms" or "doctrine."[82] We can call it a strictly procedural reason if we wish,[83] but that just lands us within and not beyond constitutional contractarian thought. It is to say that the acceptability of the law can flow only from a discursively validatable constitutional agreement, at all times visibly established by law, regarding the rights here and now required to set up and maintain a radically democratic political practice.[84]

Apparently standing squarely athwart that possibility is pragmatism. Günther's proposal, other merits aside, apparently offers no way through. I do not say there may not be others.

Notes

1   John Rawls, *Political Liberalism*, New York, Columbia University Press, 1993, pp. 36–7.
2   "Burdens of judgment" encompass sundry causes of obdurate disagreement about justice among persons who, as reasonable, all observe and report honestly, argue cogently, and share a "a desire to honor fair terms of cooperation" (*ibid.* p. 55). Among these causes Rawls lists the likelihood that

> the way we assess evidence and weigh moral and political values is shaped by our total experience, our whole course of life up to now; and our total experiences must always differ. Thus, in a modern society with its numerous offices and positions, its various divisions of labor, its many social groups and their ethnic variety, citizens' total experiences are disparate enough for their judgments to diverge, at least to some degree, on many if not most cases of significant complexity.
>
> (*Ibid.* p. 57)

For exploration of some consequences of the fact of "reasonable interpretive pluralism," see Frank I. Michelman, "Human rights and the limits of constitutional theory," *Ratio Juris* 13 (2000): 63.

3 If it matters, I am strongly drawn to it myself.

4 Jürgen Habermas, "Struggles for recognition in the democratic constitutional state," in Habermas, *The Inclusion of the Other*, edited by Ciaran Cronin and Pablo De Grieff, Cambridge, Mass., MIT Press, 1998, p. 225 (emphasis supplied).

5 For pertinent expression of the pragmatist view I have in mind, we may look to Margaret Jane Radin's study of Ludwig Wittgenstein's view of rules and rule-following, Margaret Jane Radin, "Reconsidering the rule of law," *Boston University Law Review* 69 (1981): 781. Radin surely is correct to associate Wittgenstein's view with the general pragmatist outlook and temper: empiricist, experimentalist, nominalist, social-constructionist, pluralist, particularist, and altogether hostile to the thought that "general propositions" can ever possibly "decide concrete cases." *Lochner v. New York*, 198 US 45, 76 (1905) (Holmes, J., dissenting). (On Holmes's relation to pragmatism, see e.g. Philip Wiener, *Evolution and the Founders of Pragmatism*, Cambridge, Mass., Harvard University Press, 1949.)

6 Richard Posner, for example, treats Habermas's membership in the guild as going almost without saying. See Richard Posner, *Overcoming Law*, Cambridge, Mass., Harvard University Press, 1995, p. xx.

7 See my "Human rights and the limits of constitutional theory," *Ratio Juris* 13 (2000): 63; "Morality, identity, and 'constitutional patriotism,'" *Denver University Law Review* 76 (1999): 1009; and "Democracy and positive liberty," *Boston Review* 21(1996): 3.

8 Rawls, *Political Liberalism*, p. 217.

9 *Ibid.*

10 *Ibid.*

11 To that extent and in that sense, *individualism* remains constitutional contractarianism's quintessential premise. True, as Charles Larmore explains, political liberalism, in a post-Romantic age, has had to cut its ties to "individualist" views about "the ends of life," meaning views that make value dependent entirely on choice after "critical reflection," and not at all on "sentiment of belonging." See Charles Larmore, "The moral basis of political liberalism," *Journal of Philosophy* 96 (1999): 599, 603–5, 623. But as Larmore further explains, what has required this retrenchment of liberalism from individualism in *that* sense is liberalism's own, historic, core commitment to a "principle of respect for persons" (*ibid.* p. 607), to which corresponds an "individual right" of every person "to be bound only by principles whose justification he can rationally accept" (*ibid.* p. 621). "Respect for persons," as Larmore neatly writes, "lies at the heart of political liberalism, not because looking for common ground we find it there, but because it is what impels us to look for common ground at all" (*ibid.* p. 608).

12 Habermas, *Inclusion*, p. 31; see *ibid.* pp. 89–90.

13 See Habermas, *Inclusion*, pp. 95–6. True, Habermas maintains that only the *actual* conduct of a properly structured democratic debate can provide an adequate basis for belief that the arrangements in question do satisfy a test of (hypothetical) universal acceptability, but that is another matter. See *ibid.*; Jürgen Habermas, *Between Facts and Norms: Contributions to a Discourse Theory of Law and Democracy*, Cambridge, Mass., MIT Press, 1996, trans. William Rehg, pp. 296, 448.

14 Cf. Larmore, "Moral basis," pp. 600, 602 ("[R]easonableness for Rawls denotes a moral response to the predicament, the profusion of disagreement about the

human good, that arises from" the disposition of people to "think and convers[e] in good faith, and apply, as best [they] can, the general capacities of reason that pertain to every domain of inquiry").

15 See Rawls, *Political Liberalism*, pp. xliv, xlvi, 226–7; John Rawls, "The idea of public reason revisited," in *Collected Papers*, edited by Samuel Freeman, Cambridge, Mass., Harvard University Press, 1999, pp. 573, 576–9, 581, 605–6.

16 Cf. Larmore, "Moral basis," p. 606, n. 8.

17 See Samuel Freeman, "Original meaning, democratic interpretation and the Constitution," *Philosophy and Public Affairs* 21 (1992), cited approvingly by Rawls, *Political Liberalism*, p. 234, n. 19. Cf. John Rawls, *A Theory of Justice*, Cambridge, Mass., Harvard University Press, 1993, pp. 195–201 (on "the four-stage sequence"). This means that your finding particular ordinary laws unjust gives you no ground for resort to unlawful force, not that it gives you no ground for denunciation, civil disobedience, or conscientious refusal.

18 An essential constitutional agreement may also be over-full in another way, which I do not examine here – that is, by including requirements that defeat the ability of anyone to know that actual practice really does conform to the essential constitutional agreement. For discussion, see Frank I. Michelman, "Rawls on constitutionalism and constitutional law," in Samuel Freeman (ed.) *The Cambridge Companion to John Rawls*, Cambridge, Cambridge University Press, forthcoming.

19 Needless to say, this is not a new discovery. See e.g. Mark Tushnet, "An essay on rights," *Texas Law Review* 62 (1984): 1363.

20 See Rawls, *Political Liberalism*, pp. 295–6.

21 We're envisioning a constitution much like the one contemplated by Mark Tushnet's idea of the "thin" constitution. See Frank I. Michelman, "Populist natural law (reflections on Tushnet's 'thin constitution')", *University of Richmond Law Review* 34 (2000): 461, 462–4, 483–7 (discussing Mark Tushnet, *Taking the Constitution Away From the Courts*, Princeton, Princeton University Press, 1999).

22 See text above, accompanying Note 1.

23 See Frank I. Michelman, "Always under law?" *Constitutional Commentary* 12 (1995): 227, 235–8.

24 Habermas, "Struggles for recognition," p. 134.

25 Before going on, I had better say a word about what it means, in this context, to say we "can know" the spirit or terms in which the body politic or the judiciary will address a question – can know the question will be addressed in the terms and spirit of what Rawls calls both "reciprocity" and "public reason." How, realistically, can we ever feel assured of any such thing?

For Rawls, after all, the notion of public reason often figures as a strictly normative or counterfactual ideal, and one that is potentially highly critical of actual political practice anywhere on earth. His point, then, is that *if* the constraint of public reason is *not*, in fact, sufficiently honored in a given society's actual practice, the liberal principle of legitimacy (see text above, accompanying Note 10) will not be met in that society, and exercises of coercive political power will not, then, in that society, be morally supportable.

But Rawls also explains public reason as what he calls a "realistically utopian" idea. He means that the actual history of constitutional-democratic countries, combined with reasonable psychological and sociological speculation, gives a basis for belief that the public-reason ideal *can* be realized adequately in practice, "taking men as they are and laws as they might be." See John Rawls, *The Law of Peoples*, Cambridge, Mass., Harvard University Press, 1999, pp. 11–13 (quoting Jean-Jacques Rousseau, *The Social Contract*). We have, Rawls argues, a strong enough basis for belief in this possibility to make constitutional contractarianism the best approach to the pursuit of political justice, at least for a society whose political culture already falls generally within the constitutional democratic tradition.

26 Compare Habermas, *Between Facts and Norms*, p. 220:

> Procedural rights guarantee each legal person the claim to a fair procedure that in turn guarantees not certainty of outcome but a discursive clarification of the pertinent facts and legal questions. Thus affected parties can be confident that in procedures issuing in judicial decisions only relevant reasons will be decisive, and not arbitrary ones. If we view existing law as an ideally coherent system of norms, then this *procedure-dependent certainty of law* can satisfy the expectations of a legal community intent on its integrity and oriented toward principles, such that each is guaranteed the rights to which he or she is entitled.

27 See Michelman, "Rawls on constitutionalism."

28 Rawls, *Political Liberalism*, p. 297.

29 See *ibid.* pp. 229, 296.

30 Compare Habermas, *Between Facts and Norms*, p. 116:

> [I]f precisely those norms are valid that deserve the rationally motivated agreement of all under the condition that actual compliance with the norm is *universal*, then no one *can reasonably be expected* to abide by valid norms insofar as this condition is not fulfilled. Each must be able to expect (*erwarten*) that everyone will observe valid norms. Valid norms represent reasonable expectations only if they can be actually enforced against deviant behavior.

31 *Ratio Juris* 2 (1989): 155.

32 See *ibid.* p. 164.

33 See e.g. Habermas, *Between Facts and Norms*, p. 107.

34 See Günther, "Normative conception," p. 164.

35 *Ibid.* p. 156.

36 *Ibid.* p. 156.

37 *Ibid.*

38 *Ibid.*

39 Cf. Radin, "Rule of law," p. 801. Habermas expressly approves this "Aristotelian insight." See *Between Facts and Norms*, p. 198.

40 At one point, Günther apparently demurs to the question whether it is finally possible for "the proponent who defends the applicability of a norm to a situation" to demonstrate an "identity of meaning" between "those expressions included in the norm" and "those included in a description of the case" (*ibid.* pp. 160–1). Elsewhere, though, with a particular case under consideration, he brushes aside any "doubt" about "the identity of meaning between the predicates included in the norm and the description of the case" (*ibid.* p. 162).

41 Radin "Rule of law," p. 801.

42 The idea of a perfect norm "subsume[s] the concept of appropriateness [of application] under the concept of validity" (*ibid.* p. 159).

43 *Ibid.*

44 See "A pragmatic construction of the problem", above.

45 See "The pragmatist worry extended: public reason", above.

46 But see generally Larmore, "Moral basis."

47 "Which consequences and effects will generate from a general following of a rule in circumstances being equal we are normally able to foresee by means of our given knowledge in a limited space of time" (*ibid.* p. 159).

48 "The violated interest can be identified without taking into account the situation in which the participants are. They have only to refer in a reciprocal manner to those effects which are expected to take place in those circumstances which are equal in every case" (*ibid.* p. 157).

49 *Ibid.* p. 158.

50 See *ibid.* pp. 159–60.

51 "In a discourse on validity, we are only able to examine those features of the description of a situation which are *equal* in every case of application. The validity depends only on this examination" (*ibid.* p. 158).

52 *Ibid.*

53 "The validity of a norm does not contain its applicability to every case" (*ibid.* p. 157). See also *ibid.* p. 159.

54 See *ibid.* p. 161.

55 *Ibid.* p. 163. As Günther says, "we attain the idea of a perfect norm *via indirecta.*"

56 See *ibid.* p. 160.

57 "[W]e will never attain to this ideal of a coherent system of all valid norms" (*ibid.* p. 163) which actual legal practice can only "represent" (*ibid.* p. 164).

58 *Ibid.* p. 163.

59 *Ibid.* p. 163.

60 *Ibid.*

61 *Ibid.*

62 *Ibid.*

63 See "The pragmatist worry extended: public reason", above.

64 Günther, "Normative conception," p. 163.

65 See text above, accompanying Notes 43–6.

66 See Günther, "Normative conception," p. 164.

67 *Ibid.*

68 *Ibid.*

69 *Ibid.*

70 *Ibid.* pp. 164–5.

71 *Ibid.* pp. 163–4.

72 Habermas may doubt the possibility of that. See e.g. *Between Facts and Norms*, p. 223 (in order to "guarantee a sufficient measure of legal certainty," a "paradigmatic preunderstanding of law" must be "intersubjectively shared by *all* citizens and express a self-understanding of the legal community as a whole").

73 For fuller treatments, see my "Human rights and the limits of constitutional theory," *Ratio Juris* 13 (2000): 63; "Morality, identity, and 'constitutional patriotism,'" *Denver University Law Review* 76 (1999): 1009; and "Democracy and positive liberty," *Boston Review* 21(1996): 3.

74 See e.g. Habermas, *Between Facts and Norms*, p. 126 ("[As] legal subjects, [the citizens] achieve autonomy only by both understanding themselves as, and acting as, authors of the rights they submit to as addressees").

75 See e.g. *ibid.* pp. 126–7 ("[T]he legal code is given to legal subjects in advance as the only language in which they can express their autonomy. The idea of self-legislation must be realized in the law itself").

76 See Note 31, above; Michelman, "Constitutional patriotism," pp. 1024–8.

77 Habermas, *Between Facts and Norms*, p. 219. At *ibid.* pp. 162, 218–21, 260–1, Habermas restates the proposal in terms departing in no significant respect from Günther's, while quoting from Günther extensively.

78 *Ibid.* p. 197.

79 *Ibid.* p. 198.

80 *Ibid.* pp. 198–9. Compare text above accompanying Notes 64, 65, 70, 71.

81 See e.g. Note 72, above; Habermas, *Between Facts and Norms*, pp. 200, 209 ("In a pluralistic society in which various belief systems compete with each other, ... [w]hat counts for one person as a historically proven topos is for others ideology or sheer prejudice ... [T]he practice of interpretation requires a point of reference beyond settled legal traditions"); *ibid.* p. 223 (a "suspicion of ideology" hangs over every claim of a universally shared "background understanding").

82 *Ibid.* p. 232.

83 See *ibid.*

84 "If we follow a procedural theory, the legitimacy of legal norms is gauged by the rationality of the democratic procedure of political legislation" (*ibid.*). See my articles cited in Note 73.

Part III

LANGUAGE AND
AESTHETIC EXPERIENCE

7

RECONSTRUCTING THE FOURTH DIMENSION

A Deweyan critique of Habermas's conception of communicative action

Lenore Langsdorf

Two tasks of communicative action, dependent upon very different conceptions of communication, can be discerned within our intellectual history. The more valorized conception is of communicative action as a process of representation and transmission. What's implied here is the presence of a given – whether objects, events, or sense-data – that is identified in language. Communicative action's task, then, is accurate representation of that given, in language that can be used in deductive or inductive reasoning toward an epistemic goal. This is an objectivistic orientation, in that it focuses on objects and seeks to minimize, if not dismiss, the influence of communicating subjects upon their knowledge. I identify this orientation as ontological, because it concentrates on the "what" of a situation, investigated as linguistic content that's substantial and static.

Certain epistemic practices follow from this ontological orientation. They are perhaps most evident in a Cartesian method that advocates dividing complex subject matter into its simplest components, or in Russell's (and the early Wittgenstein's) logical atomism. However, I find these practices embedded (most often, tacitly) in contemporary philosophical and everyday beliefs about knowing and the known. In order to provide an accurate portrayal of the known, communication is to use one linguistic designator (symbol) for each object (thing or fact) together with connectives that represent rules for ordering those designators in assertoric sentences that express propositions. Insofar as it serves epistemic ends, then, communication must eschew metaphoric, narrative, poetic, and rhetorical modes of language. These may serve to inspire thought and relate thinkers to one another; but they retard procedures that enable rational justification of beliefs about what is the case; about what objects must be. The assumed or stipulated static and substantial nature of those objects means that certain procedures can accomplish uniformity of belief: Since what there is, ultimately, is one way rather than another, and given that communicating subjects can come to understand that things are one way or another, they can formulate arguments for that one way (or another) and so reach agreement. Coherence among beliefs then suggests correspondence of what's believed with the way things truly are. In other words, uniformity of belief implies that argument has reached the truth of things: has revealed what every knower must believe, if she or he is to avoid being labeled (by the common sense of the community) as irrational.

A pragmatically informed understanding of communication can expand upon this ontologically dominated orientation by taking up the second task of communicative action (or, more broadly conceived, communicative experience), interaction, and the very different conception of communication that it entails. "Pragmatic" here refers either to pragmatism as variously espoused by Dewey, James, Mead, and Peirce, within the tradition often called classical American pragmatism; or, to theories of language and knowing – such as those of Austin, Searle, and Habermas – that focus upon the pragmatic, in contrast to syntactic or semantic functions of language. The former is amenable to a constitutive conception of communication that understands its task as interaction; the latter, to an ontological orientation toward communication that understands its task as representation.

In what follows, I propose using John Dewey's constitutive conception of communication, emphasis upon communicative experience's interactive task, and theory of aesthetic experience, to reconstruct Jürgen Habermas's ontological preoccupation and his related retention of the primacy of an epistemic task that relies upon accurate representation. The great contribution of Habermas's theory of communicative action, I believe, is his recognition that validity claims can be made within four dimensions of communicative action: They can be made about the rightness of normative claims within the context of moral and legal interaction ("'our' moral world"), and about the truthfulness of subjects' expressive claims in relation to their attitudes or intentions ("'my' personal world"), as well as about the truth of propositions about things in the environment ("'the' world of nature").[1] From the very beginning of his attention to communication, a fourth dimension – initially characterized as "language," which makes the validity claim of "comprehension" – lurks about the fringes of these three. It remains unexplicated and relatively ignored, although its character does shift to "aesthetic–practical rationality" and "dramaturgical action" relatively early in the evolution of the theory of communicative action.[2] Habermas's understanding of that category remains within a relatively narrow and traditional sense of "the artistic," and thus is quite different from Dewey's sense of "aesthetic experience." Before turning to exposition of both Habermas and Dewey, and to arguing for the benefit of reconstructing that fourth dimension along lines provided by Dewey's conception of "aesthetic experience," we need to consider the second of the two tasks of communicative experience that I mentioned at the start of these introductory remarks.

142

The second task of communicative experience scarcely is recognized as such in academic as well as everyday reflection – perhaps because its conceptual basis is in such strong opposition to the ontological focus I've described. This second task is dependent upon a conception of communication as constitution – which is to say, as shaping, forming, or crafting the subject-matter that emerges within any communicative event. What communicative experience does, in other words, is bring to presence (for those who participate in that experience) a coherent subject-matter. This is not to deny that communicative experience occurs within an already present cultural, economic, physical, social, and political environment. But it is to say that what communicative experience does is craft that environment in dynamic and even unanticipated ways, rather than transmit it as linguistically represented objects.

This is an interactional, rather than objectivistic, orientation, in that it focuses on how subject-matter emerges in the course of interaction among the multiplicity of diverse vectors and agents engaged in communication. Recognizing the efficacy of communication in performing this task is difficult, I suspect, because to do so we must abandon a deeply embedded and tacitly held assumption: namely, that the environment is furnished with objects that react to one another as a result of external (to those objects) forces. A constitutive (rather than representational) conception of communication, however, explicates objects as the results (rather than the givens) of communicative experience. It therefore focuses on praxeology rather than ontology: on *how* those objects come to be (and cease to be) as they are experienced, rather than on *what* they are, prior to their representation in communicative experience. Thus it can inquire into how things *could be* – rather than limiting its activity to asserting what they *are*. Insofar as that inquiry takes a critical turn, it adds concern for how things *should* be – and even (although problematically) how they *must* be.

Although there are epistemic practices that are useful for discerning constitutive processes at work, they are very different from what our intellectual history certifies as epistemically acceptable. Most commonly, they are ridiculed or denied, if not simply ignored. Although there are many reasons for the recent ascendancy of modes of philosophizing called "analytic" and "Euroamerican" (hermeneutic, phenomenological, or deconstructive), and the correlative low profile of pragmatism, I suspect that classical American pragmatism's failure to supply acceptable (by traditional standards) epistemic practices has been a contributing factor. Rather than argue for alternative epistemic practices here, I want to direct attention to the experience in which knowing happens. Following Dewey, I take this to be communicative engagements with an environment that transform it into objects within a context, rather than representing it as things that can be named in abstraction from their contexts. More particularly, I use Dewey's explication of that mode of experience as the basis for reconstruction of

Habermas's conception of communication. Dewey's label for that mode, "aesthetic," is pervasively troublesome, since the traditional associations of that term as well as its contemporary use in the context of an "aesthetic turn" in philosophy present much the same difficulties that Dewey encountered when he tried to use his inherited philosophical vocabulary (perhaps most notoriously, "experience" and "metaphysics") in new ways that would enable readers to understand what he had discerned.

Yet another disclaimer is needed at the outset: I can offer some description of the constitutive efficacy of what Dewey calls "aesthetic experience." But going beyond description, to recognizing the extent of that efficacy, requires somatic (or at least imaginatively somatic) participation – rather than the distanciated, disengaged, and mentalistic ways of knowing that are traditionally accepted in our intellectual history and current academic setting. There are tasks for which those traditional ways of knowing (loosened from untenable presuppositions inherited from traditions of realism and idealism) are appropriate: We can learn much about the cognitive, moral/legal, and expressive (propositional, sociopolitical, and personal) dimensions of experience that are predominant in Habermas's theory of communicative action by using those more academically acceptable ways of knowing. But the reconstruction of Habermas on communicative action that I want to propose here concerns what his theory does not do – namely, investigate and integrate what I explicate as the fourth dimension of communicative experience – and the consequences of that lack. At the core of this reconstruction is the need for a different conception of knowing than those traditionally accepted ways. In Dewey's language, this is inquiry: knowing in doing, which is quite opposed to distanciated, contemplative knowing. Others speak of "tacit knowing" (Michael Polanyi) or "knowing of a third kind ('from within' conversational situations)" – in addition to "knowing that" and "knowing how" (John Shotter). Perhaps the best term is "performative inquiry," which takes up clues from both Dewey and contemporary performance theory, but discussion of that theme lies beyond the scope of this chapter.[3]

I've introduced this reconstructive proposal by thematizing these two tasks of communication and this additional sense of knowing as inquiry for two reasons that have to do with the nature of the phenomenon. As it turns out, the three domains of communicative action that Habermas theorizes are all primarily involved in the task of representing objects, while the fourth domain that he leaves untheorized is a pre-objective one; a processual, rather than substantive, dimension in which communicative *experience* constitutes the objects of communicative *action*. Furthermore, the nonobjective character of this fourth domain means that inquiry from within situations, rather than knowing as traditionally conceived, is the appropriate epistemic procedure. Most importantly, reconstructing the fourth domain may further our capacities for inquiry into the way things are and could be as the basis for a critical social theory that serves pragmatism's meliorative goals.

In what follows, I summarize Habermas's explication of the domains of communicative action with particular attention to his comments on the fourth domain – now appreciated as a dimension within all communicative experience – against the background of his emphasis on language. I then turn to Dewey's conception of aesthetic experience, and finally, to my proposal that using Dewey's conception enables us to understand how the fourth dimension works. A praxeological (in contrast to epistemic) understanding enables appreciation of the aesthetic dimension as the source of change in the lifeworld, and so increases the value of this reconstructed Habermasian critical theory for meliorative endeavors.

Habermas's theory of communicative action

> What raises us out of nature is the only thing whose nature we can know: language. Through its structure, autonomy and responsibility are posited for us.[4]

> Today the problem of language has replaced the traditional problem of consciousness; the transcendental critique of language supersedes that of consciousness.[5]

> We can think of the lifeworld as represented by a culturally transmitted and linguistically organized stock of interpretive patterns ... Culture [is] those patterns of interpretation transmitted in language ... The contents of tradition persist only in symbolic forms, for the most part in linguistic embodiment.[6]

Jürgen Habermas turned in the early 1970s from the critique of institutions (in continuation of the program of Frankfurt School Critical Theory) to the study of interactions, and more precisely, of linguistic interaction. He theorized the latter in a "formal pragmatics" that investigates the correlation between three types of speech acts and three domains of reality. Although he presents this investigation as a theory of communicative action, I have argued elsewhere that this is a misnomer: Habermas develops, instead, a theory of linguistic action.[7] His theory expands upon traditional accounts of language's representational task in the service of justifying beliefs about physical reality, for it identifies two additional domains of reality – the social and the personal – about which validity claims may also be made. Thus, Habermas's theory is considerably more useful for social theory than are traditional investigations of language use, which focus on that first domain (physical reality). Its representational orientation, however, forbids consideration of how these three domains come to be present. In other words, it adopts the culturally embedded presumption that " 'the' world of external nature" is given to human beings as such, and adds two further givens: " 'our' world of society" and " 'my' world of internal nature." The fourth domain in the theory is "language," which "remains in a peculiar half-transcendence in the performance of our communicative actions and expressions" and so "presents itself to the speaker and the actor (precon-sciously) as a segment of reality sui generis."[8] This domain remains undertheorized throughout the evolution of Habermas's theory of formal pragmatics, although its scope is broadened from the functioning of a communicative medium – and in particular, language – that provides "comprehensibility." The initial separations and relations of these elements are shown most clearly in Table 7.1, which reproduces the table given at the conclusion of Habermas's introduction of formal pragmatics.

Table 7.1 Domains of reality and modes of communication

Domains of reality	Modes of communication		
	Basic attitudes	*Validity claims*	*General functions of speech*
"The" world of external nature	Cognitive: objectivating attitude	Truth	Representation of facts
"Our" world of society	Interactive: conformative attitude	Rightness	Establishment of legitimate interpersonal relations
"My" world of internal nature	Expressive: expressive attitude	Truthfulness	Disclosure of speaker's subjectivity
Language	——	Comprehensibility	——

Source: J. Habermas, "What is universal pragmatics?" p. 68

Three aspects of this conception are particularly important for my recon-struction of the fourth domain. First, this table analyzes "communicative action" which supports understanding (and ultimately, consensus) as strictly separated from Habermas's dispreferred use of language, "strategic action." He characterizes the latter as oriented toward success; toward furthering the goals of a speaker at the expense of reaching consensus on the truth, right-ness, or truthfulness of a speech act. This characterization repeats an ancient pattern: philosophy understands itself as discovering truth (about prelin-guistic things) and upholding it against the inroads of poetic and rhetoric, which use language to discover things hidden (and perhaps concealed) by established usage – and thus, to propose alternative accounts of what truths

146

there might be. Implicit in Habermas's choice to take up philosophy's story of truth is a valorization of disinterested knowledge and neutral language that transmits truth, in contrast to engaged inquiry based upon particular human interests that constitute (form, shape, craft) situations within which truth is emergent. Granted, these interests need to be identified and assessed, and reversing that choice (i.e. recognizing that "strategic" is intrinsic to "communicative" action) entails going beyond Habermas's reliance upon traditional modes of argumentation to search for alternative modes that are inclusive of the diverse convictions that make for dissensus, rather than those aimed at excluding some convictions (arguments that "lose") in order to establish consensus on the truth or rightness of others (arguments that "win").[9]

The thoroughgoing representationalism of Habermas's conception is the second aspect of concern, for it encourages a theory that is unable to appreciate the power of communication to constitute novelty — and especially, to actualize, within a community, possibilities which may have a meliorative effect on the present. This is not to deny that language symbolically represents and transmits patterns of conduct and belief that reinforce the status quo; it is to point to the irony of Habermas's choice to valorize and advocate only this use of language within a critical theory. Although this preference for re-presenting what is given to communicative experience is most evident regarding the cognitive function of language — which is oriented to objects and facts — it is no less present as linguistic action occurs within the other two domains. For Habermas holds that language use is "right" when it conforms to established modes of interpersonal relations; that is, when it re-presents extant social and legal norms. The expressive dimension carries a still more implicit representational burden, for its function is to re-present, to the external and social world, what is already present as the speaker's "subjectivity." This restriction of communication to representation supports Habermas's construal of communicative activity as language use, for it denies communicative status to the many ways in which people (and animals) somatically develop their interaction with their environments (e.g. chronemics, haptics, kinesics, proxemics, and vocalics) in ways that cannot be represented, but must be performed by communicating bodies. Accordingly, Habermas's theory is based in what he acknowledges is an "assumption" that pragmatics can be investigated from a basis that "single[s] out explicit speech actions" and "ignore[s] nonverbalized actions and bodily expressions."[10] However, communication research finds that what is "ignore[d]" is particularly efficacious in presenting diverse and unrepresented (indeed, as yet unverbalizable) goals, including those that Habermas excludes as "strategic" rather than "communicative."

The third (and closely connected) aspect of concern is Habermas's choice of linguistics as the model for his pragmatism. Here again, an ancient pattern is invoked: knowledge requires a stable object. The line of linguistic research upon which Habermas builds his formal pragmatics begins with Saussure's struggle to extract such an object from the "confused mass of heterogeneous and unrelated things" comprising speech (*le langage*). He succeeded in doing so by differentiating, within that domain of human activity, a relatively stable object (language; *la langue*) and an intrinsically dynamic process (speaking; *la parole*), and choosing the former for his science's object of investigation: "we must put both feet on the ground of language [*la langue*] and use language as the norm of all other manifestations of speech [*le langage*]."[11] There are other possibilities for resolving this struggle: as a "good pragmatist,"[12] Habermas could have taken up the processual orientation that is strong in Dewey's work, and pervasive in his understanding of communicative experience. This possibility is the one chosen by ethnomethodology: as Habermas notes, "ethnomethodologists stress the "processual character and ... .context-dependency of everyday communication," and to the extent that ethnomethodology offers "a theory in its own right, the outlines of a program of formal pragmatics become visible."[13] The difference that such a choice could have made for his theory is suggested by Stephen Levinson: "Conversation is not a structural product in the same way that a sentence is – it is rather the outcome of the interaction of two or more independent, goal-directed individuals, often with divergent interests."[14]

Much more could be said about the influence of these three choices and the limited conception of communication that they motivate.[15] There are clues throughout the later evolution of Habermas's formal pragmatics of the difference that a radically different basis – that is, one grounded in communication, rather than language – might have made: e.g. Thomas McCarthy's observation that "Habermas's entire project ... rests on the possibility of providing an account of communication that ... [can] articulate and ground an expanded conception of rationality."[16] However, I want to limit further summarizing of Habermas's theory to its fourth domain.

In Habermas's continued development of his theory of formal pragmatics the fourth domain is present as an "aesthetic–practical," "dramaturgical" domain in which the "model of transmitted knowledge" is "works of art."[17] This domain can present a distinct sort of "validity claim" that, when "incorporated into the context of individual life-histories ... reaches into our cognitive interpretations and normative expectations and transforms the totality in which those moments are related to one another."[18] He grants, then, that "a certain type of 'knowing' is objectified in art works, albeit in a different way than in theoretical discourse or in legal or moral representations," for it concerns their "unity (harmony) ... authenticity, and the success of their expressions."[19] This shift is ratified by Habermas's observation that

> McCarthy correctly notes [that] what accumulates [from the "trans-
> formations" that are "the works of art themselves, and not the
> discourses about them"] are not epistemic contents, but rather the
> effects of the inner logical differentiation of a special sort of experi-
> ence: precisely those aesthetic experiences of which only a
> decentered, unbound subjectivity is capable.[20]

His more recent work shows increased recognition that language has a
"world-constituting, world-disclosing function" in "aesthetic experiences"
that are closely associated with the subjective world of "inner nature," as it
influences the world of "society":

> When experiences of inner nature ... gain independence as aesthetic
> experiences, the ensuing works of autonomous art take on the role
> of objects that open our eyes, that provoke new ways of seeing
> things, new attitudes, and new modes of behavior.[21]

However (he immediately goes on to say), these experiences are "not
forms of everyday practice" and "do not refer to cognitive–instrumental
skills and moral ideas."[22]

Habermas's renewed stress on the separation of the fourth domain from
the cognitive, moral/legal, and expressive domains may be occasioned by a
threat he sees in contemporary theory, namely, the "aesthetizing of
language" that occurs in the "leveling of the genre distinction between
philosophy and literature" which he identifies in the work of Jacques
Derrida and Richard Rorty.[23] He argues that their theories conflate aesthetic
and cognitive rationality, and so threaten the "problem-solving capacities" of
"science, morality, and law" through their privileging of the "capacities for
world-disclosure" offered by "art and literature."[24] In resistance to that
conflation, he insists on the need for a "polar tension" between those
"problem-solving" and "world-disclosure" capacities, and holds that the
latter "are specialized for experiences and modes of knowledge that can be
shaped and worked out within the compass of one linguistic function and
one dimension of validity at a time."[25]

What even this very brief indication of Habermas's conception of the
fourth domain suggests is an increasing recognition of its efficacy, which
turns into a resistance to the claims of the aesthetic that he identifies in
contemporary theory. I want to propose, in the final section of this chapter,
that this choice between separation and conflation is unnecessary, if the
aesthetic is theorized within a Deweyan conception of communicative experience as transformative, rather than within a conception of communicative
action that is (as I have argued) a theory of linguistic action as representational. Dewey's conception of aesthetic experience is quite different from

Habermas's, however, and so I turn now to summarizing Dewey's under-standing of "art as experience."

Dewey's conception of aesthetic experience

> Of all affairs, communication is the most wonderful. That things should be able to pass from the plane of external pushing and pulling to that of revealing themselves to man, and thereby to themselves; and that the fruit of communica-tion should be participation, sharing, is a wonder by the side of which transubstantiation pales. When communication occurs, all natural events are subject to reconsideration and revision; they are re-adapted to meet the requirements of conversation, whether it be public discourse or that prelimi-nary discourse termed thinking. Events turn into objects, things with a meaning.
>
> (LW 1: 132)[26]

> Communication is not announcing things ... [it] is the process of creating participation, of making common what had been isolated and singular ... The expressions that consti-tute art are communication in its pure and undefiled form.
>
> (LW 10: 248–9)

> Art is a process of production in which natural materials are re-shaped in a projection toward consummatory fulfillment through regulation of trains of events that occur in a less regu-lated way on lower levels of nature ... Art thus represents the culminating event of nature as well as the climax of experience ... science as method is more basic than science as subject-matter ... scientific inquiry is an art, at once instrumental in control and final as a pure enjoyment of mind.
>
> (LW 1: 8)

Dewey's oft-repeated encomium for communication is not occasioned by its task of representation or by according any privileged status to the epistemic and objectivistic focus which motivates that task. Rather, it's occasioned by how communication works to constitute objects within the evolving continuum that begins with the experience of physical organisms interacting with their environment and culminates in aesthetic experience. "To esthetic experience," says Dewey, "the philosopher must go to understand what expe-rience is"; thus he urges us to allow that experience to "tell its own tale" (LW 10: 278–9). But we are more apt to understand that tale if we begin prior to it – even prior to communication – and trace the levels of experience that begin with interaction and end with the particular sort of transaction that he calls aesthetic experience. It's important to emphasize at the outset, however, that these "levels" are not ontological posits. Rather, they are abstracted "plateaus" in the evolution of a physical, psychophysical, and communicative continuum (*LW* 1: 208): "Experience is the result, the sign, and the reward of that interaction of organism and environment which, when it is carried to the full, is a transformation of interaction into participation and communication" (*LW* 10: 28).

Even the barest interaction of organism and environment (Dewey's "physical" plateau) is one in which an embodied mind interacts with physical surroundings informed by the complex of economic, cultural, social, and political vectors that can be called, collectively, a lifeworld. This experience is a complex affair of doing and undergoing (or, engagement and response) that is "felt" rather than "known" (*LW* 1: 198). It is not reducible to its elements (qualities and relations); rather, those elements are abstractions from experience that may be useful for inquiry. In its "primary integrity" – that is, absent those abstractions – it "recognizes ... no division between act and material, subject and object, but contains them both in an unanalyzed totality" (*LW* 1: 18).

At the psychophysical level, this dynamic engagement articulates the "contextual wholes" that Dewey calls "situations" (*LW* 12: 72). These are not formed causally, but in transaction; which is to say that they are constituted in events of mutual participation of particular potentialities for shaping space and time. The "qualities" we recognize in situated things within those situations are not in the organism or in the environment, but "always were qualities of interactions" (*LW* 1: 198). "Mind," Dewey holds, "is an added property assumed by a feeling creature, when it reaches that organized interaction with other living creatures which is language, communication" (*LW* 1: 198). At that level of the continuum, "Events turn into objects, things with a meaning" (*LW* 1: 132; quoted above in context). Also, the ongoing activity which is experience can be delineated, which is to say that the practical/moral, cognitive, and expressive qualities of "an experience," a complete and yet dynamic whole, can be described in terms of their consequences, and thus its meliorative value can be assessed.

Dewey's elucidation of the organism's response to its conditions displays an equitable valuation of body and mind (activity as well as thought; somatic as well as cognitive contributions) throughout these levels. It thus affronts the pervasive valorization of the mental – and in particular, the linguistic – in the dominant Euroamerican intellectual context. Its thoroughgoing focus on process rather than substance confounds our usual ways of thinking in both everyday and scholarly domains. Furthermore, Dewey finds that the aesthetic can mark any experience: it is "no intruder from without," but is "the clarified and intensified development of traits that belong to every normally complete experience" (*LW* 10: 52–3). Thus Dewey's conception denies traditional aesthetic theory's separation of art from everyday, moral, and scientific doings and makings. There is one further divergence from dominant modes of thought that adds to the intensity of resistance that's apt to greet any advocacy for a Deweyan reconstruction: Deweyan pragmatism is concerned primarily with *how* any process aids in melioration, rather than with *what* may be demonstrated about the nature of its components. Accordingly, Dewey's aesthetic theory is interested in how art works throughout human life in the service of meliorative goals, rather than in what it is, apart from life's everyday and specialized domains. Thus the subject-matter of pragmatic aesthetics differs from that of traditional, analytic aesthetics: it concerns the *work* of art, rather than the art *object*; the dynamic experience that is artistic creation, rather than the static product of that activity; the consequences of art for the improvement of life, rather than "art for art's sake."

Given these profound differences, it's little wonder, as Richard Shusterman notes, that pragmatist aesthetics "began with John Dewey – and almost ended there."[27] Every attempt to explicate this divergent and novel conception runs afoul of embedded meanings and associations that distort it. What's needed here is imagination – "the conscious adjustment of the new and the old" (*LW* 10: 276); of grasping (new) possibilities within (old) actualities, and incorporating them in a continuity of inquiry that grows past prior understanding. Expanding comprehension in this way calls upon a constitutive rather than representative understanding of communicative experience's task, in order to direct participants toward the unsayable: to what cannot be transmitted, because there is no antecedent to transmit. It requires calling upon the enduring presence of nondiscursive, somatic experience to expand our discursive parameters, and so relies upon Dewey's thesis that somatic experience – which is "had" but not "known" (*LW* 1: 198) – continues its efficacy throughout all modes of communication. Otherwise stated, expanding comprehension in this way requires rejection of claims that the limits of language (in the sense of established meanings) are the limits of thought and experience. "Language fails," Dewey wrote in his "Qualitative thought" essay, "not because thought fails but because no verbal symbols can do justice to the fullness and richness of thought" (*LW* 5: 250). Granted, "there is something artificial and repellent in discoursing about any consummatory event or object. It speaks so completely for itself that words are poor substitutes ... translation into explicit terms gives a partial and inadequate result" (*LW* 5: 250). However, Dewey's continuity principle encourages starting with that partiality and inadequacy and directing inquiry toward communication as constitutive; as the "process of creating participation, of making common what had been isolated and singular" (*LW* 10: 248). That alternative orientation enables comprehending (Deweyan) aesthetic experience as a potentiality within all forms of experience – and in particular, across Habermas's cognitive, interactive, and expressive domains of communicative action.

152

The distinction that is basic for this alternative mode of inquiry is that between a work of art and the product of that work, an art object: "Art is a quality of doing and of what is done ... The product of art – temple, painting, statue, poem – is not the work of art" (*LW* 10: 218). The relation between these two is transactional, rather than causal: "the actual work of art is what the product does with and in experience" (*LW* 10: 9) and "aesthetic" designates an orientation within experience that appreciates that doing. This focus on the work of art privileges creative process over static object (creative activity over its product). Only the latter is available for commodification on the market and fetishization in the museum. This is a focus that affronts dominant epistemic and economic values: we cannot know, or sell, what is in constant change; what never leaves the production process. Aesthetic value certainly is other than the economic and epistemic values that are pervasively transmitted in everyday and scholarly life. Given the domination of these values in Euroamerican culture, we can understand the isolation and frequent deprecation of that dimension of communicative experience that is art and aesthetic experience, in Dewey's sense.

It's against this background that Dewey develops the radical alternative of understanding communicative experience as potentially aesthetic; i.e. as harboring potential for innovative transformation. In his words: "Art is a quality that permeates an experience; it is not, save by a figure of speech, the experience itself." (*LW* 10: 329). A "body of matters and meanings" becomes aesthetic "as they enter into an ordered rhythmic movement toward consummation" (*LW* 10: 329). The diversity of this plurality (matters, body; meanings, mind) assures that the unity of a work of art is not a uniformity: it is a dramatically harmonious blending of differences, rather than a reduction or purification to one stuff. Neither is it a static unity:

> experience is a matter of the interaction of the artistic product with the self. It is not therefore twice alike for different persons ... It changes with the same person at different times as he brings something different to a work.
>
> (*LW* 10: 334)

Even the consummatory closure that marks a work of art is but a temporary stasis: "Every movement of experience in completing itself recurs to its beginning ... But the recurrence is with a difference ... Every closure is an awakening, and every awakening settles something. This state of affairs defines organization of energy" (*LW* 10: 173–4). This consummatory moment, then, is one that produces a felt sense of unity in configuring space (phenomenal features) and time (the past, present, and future) and so unites the instrumental and final aspects of an experience. Shusterman emphasizes the temporality of this "moment" in his explication of the term:

> The sense of the consummatory is gradually transformed from a
> feeling of immanent possibility, of the ideal capacity of the experi-
> ence, to one of progressive realization. The end of the work does not
> lie outside it but within it as a moving force, the entelechy rather
> than the terminus.[28]

Understood in this way, the character of a work of art (in contrast to an art object) is much like the character of selfhood as explicated by Paul Ricoeur. Its form (pattern of dynamic organization) is "ipseity": an inter-weaving of "act and potentiality" within which "constancy" of responsibility for consequences, functioning throughout dynamic multiplicity, enables constancy to be formed within change – rather than its form being "idem," a static sameness of substance.[29]

This alignment of Dewey's conception of art with selfhood provides an alternative way of interpreting Foucault's observation that "in our society, art has become something that is related only to objects and not to individuals or to life ... art is something that is specialized or done by experts who are artists." He then goes on to ask: "But couldn't everyone's life become a work of art? Why should the lamp or the house be an art object but not our life?"[30] A pragmatist aesthetics can respond: each life *is* becoming a work of art (in consummatory engagement with the environment). We typically fail to notice that intrinsic aesthetic dimension within everyday life for at least two reasons. First, dominant cultural values (epistemic and economic) encourage an everyday understanding of each life as an object that has particular value on the market, and a theoretical understanding of each life as both an object of and a producer of knowledge. Also, the economic, polit-ical, and social reality of the situations in which many of us live our lives operates to limit the freedom of the aesthetic dimension and to conceal its work. Given that reality, recognizing that strategic crafting of the environ-ment is creating a work of art is not claiming that all lives allow of equal aesthetic experience. It does, however, suggest the pervasiveness of the aesthetic dimension within the cognitive–instrumental, moral–practical, and expressive dimensions that are extensively theorized in Habermas's theory. Engaging in artistic work – not in isolation from the unique circum-stances and limitations of the situations within which each organism interacts with the environment, but as a crafting of those circumstances that can succeed in expanding those limitations – is engaging in an art that is life, in "art as experience."

Reconstructing the fourth dimension

> The social sciences take human and nonhuman nature in its
> entirety as given and are concerned only with how relation-
> ships are established between man and nature and between

154

man and man. However, an awareness of this relation ... is not enough to bring the concept of theory to a new stage of development. What is needed is a radical reconsideration ... of the knowing individual as such.[31]

We wish to proceed ... by asking after the how of the world's pregivenness ... As such we now consistently make the world our subject of investigation, i.e., as the ground of all our interests and life-projects, among which the theoretical projects of the objective sciences make up only a particular group ... to be in no way privileged.[32]

A thing is more significantly what it makes possible than what it immediately is.[33]

I want to examine a few of the transitions from the formal pragmatic level of analysis to empirical pragmatics, and ... explain why the concept of communicative action has to be completed through a concept of the lifeworld.[34]

From the idea that the self is not given to us, I think there is only one practical consequence: we have to create ourselves as a work of art.[35]

These remarks by Max Horkheimer, Edmund Husserl, John Dewey, Jürgen Habermas, and Michel Foucault (respectively) point out the reconstructive direction I sketch here. Dewey's understanding of communication as both constitutive and representational, and aesthetic experience as the creative epitome of constitutive communication, enables reconstructing the fourth domain of Habermas's theory of communicative action as a dimension of creative potential within the cognitive, moral/legal, and expressive dimensions of communicative experience. There are two potential reservations about this endeavor, which I will discuss after sketching the evolution in Habermas's theory that encourages this reconstruction. The first concerns whether the massive rethinking of what's involved in aesthetic, cognitive, and ethical experience – which is what this reconstruction advocates – could be accomplished. The second is why this reconstruction of Habermas's theory of communication action is useful for social theorists and activists who work towards the meliorative goals espoused by Deweyan pragmatism.

Although there's been considerable evolution in Habermas's theory, the conception of the four domains of communicative action that he introduced in "What is universal pragmatics?" (summarized in Table 7.1) is still present in his contemporary work. It has not remained static, however, and the reconstruction that I propose here is by way of further evolution, rather than rejection or refutation, of Habermas's considerable step forward (from consciousness to experience, albeit linguistic experience) in social theory.

Considerable evolution is evident in the table he published just five years after Table 7.1, which is presented here as Table 7.2.[36]

Table 7.2 Rationalization complexes

Basic attitudes	Worlds			
	1 Objective	2 Social	3 Subjective	1 Objective
3 Expressive	Art			
1 Objectivating		Cognitive–instrumental rationality Science Social Technology Technologies		
2 Normative	X		Moral–practical Rationality Law Morality	
3 Expressive		X		Aesthetic–practical rationality Eroticism Art

Source: J. Habermas, *Theory of Communication Action, Volume 1*, p. 238; modified from the original

Three features in this evolution call for specific comment. First, Table 7.2 speaks of "Worlds," which is considerably more open to metaphoric understanding and less demanding of a problematic ontology than is Table 7.1's "Domains of reality." I exploit this change in reconstructively theorizing communicative experience as embodying four dimensions, rather than being divisible into four domains. Also, "Language," which was not associated with any "Basic attitude" or "General function of speech" in Table 7.1, no longer appears as a fourth domain that simply serves the task of "Comprehensibility." Instead, the fourth place is given to "Art" and "Aesthetic–practical rationality," which present "Expressive" attitudes in the "Objective" and "Subjective" "worlds," respectively. (Habermas's linking of the "Subjective" aesthetic–practical with "Eroticism" is a complex issue that I lack space to discuss here, other than to suggest that it connects with his current criticism, mentioned earlier, of current "aesthetizing of language" – and thus provides a counter-force to the integrative movement that I emphasize here.) Third, the theoretical context that Habermas cites as supportive of the Table 7.1 conception is primarily populated by linguists, logicians, semanticists, and speech act theorists.[37] The correlative context for Table 7.2, however, is populated (again, primarily) by social theorists and philosophers – and predominantly influenced by Max Weber. The topic is still "formal–pragmatic relations," and more precisely, relations "between actors and their external or internal environments."[38] This shift in intellectual background may be influential in linking "Art" to the "Objective" category and "aesthetic–practical rationality" to both the "Objective" and "Subjective" categories of "World," rather than retaining it as a separate dimension. Still, Habermas's remarks about "Art" (in its "Subjective" rather than "Objective" form; i.e. as artistic process, rather than art product) as well as about "aesthetic experience" confirm his adherence to a theory of knowledge that valorizes accumulation of facts about "'the' world of nature": "nothing can be learned in an objectivating attitude about inner nature qua subjectivity"; "the production of knowledge" about "aesthetic–practical rationality" yields, at best, "authentic interpretations of needs ... that have to be renewed in each historically changed set of circumstances."[39] Habermas's valorization of "cognitive–instrumental" and "moral–practical" rationality is thereby tenuously extended into art and aesthetic experience. But only insofar as the latter produce objects that may be accumulated – analogously to the facts, norms, and laws of the former domains, which may be accumulated as linguistic objects – are they to be accorded a place within rationality.[40]

This conception of learning and knowing stands in sharp contrast to Dewey's correlative conceptions of productive doing and receptive undergoing: of learning through doing, and inquiry "from within" the situations we undergo (and make, within historically and socially constrained production systems).[41] Thus, this close examination of Habermas's addition of art and aesthetic experience to his conception of formal pragmatics reveals two important differences. First, Habermas's ontological orientation supports his valorization of art *objects* (products with market value), while Dewey's processual orientation supports his valorization of art *works* (transformative experiences). Also, Habermas values aesthetic experience insofar as it produces validity claims that can be adjudicated along the lines of claims about "external" and "internal" nature, i.e. through argumentation that presumes consensus as its goal. Dewey, however, values aesthetic experience insofar as it transforms the lifeworld (the process of culturally, economically, physically, politically, and socially forming an environment), and so produces a diversity of experiential means that can be strategically exploited for meliorative ends. Art works, in other words, to transform situations: to instigate change in the status quo, rather than to solidify knowledge about it.

Continued evolution in Habermas's theory opens a path that motivates my use of Dewey's conception of art as experience to reconstruct his theory's fourth dimension as the core of a more insightful theory of communicative experience – and thus, a more powerful social theory. Largely (it seems) through conversation with his critics, Habermas comes to acknowledge the possibility of conditions under which "art enters into ... everyday communicative practice" and "transforms the totality" of "cognitive interpretation and normative expectations" in that practice.[42] "The aesthetic 'validity' or 'unity' that we attribute to a work," he goes on to say, "refers to its singularly illuminating power ... to disclose anew an apparently familiar reality" and so provide a "'truth potential' [which] may not be connected to (or even identified with) just one of the three validity claims." Rather, he concludes, the "normative validity claim raised in regulative speech acts is not a proper model for the relation for ... the transformed relations between self and world stimulated by aesthetic experience."[43] The effect of this acknowledgment is to encompass a broader spectrum of actual communicative experience, and so expand upon the objectivistic and epistemic focus of Habermas's theory by opening it to Dewey's sense of aesthetic experience. The result is a social theory that is more applicable to analyzing actual communicative experience, as well as to developing a critique of that experience based in recognizing the triumphs and failures that occur as people living within oppressive conditions devise means of bringing about change in their circumstances.[44]

I turn now to the two reservations about this reconstructive endeavor that I mentioned at the start of this section. First: can the rethinking of aesthetic, cognitive, and ethical experience that's required if Dewey's understanding of those facets of experience is to be integrated with Habermas's, be accomplished? For what's needed here is nothing less than overturning a set of embedded assumptions that originate with Plato's separation of art from life, and particularly, from the good life epitomized by the philosopher's dwelling with the Forms. Plato valued craft (techne) insofar as it produced useful things that served as means for the end of that good life, but not as an end in itself. He derided art (visual, verbal, or auditory) as a most unworthy pursuit, removed from the practical concerns of civic life as well as the pursuit of wisdom. Aristotle's identification of praxis (productive doing) as containing its own end, but poiesis (creative making) as independent of its end, reinforced that hierarchy. A case could be made, however, in honor of poiesis for not determining or dominating – and thus, in a sense, not "containing" – its creations.[45]

This Platonic and Aristotelian heritage still thrives within Euroamerican culture and theory as a hierarchy of reason/knowing (episteme), action/doing (praxis), and creating/making (poiesis); or science (cognitive reason), ethics/politics (practical reason; phronesis) and art (aesthetic – typically denied the honorific of "reason," although often granted "taste" or "feeling"). Those within this heritage who value art and aesthetic experience typically do so because of its separation from life, or because it provides an exotic species of knowledge accessible to an elite few. What remains unacknowledged as a type of aesthetic experience – even remains unnoticed, given the hegemony of this heritage – is the strategic crafting (techne) informed by poiesis (imaginative remaking of a situation's possibilities accomplished in constitutive communication) which is at work as people devise means of improving their lot. This does not occur solely within the "fine" arts; nor is it limited to humans' impressive record of technological advancement. As Larry Hickman notes,

> Dewey's insistence that from the standpoint of production and appreciation no meaningful distinction can be made between the "fine" and the "useful" arts is to this day a radical position ... there are still treatments of modern art that bifurcate "art" and "technology," as if art objects were not examples of productive skill and as if "technology" were somehow the enemy of "art."[46]

Refusing that bifurcation is a crucial first step toward recognizing the pervasiveness of the fourth dimension within communicative experience.

Dewey's theory opposes this Platonic and Aristotelian hierarchy, and thus enables recognition of the extent of communication's constitutive task. He proposes that art is a form of experience, and that it is to aesthetic experience – the very best, complete, and most satisfying mode of experience – that we must turn if we are to understand experience at all: "Artistic thought ... only shows an intensification of a characteristic of all thought." (*LW* 5: 251–2). Thus, it is intrinsic to, not separated from, life; accessible to all as the means for actualizing more of the multiple possibilities intrinsic in any situation (i.e. in knowing and doing, as well as making), and thus, expanding upon the given – perhaps in meliorative ways – rather than simply re-presenting it. Dewey is able to overturn our inherited hierarchy of knowing, doing, and making, I suspect, because he focuses not on the product of art, or on the criticism of art, but on the very process in which art comes to be. Rather than accept Aristotle's dictum that doing (praxis) includes its end (the activities of the agent who accomplishes that doing) within itself, whereas making (poiesis) has only an external end (an "art object"), Dewey looks anew at what has been looked at many times, and appreciates what was always overlooked or underestimated: the very engagement in aesthetic experience is a creative shaping (crafting; constituting) of space and time that includes the shaping of the creator ("agent"). This insight – readily verifiable by anecdotal evidence as well as social scientific studies of the creative process – confirms that communicative experience is both a doing and a making.[47] It creates a product that fits the Platonic and Aristotelian dictum, in that it is independent of its creation and takes on market value for reasons quite extrinsic to the shaping process that made it. But it also transcends any such particular process and cumulatively shapes its shaper. In other words: in the process of shaping (constituting) space and time into an art *object*, the creative process also constitutes a *work* of art, namely its maker. The double efficacy of aesthetic experience accomplishes, in Foucault's words (quoted earlier), this "practical consequence": We "create ourselves" as we perform divergence (only some of which is linguistically crafted as explicit dissent) from what is given as our lot.

Dewey's method for rethinking this traditional hierarchy of knowing, doing, and making – and the conception of communication as re-presentation (doing, rather than both doing and making) which supports that hierarchy – relies upon the basic pragmatist test for the truth of a claim: seek out the empirical evidence that would confirm or confound it. I adopt that method for responding to the question of whether entrenched ways of thinking, in both everyday and theoretical contexts, may be overturned. Many affirmative examples come immediately to mind: the earth's flatness and fixed position under heaven, the rightness of Latin as the only language for prayer and scholarship, the divine right of kingship, the nonsexuality of children and the elderly, the wrongness of dressing young males in long pants or females of any age in pants at all, the impossibility of democracy, the efficacy of draining blood to cure disease, the inferiority of a particular gender or race, the inability of non-human animals to use (much less develop and teach) language, the justification of slavery, the dangers to health of leaving windows open at night ... Although I do not minimize the difficulty of revising entrenched ways of thinking, our embedded beliefs as to the nature and goal of communicative experience, and thus of the aesthetic experience that is its most creative form, do not seem any less impervious to change than the beliefs on this list.

The second potential reservation about this reconstructive endeavor concerns how, and even whether, reconstructing Habermas's theory of communication action is useful for social theorists and activists who are concerned to further the meliorative action that Dewey's pragmatism advocates. My response to this reservation begins in rethinking the relation between the first three categories and the last category in Tables 7.1 and 7.2. As I mentioned earlier, Habermas shifted from understanding the category of "language" as a "domain of rationality," to recognizing the "expressive" as a "basic attitude" present throughout the other three domains. However, he continued to theorize what is expressed within an objectivistic orientation which assumes that communication's task is to linguistically re-present the status quo within all three "domains of reality." This reduction of constitutive communicative experience to representational linguistic action disables his theory, insofar as it conceals the somatically performed strategies (such as body configurations, postures and movements, clothing preferences, and spatial manipulation) as well as non-argumentive uses of language (e.g. legends, maxims, myths, pledges, poems, prayers, songs) that people devise and employ to further their interests in subverting or solidifying the status quo.

Dewey's understanding of communicative experience's task as transforming, rather than representing, encourages us to look to performances of these non-argumentative and even non-linguistic modes of communication as sites of melioration. For what we somatically do and strategically say can surpass the limitations of our "linguistically organized stock of interpretive patterns"[48] and so realize possibilities of making things other than they are (and even, seem always to have been). Rather than expecting melioration to come from what some say to others, then, we would look for it to emerge from how those who live within situations that call out for the alleviation of oppression craft doings and undergoings that make change happen.

Notes

1 Jürgen Habermas, "What is universal pragmatics?" in *Communication and the Evolution of Society*, Thomas McCarthy (trans.), Boston, Beacon Press, 1979, p. 68.

2 J. Habermas, *The Theory of Communicative Action* vol. I, Thomas McCarthy (trans.), Boston, Beacon Press, 1984, pp. 236–40.

3 For a discussion of inquiry within "performative" in contrast to "productive" praxis, see my "In defense of poiesis: the performance of self in communicative praxis," in *The Task of Philosophy after Postmodernity*, William McBride and Martin Beck Matustik (eds), Evanston, IL, Northwestern University Press, 2002.

4 J. Habermas, "Appendix," *Knowledge and Human Interests*, J.J. Shapiro (trans.), Boston, Beacon Press, 1971, p. 314.

5 J. Habermas, *On the Logic of the Social Sciences*, Shierry Weber Nicholsen and Jerry A. Stark (trans.), Cambridge, MIT Press, 1988, p. 117.

6 J. Habermas, *The Theory of Communicative Action* vol. II, Thomas McCarthy (trans.), Boston, Beacon Press, 1987, pp. 124–5.

7 L. Langsdorf, "The real conditions for the possibility of communicative action," in *Perspectives on Habermas*, Lewis E. Hahn (ed.), Peru, IL, Open Court, 2000. A condensed version was presented at the annual meeting of the Society for Phenomenology and Existential Philosophy, University of Colorado at Denver, October 1998.

8 J. Habermas, "What is universal pragmatics?" p. 67.

9 For discussion of this need for alternate conceptions, see my "Argument as inquiry in a postmodern context," *Argumentation* 11 (1987), pp. 315–27.

10 J. Habermas, "What is universal pragmatics?" p. 1.

11 F. de Saussure, *Course in General Linguistics*, Charles Bally and Albert Sechehaye (eds), Wade Baskin (trans.), New York, McGraw Hill, 1959, pp. 8–9, 14.

12 J. Habermas, "Questions and counterquestions," in *Habermas and Modernity*, Richard J. Bernstein (ed.), Cambridge, MIT Press, 1985, p. 198.

13 J. Habermas, *Theory of Communicative Action* vol. I, pp. 124, 127–8.

14 S.C. Levinson, *Pragmatics*, Cambridge, Cambridge University Press, 1983, p. 294.

15 For further discussion of these choices and limitations, see Darrin Hicks and Lenore Langsdorf, "Proceduralist theories of public deliberation: implications for the production of citizens," *Argumentation* 13, 2 (1999), pp. 139–61, and my "The real conditions for the possibility of communicative action."

16 T. McCarthy, *The Critical Theory of Jürgen Habermas*, Cambridge, MIT Press, 1978, p. 272.

17 J. Habermas, *Theory of Communicative Action* vol. I, p. 334; cf. pp. 238, 329.

18 J. Habermas, "Questions and counterquestions," pp. 202–3.

19 J. Habermas, "Questions and counterquestions," p. 200.

20 J. Habermas, "Questions and counterquestions," p. 200.

21 J. Habermas, "Actions, speech acts, linguistically mediated interactions, and lifeworld," in *On the Pragmatics of Communication*, Maeve Cooke (ed.), Cambridge, MIT Press, 1998, pp. 245–6.

22 J. Habermas, "Actions, speech acts," p. 246.

23 J. Habermas, "On leveling the genre distinction between philosophy and literature," in *The Philosophical Discourse of Modernity: Twelve Lectures*, Frederick G. Lawrence (trans.), Cambridge, MIT Press, 1987, pp. 205, 208–9.

24 J. Habermas, "On leveling the genre distinction," p. 207.

25 J. Habermas, "On leveling the genre distinction," p. 207.

26 All quotations from Dewey are taken from the standard edition published by Southern Illinois University Press as *The Early Works*, *The Middle Works*, and *The Later Works*. They are identified parenthetically in the text as *EW*, *MW*, or *LW*, followed by volume number and page.

27 R. Shusterman, *Pragmatic Aesthetics: Living Beauty, Rethinking Art*, Oxford, Blackwell, 1992, p. ix.

28 Shusterman, *Pragmatic Aesthetics*, p. 212.

29 P. Ricoeur, *Oneself as Another*, Kathleen Blamey (trans.), Chicago, University of Chicago Press, 1992, pp. 295–6. For discussion of this conception in relation to the self as constituting and constituted, see my "The doubleness of subjectivity," in *Ricouer as Another: The Ethics of Subjectivity*, Richard A. Cohen and James L. Marsh (eds), Albany, New York, SUNY Press, forthcoming.

30 M. Foucault, *Ethics: Subjectivity and Truth* (*The Essential Works of Michel Foucault, 1954–1984* vol. I), Paul Rabinow (ed.), New York, New Press, 1997, p. 26. For discussion of this conception in relation to refusing concepts of the self as object, see my "Refusing individuality," *Communication Theory* 7, 4 (1997), pp. 321–42.

31 M. Horkheimer, "Traditional and critical theory," in *Critical Theory: Selected Essays*, Matthew J. O'Connell and others (trans.), New York, Seabury Press, 1972, p. 199.

32 E. Husserl, *The Crisis of European Sciences and Transcendental Phenomenology* (original German publication 1954; written 1934–7), David Carr (trans.), Evanston, IL, Northwestern University Press, 1970, p. 154.

33 J. Dewey, *LW* 1: 105 (see Note 26 for explanation of references to Dewey's work).

34 J. Habermas, *Theory of Communicative Action* vol. I, p. 279.

35 M. Foucault, *Ethics, Subjectivity and Truth*, p. 261.

36 J. Habermas, *Theory of Communicative Action* vol. I, p. 238.

37 J. Habermas, "What is universal pragmatics?" p. 7; this "primarily" allows for his references to Karl-Otto Apel (pp. 1, 5–6), Jean Piaget (p. 25), analytic action theorists (p. 7) and (of course) Immanuel Kant.

38 J. Habermas, *Theory of Communication Action* vol. I, pp. 236–7.

39 J. Habermas, *Theory of Communicative Action* vol. I, pp. 235–6.

40 J. Habermas, *Theory of Communicative Action* vol. I, p. 239.

41 Paulo Freire's contrast between "banking" and "problem-posing" concepts of education, and Michael Arbib's contrast between "schema" and "container" concepts of knowing, offer helpful contemporary developments of this contrast. Current pedagogical interest in these conceptions is a fitting continuation of Dewey's enduring determination to apply his philosophical work to educational practice.

42 J. Habermas, "Questions and counterquestions," p. 202.

43 J. Habermas, "Questions and counterquestions," p. 203.

44 For further discussion of instances in which this occurs, see Dwight Conquergood, "Ethnography, rhetoric, and performance," *Quarterly Journal of Speech* (1992), pp. 80–123.

45 For one such case, see my "In defense of poiesis: the performance of self in communicative praxis."

46 L. Hickman, *John Dewey's Pragmatic Technology*, Bloomington, Indiana University Press, 1990, p. 68.

47 I discuss this dual function in "In defense of poiesis" and in "Philosophy of language and philosophy of communication: poiesis and praxis in classical pragmatism," in *Recovering Pragmatism's Voice: The Classical Tradition, Rorty, and the Philosophy of Communication*, Lenore Langsdorf and Andrew R. Smith (eds), Albany, New York, SUNY Press, 1995. The latter (1995) analysis is confused, however, by a terminological error that is most explicit on p. 206: discussion of poiesis as "creative doing" and praxis as "productive making" should have been, respectively, "creative making" and "productive doing."

48 J. Habermas, *Theory of Communicative Action* vol. II, p. 124; quoted above in context.

Bibliography

Arbib, Michael A. "The schema theory of minds: implications for social sciences," in *Rethinking Knowledge: Reflections Across the Disciplines*, ed. Robert F. Goodman and Walter R. Fisher. Albany, New York, SUNY Press, 1995.

Conquergood, Dwight. "Ethnography, rhetoric, and performance," *Quarterly Journal of Speech* (1992): 80–123.

Dewey, John. *Experience and Nature* (1925; revised 1929). *Later Works* vol. I. Carbondale, Southern Illinois University Press, 1981.

——"Qualitative thought" (1930). *Later Works* vol. 5. Carbondale, Southern Illinois University Press, 1984.

——*Art as Experience* (1934). *Later Works* vol. 10. Carbondale, Southern Illinois University Press, 1987.

——*Logic: The Theory of Inquiry* (1938). *Later Works* vol. 12. Carbondale, Southern Illinois University Press, 1991.

Foucault, Michel. *Ethics: Subjectivity and Truth (The Essential Works of Michel Foucault, 1954–1984* vol. 1), ed. Paul Rabinow. New York, New Press, 1997.

Freire, Paolo. *Pedagogy of the Oppressed* (written in Portuguese, 1968), trans. Myra Bergman Ramos. New York, Continuum, 1983.

Habermas, Jürgen. *On the Logic of the Social Sciences* (original German publication, 1967), trans. Shierry Weber Nicholsen and Jerry A. Stark. Cambridge, MIT Press, 1988.

——*Knowledge and Human Interests* (original German publication, 1968), trans. J.J. Shapiro. Boston, Beacon Press, 1971.

——"What is universal pragmatics," in *Communication and the Evolution of Society* (original German publication, 1976), trans. Thomas McCarthy. Boston, Beacon Press, 1979.

——*The Theory of Communicative Action* vol. I (original German publication, 1981), trans. Thomas McCarthy. Boston, Beacon Press, 1984.

——*The Theory of Communicative Action* vol. II (original German publication, 1981), trans. Thomas McCarthy. Boston, Beacon Press, 1987.

——"Questions and counterquestions," in *Habermas and Modernity*, ed. Richard J. Bernstein. Cambridge, MIT Press, 1985.

——*The Philosophical Discourse of Modernity: Twelve Lectures*, trans. Frederick G. Lawrence. Cambridge, MIT Press, 1987.

——*On the Pragmatics of Communication*, ed. Maeve Cooke. Cambridge, MIT Press, 1998.

Hickman, Larry A. *John Dewey's Pragmatic Technology*. Bloomington, Indiana University Press, 1990.

Hicks, Darrin and Lenore Langsdorf. "Proceduralist theories of public deliberation: implications for the production of citizens," *Argumentation* 13, 2 (1999): 139–61.

Horkheimer, Max. "Traditional and critical theory," in *Critical Theory: Selected Essays*, (original German publication 1937), trans. Matthew J. O'Connell and others, New York, Seabury Press, 1972.

Husserl, Edmund. *The Crisis of European Sciences and Transcendental Phenomenology* (original German publication 1954; written 1934–7), trans. David Carr. Evanston, IL, Northwestern University Press, 1970.

Langsdorf, Lenore. "Argument as inquiry in a postmodern context," *Argumentation* 11 (1987): 315–27.

——"Refusing individuality," *Communication Theory* 7, 4 (1997): 321–42.

——"Epistemology, tropology, hermeneutic and the 'essence of language'," in *The Transversal Resources of Communicative Praxis*, ed. Ramsey Eric Ramsey and David James Miller. Albany, New York, SUNY Press, forthcoming.

——"In defense of poiesis: the performance of self in communicative praxis," in *The Task of Philosophy After Postmodernity*, ed. William McBride and Martin Beck Matustik. Evanston, IL, Northwestern University Press, 2002.

——"The doubleness of subjectivity," in *Ricoeur as Another: The Ethics of Subjectivity*, ed. Richard A. Cohen and James L. Marsh. Albany, New York, SUNY Press, forthcoming.

——"The real conditions for the possibility of communicative action," in *Perspectives on Habermas*, ed. Lewis E. Hahn. Peru, IL, Open Court, 2000.

Levinson, Stephen C. *Pragmatics*. Cambridge, Cambridge University Press, 1988.

McCarthy, Thomas. *The Critical Theory of Jürgen Habermas*. Cambridge, MIT Press, 1978.

Polanyi, Michael. *Personal Knowledge: Towards a Post-Critical Philosophy*. London, Routledge and Kegan Paul, 1958.

Ricoeur, Paul. *Oneself as Another*, trans. Kathleen Blamey. Chicago, University of Chicago Press, 1992.

Saussure, Ferdinand de. *Course in General Linguistics*, ed. by Charles Bally and Albert Sechehaye, trans. Wade Baskin. New York, McGraw-Hill, 1959.

——*Cours de Linguistique Générale* (original French publication 1915), ed. Charles Bally, Albert Sechehaye and Albert Riedlinger. Paris, Payot, 1960.

Shotter, John. *Conversational Realities: Constructing Life through Language*. London, Sage, 1993.

Shusterman, Richard. *Pragmatist Aesthetics: Living Beauty, Rethinking Art*. Oxford, Blackwell, 1992.

8

HABERMAS, PRAGMATISM, AND THE PROBLEM OF AESTHETICS[1]

Richard Shusterman

I

There are several likely ways to approach Habermas's pragmatism. We could show his theoretical affinities to themes in the classical pragmatism of Peirce, James, Dewey, and Mead. Or we could also trace the important ways he explicitly uses the writings and arguments of Peirce and Mead to advance some of his own central doctrines. Yet another option would be to explain the specificity of Habermas's pragmatism in comparison to other European appropriations of pragmatism (for instance Karl-Otto Apel's or Pierre Bourdieu's). Promising as these approaches may be, my paper instead adopts the strategy of considering Habermas in the context of contemporary American pragmatism by comparing his work to Richard Rorty's.

I choose Rorty as the comparative partner not only because he is probably (for better or for worse) the living American philosopher most widely known for advocacy of pragmatism, but also because Rorty clearly seems to be the American pragmatist with whom Habermas has engaged in the most extensive relationship of critical dialogue. For more than a decade, the ongoing Habermas–Rorty debate has been portrayed, at least in Europe, as expressing a radical philosophical opposition of deep and dramatic significance. They seemed to be locked in crucial contention over such profound principles as the public versus the private, universalism versus historicist contextualism, invariance versus contingency, reason and truth versus ironist play and aesthetic creativity, modernity versus postmodernity.

The perceived world-historical import of the Habermas–Rorty debate has not only issued in a wealth of published commentary and exchange, but has also been thought worthy of costly conference events designed to bring these philosophers (and also sometimes their cohorts) together in a critical face-off where they could thrash out their differences before an avid, admiring public in the hope that some momentous philosophical breakthrough or verdict might be reached. Even skeptical spirits who doubted that the debate would reveal any final answers could not resist the seductive promise and drama of such events. For in the strangely primitive sense of gladiatorial ritual from which philosophy seems hardly to differ from boxing, there was an avid curiosity to see if one of these world-class heavyweights would score a knockout on the other, or at least produce a knockdown argument.

I first met Jürgen Habermas at one of these dramatic encounters in July 1993. Entitled: "La Modernité en question: chez J. Habermas et R. Rorty," the conference was staged in the attractive yet austere Château of Cerisy la Salle, stunningly set in the .olling hills of Normandy, only a short drive from the beaches of the D-Day invasion.[2] It was clear that many of the French hosts were sensitive to this symbolic location, for some viewed this Habermas–Rorty encounter in metonymic terms as a battle between German critical theory with its commitment to modernity's rationalist ideals (represented by Habermas) and, on the other hand, American pragmatism (as symbolized by Rorty), which seemed critical of reason's rigid rule and seemed hospitable to some postmodern bendings.

Invoking this sense of the debate's *mise en scène* is apt to provoke a complaint I have often heard from Habermas (and indeed sometimes against my own work). This complaint is typically captured in a single word that Habermas solemnly intones with considerable power, as if it served him as incontrovertible critical mantra: "*Ästhetisierung*!" But the notion of staging is most appropriate to this paper's central concerns. For I wish to consider not only why aestheticization seems such a danger for Habermas, but also to examine to what extent the perceived gravity of the Habermas–Rorty debate is largely a dramatic effect – the product of dramatizing minor differences to give the sense of compelling contrasts so as to make their debate seem more radical and culturally portentous. This chapter aims to penetrate beyond the dramatized show of minor differences to show the deeper agreement they mask. But my aim is not reconciliation. For I also want to underline what I see as the most substantive differences between Habermas's and Rorty's pragmatisms. Still more important, I want to underline some crucial differences between their philosophies and the pragmatist aesthetics that I have tried to develop by building more on the experiential tradition of pragmatism.

It is by now hard to see the debate between modernity and postmodernity as a deep and influential difference between Habermasian and Rortian pragmatism. This is not only because the terms "modernity" and "postmodernity" are so difficult to define and because Rorty now seems to have disavowed his use of the term "postmodern".[3] It is also because when they theorize the postmodern, both have done so essentially in terms of philosophical narrative (rather than by socio-economic, political, or stylistic features). Moreover, both Habermas and Rorty have portrayed the narrative of postmodernity's challenge to modernity as essentially a challenge by aesthetics to the reign of reason.

As the project of modernity (with its Enlightenment roots and its rationalizing principle of differentiation of cultural spheres) is identified with reason, so the postmodern is contrastingly characterized as dominantly

166

aesthetic. But, from my pragmatist perspective, the rational/aesthetic and modernity/postmodernity oppositions must not be taken too rashly. Modernity clearly has its aesthetic, while postmodernism has its reasons. As art typically displays a rationality of order, unity, and purpose, so reason reveals its own deep aesthetic dimension. For many of reason's central notions (coherence, balance, proportion, completeness, simplicity, fairness) not only have aesthetic connotations but, even when mechanically defined, require a kind of cultivated aesthetic perception or taste for their proper understanding and application.

Since both Rorty and Habermas insist on the primacy of language, it is there that their reason/aesthetic debate is ultimately focused. Thus Habermas criticizes Rorty for "aestheticizing" language by privileging metaphor and rhetoric as more central to meaning than truth and argument. This leads to a disastrous "leveling [of] the genre distinction between philosophy and literature" in which philosophy's long-standing commitment to truth and the rational consensus of problem-solving is replaced by the poetic quest for exciting new metaphors.[4] Rorty responds not only by questioning the "universalism" implicit in Habermas's theory of communicative reason, but by challenging the very distinction "between rationality and irrationality" as an "obsolete and clumsy" piece of rhetoric. Despite Habermas's claims to historicize reason by embedding it in pragmatic contexts, Rorty finds the ideal of reason still too abstract, general and metaphysical. It represents, he claims, a restrictive remnant of religion's need to supply a redeeming unity of human essence, while what we need instead is to give free play to aesthetic "fantasy" and its enriching multiplicities. Opposing modernity's "Enlightenment hope" for rationalized society, Rorty advocates that "culture as a whole ... be 'poeticized'."[5]

Through such polemics, Habermas and Rorty project a misleading dualism between reason and aesthetics that seems inconsistent with pragmatism's pluralist stance and its resistance to dichotomies. This troubling dualism can be weakened by showing that its dueling theorists actually agree on far more than they differ, though their agreement is concealed by the rhetoric of contrast so central to our habits of philosophical thinking and reinforced by the institutional frameworks that thrive on the drama of debate. We can begin with their convergent narratives of the path to postmodernity, which both see in terms of aesthetics' challenge to the sovereignty of reason.

II

For Habermas, the story starts with Schiller's and Hegel's dissatisfaction with the tradition of subject-centered reason and its philosophy of reflection, a tradition that stems from Descartes and reaches its apotheosis in Kant. This concept of reason could not escape the self-referential dilemma of having to reflect critically on the subject's knowledge while basing such criticism wholly on the subject's own reason. Moreover, in focusing on the individual subjects and thus neglecting the communicative dimension of human understanding, it heightened social fragmentation and prevented philosophy from fulfilling the role of promoting cultural unity, which it had inherited from religion (*PDM* 19–22). Yet, for Habermas, reason – properly understood as communicative – constitutes "the ultimate power of unification" (*PDM* 32). Philosophy's failure to grasp the idea of reason not in terms of subjectivity but in terms of communicative intersubjectivity – an idea implicit in Schiller's and the young Hegel's view of *art* "as the genuine embodiment of communicative reason" and a non-coercive unifier – constitutes for Habermas the philosophical catastrophe of our epoch (*PDM* 48).

Blindness to this alternative model of reason has locked us in the relentless self-critique of subject-centered reason, so that we have become suspicious of reason altogether. To escape this divisive dialectic of enlightenment – the self-critique of reason by its own immanent activity (complemented by its repressive self-control of the rational subject), Nietzsche turned instead to the aesthetic as "reason's absolute other" (*PDM* 94). Since Habermas affirms "the internal relationship between modernity and rationality" (*PDM* 4), he sees Nietzsche's aestheticism as "the entry into postmodernity," and characterizes this aesthetic as an anti-rational, Dionysian "decentered subjectivity liberated from all constraints of cognition and purposive activity" (*PDM* 94, 96).

Of course, already in modernity's cultural economy of aesthetic autonomy (through its tripartite division of science, ethics–politics, and art), aesthetic experience aimed at freeing subjectivity both from narrow self-centeredness and the constraints of scientific and moral–practical judgment. But here aesthetic freedom was essentially confined to the sphere of art. Hence aesthetic experience was not only directed by the rational discourse of art criticism, but also controlled in being framed by the regulative boundaries constituted by the corresponding autonomy of the more clearly reason-governed domains of science and morality. With Nietzschean postmodernism, however, the aesthetic no longer remains content with such rational limits. Displaying an irrational, limit-defying "anarchistic intention" of Dionysian will to power, it "reduces everything that is and should be to the aesthetic dimension," presenting itself as not only reason's other but its sovereign (*PDM* 95–6, 123).

Habermas's story thus contains two very different notions of the aesthetic, though he often forgets to distinguish them. (More generally, he admits that his knowledge may not "be up to the complexity" of aesthetic questions – perhaps one more reason why he seems so suspicious toward the aesthetic.)[6] In any case, the first notion of the aesthetic we find in Habermas's narrative is the rational, compartmentalized, and disciplined domain of art. Embodying communicative reason, seeking artistic progress, and providing the pleasures of meaningful form, it represents, for him, the classic aesthetic of modernity, one of "aesthetic harmony" and "artistic truth" (*PDM* 207). This is the aesthetic of autonomous modern art whose essential "truth-reference" (*Wahrheitsbezug*) and reconciling-potential (*Versöhnungspotential*) was affirmed in "the great tradition" from Hegel to Lukács (*R* 51).[7]

In contrast, what Habermas mainly identifies as the aesthetic is an anti-rational drive of unconstrained hedonism and radical transgression, an aesthetic of "body-centered experiences of a decentered subjectivity," aimed at "limit-experiences" of "mystical" "ecstasy," producing "dizzying effects ... of shock ... without any proper object," This becomes, in Habermas's polemic, the dominant aesthetic force, which he demonizes as "aesthetically inspired anarchism" and attacks as the postmodern threat to modernity's project of progressive emancipation through reason (*PDM* 5, 306–9).

Habermas traces this aesthetic challenge from Nietzsche to Georges Bataille's "aesthetically inspired" eroticism and then to Foucault's theory of bio-power. It can also be seen in their idea of limit-experiences, which decenter the rationally controlled subject experientially, just as their genealogical critique decenters it theoretically (*PDM* 211–16, 221–93). Postmodern privileging of aesthetics over reason becomes, for Habermas, still clearer in Derrida's and Rorty's advocacy of "the primacy of rhetoric over logic," "world-disclosing" literary artistry over "problem-solving" argument, and metaphor over "normal" speech: all of this captured in their vision of philosophy as just a kind of writing (*PDM* 190–207). He also finds this dangerously anti-modern aesthetic challenge in recent German philosophy. Most virulent in Heidegger's ecstatic appeal to an archaic disclosure of Being (an "ontologized art") through a poetic "thinking more rigorous than the conceptual", it can even be detected in a rational arch-modernist like Adorno, with his emphasis on the redemptive, nondiscursive truth of art's archaic "mimetic content" (*PDM* 104, 128, 136).

For Habermas, the anti-rational aesthetic derives its authority from the enormous power of aesthetic experience in modern times, particularly as it developed from Romanticism to the modernist avant-garde. By seeming to surpass reason (and overwhelm our self-possession), such experience seems to fruitfully offer an alternative to reason and an escape from the self-centered critical self. Yet such potent aesthetic experience, he argues, is only the product of modernity's progress toward avant-garde art, and therefore depends on its rational discursive structures even while purporting to oppose and transcend reason. The aesthetic experiences employed by these anti-rational theorists "are due to the same process of differentiation [and rationalization] as science and morality" (*PDM* 339). Therefore, to appropriate aesthetic experience theoretically in order to escape or outflank rationality involves a performative contradiction. Moreover, to the extent that it negates the rationality embodied in modernity's artistic tradition, radical aesthetic experience loses all its meaning; "the contents get dispersed [and] an emancipatory effect does not follow."[8]

Though plausible as *ad hominem* arguments concerning the modernist taste of anti-rational champions of the aesthetic, these arguments fail to clinch the case for the primacy of reason. For they wrongly presume that powerful aesthetic experience always needs modernity's rationalized, differentiated conception of art, that it never existed before nor is ever achievable outside the framework of modernity's aesthetics. This presumption not only unconvincingly excludes the passionate aesthetic experience of ancient Greece (so inspirational for Nietzsche), but that of contemporary African cultures where such experience is not prestructured by modernity's cultural divisions.[9]

Habermas, however, still has his master argument for the primacy of reason. There is no escaping reason, because there is no escaping language and because language is essentially and necessarily rational. Language is the medium through which we live; and it is unavoidably rational since there is "an internal connection between meaning and validity," i.e. between meaning and the rational, communicative assessment of truth claims and truth-related judgments (*PDM* 313–14).[10] Aligning himself with Peircean pragmatism, Habermas insists that this defense of communicative reason makes no appeal to a transcendent "pure reason that might don linguistic clothing only in the second place. Reason is by its very nature incarnated in contexts of communicative action and in structures of the lifeworld" (*PDM* 322).

But in viewing language as the essence of rationality and the ground of its primacy, Habermas must resist Derrida's and Rorty's deconstructive efforts to portray language as more fundamentally aesthetic, as more a matter of disseminating creativity, persuasive rhetoric, and world-making tropes than of logical validity. Their attempt to blur the distinctions between literature, literary criticism, and philosophy is likewise condemned as a strategy to undermine the primacy of reason by denying its rationalizing process of differentiation of disciplines, a differentiation Habermas sees as essential to the achievement and progress of those disciplines. "This aestheticizing of language," he claims, "is purchased with the twofold denial of the proper senses of normal and poetic discourse. Moreover, to deny all distinction between the poetic world-disclosive function of language and its prosaic innerworldly functions" obscures the crucial fact that it is ultimately on such normal "everyday communicative practice" that all "learning processes" (including those of poetic production) are based, and "in relation to which the world-disclosive force of ... language has in turn to prove its worth" (*PDM* 205).[11]

Habermas further argues that privileging the aesthetic language of innovative world-disclosure (paradigmatically expressed in "the esoteric work of art") fosters not only an "elitist contempt for discursive thought" but similar disrespect for the more ordinary, more essential lifeworld practices of problem-solving and for the ordinary people engaged in them (*PDM* 186). By endorsing the primacy of communicative reason through the ordinary linguistic practices of the lifeworld, by enlisting both pragmatism's stress on consensual practice and Anglo-American philosophy's linguistic turn, Habermas seeks to overcome the Nietzschean–postmodern aesthetic turn that pervades so much contemporary continental theory, not only in France but closer to home in Heidegger and Adorno.

III

Rorty also advocates the primacy of language, but no longer sees it as the incarnation of reason or the expression of a deep human essence. Instead, language is taken primarily as an aesthetic tool for new creation and self-fashioning; we revise science, self, and society by redescription, by retelling their respective histories through different vocabularies. Philosophy should therefore also "turn against theory and toward narrative" (*CIS* xvi). Rorty's narrative of the path to postmodernity (or "ironist culture"), is one of progressive liberation from the rule of reason through the advocacy and appeal of the aesthetic. This tale is structured on a series of parallel binary oppositions that flesh out the central contrast of reason versus the aesthetic. The oppositions can be lined up as follows: truth/metaphor, necessity/contingency, universal/particular, public/private, philosophy/poetry, inference/narrative, logic/rhetoric, discovery/creation, foundations/apologetics, deep reality/surface appearances, metaphysicians/ironists, theorists/novelists. Freedom and progress are a function of reversing the repressive privilege of the former terms.

Hegel began the aesthetic revolt against philosophy by historicizing and narrativizing it in his *Phenomenology*. However, he lapsed by taking his narrative as the final definitive story with his own philosophy as the ultimate conclusion. Nietzsche advanced the cause of freedom by highlighting the aesthetic, by advocating an uncompromising perspectivism, and by rejecting truth and metaphysics for creative interpretation and genealogical redescription. But despite Nietzsche's professed anti-metaphysical perspectivism, there lurks a vestigial metaphysics and privileged perspective in his theory of the will to power.[12] Similarly, his anti-authoritarianism masks an autocratic injunction that the only worthy life is the sublime heroic one of the creative, striving of the Overman.

Heidegger, despite his attempt to overcome all metaphysics (including Nietzsche's), still falls victim to the same metaphysical impulse of universalizing his own vocabulary and interpretive redescriptions as *the* authoritative lexicon, narrative, and destiny of Western civilization. Early Derrida makes the same mistake by presenting his notions of *différance* and "the myth of presence" as (respectively) the necessary root of all writing and the definitive interpretation of the entire history of metaphysics. Instead, he should recognize that these notions are nothing more than apt new ways to redescribe his own self and thought in relation to the past vocabularies and narratives on which he (like most of us philosophers) was raised.

This error of universalizing one's own preferred vocabulary and story as authoritative for the general public is, for Rorty, a pernicious remnant of the metaphysical claim of reason: the idea that private and public must be united through a rational grounding synthesis, the view that private ideals and beliefs are only truly valid if publicly validated, and that validity and legitimacy involves universalizability. Reason traditionally urged this standard of validity, just as metaphysics had the traditional goal of uniting our words and personal stories with something monumental, eternal and sublime: Truth, Reality, Power, Human Nature, History. But the aesthetic, for Rorty, is different. It can be satisfied with the particular and contingent, even the private, transitory and fictional. For (to use another of Rorty's contrasting pairs), it can seek beauty rather than sublimity (*CIS* 105–6). Rorty sees Habermas's commitment to the sovereignty of reason and its ideal of "universal validity" as one more case of this "craving for a sublime."[13]

Freedom is thus better served by aesthetic writers who cherish particularity and personal linguistic invention than by philosophers who want to speak for all humanity in the name and language of universal reason or even in terms of something else Big and Basic (like Power or *Dasein*). Such consciously aesthetic creators best realize Rorty's "liberal ironist" dream "to overcome authority without claiming authority": overcoming the authority of inherited narratives and vocabularies by creating a strikingly distinctive self and history in one's own terms, but doing so without claiming authority over the language and self-fashioning of others.[14] Proust (in contrast to Nietzsche and Heidegger) proves paradigmatic of the ironist's aesthetic ideal "because he had no public ambitions" that his language would determine the true meaning of modern Europe. By telling his own personal stories rather than offering general theory, he shows both the humble irony and "the courage to give up the attempt to unite the private and the public, to stop trying to bring together a quest for private autonomy and an attempt at public resonance and utility" (*CIS* 125).

The ironist aesthete can likewise escape the performative paradox that both Rorty and Habermas see as the prime stumbling block of postmodern philosophers: the problem of how to displace theory and reason without further theorizing and reasoning. The answer, for Rorty, is simply to circumvent theory's traditional claims of universal, essential truth by instead telling more personal stories for one's own individual self-constituting emancipation; in short, to privatize philosophy.

Though privileging language as constitutive of the self and lifeworld, Rorty rejects the idea of "language in general" as a substantive universal, as some "entity" or "unity," "intervening between self and reality" that constitutes the common core of human experience (*CIS* 13–15). For such an idea amounts to an essentialism about language that is no better (if indeed different) than an essentialism about reason. Instead, Rorty advocates the idea of very particular, contingent, historicized linguistic practices or vocabularies. These are simply tools for coping with experience, and their highest function is not the Habermasian one of cooperative problem-solving to promote mutual understanding and consensus, but rather the aesthetic one of individual, original creation, to 'make things new', "to make something that never had been dreamt of before." The most crucial goal is innovative "self-creation": refashioning and mastering oneself and one's structuring world "by inventing a new language" that redescribes these things in one's "own terms," so as to escape from oppressive "inherited descriptions" and free oneself from the "horror of finding oneself to be only a copy or replica" (*CIS* 13, 27–9).

Rorty's aesthetic view of language as a tool for constant novelty and individual self-expression seems challenged by the fact that language requires some stable commonalities and consensus in order to be at all effective. Wittgenstein makes this point in his famous private-language argument, and Habermas similarly urges that language-games cannot work (hence sentences cannot mean) without a linguistic community sharing to some extent the same vocabulary and "*the presupposition of intersubjectively identical ascriptions of meaning*" (*PDM* 198, italics in original).

Rorty has two strategies for meeting this objection. Adopting Donald Davidson's account of metaphoric meaning, he argues that we need no stable shared rules for linguistic understanding. We can simply proceed on intuitive predictions of meaning based on current context and our previous habits of linguistic understanding. My rejoinder is that those habits would be undermined and unprojectible if language were fully aestheticized, privatized, and innovationally protean in Rorty's recommended way.

Rorty's second strategy is to separate a public from a public use of language. While the former is fully shared to serve the needs of consensual social life, the private use need not be fully shared and indeed *should not be*, if the individual is to achieve autonomy. But this private rhetoric of self-creation can remain sufficiently anchored in shared public language so as to be comprehensible to others and thus avoid the problem of the private-language argument. Since effective communication and social functioning require some linguistic consensus and stability, Rorty admits that there can be no "culture whose public rhetoric is ironist. Irony seems an inherently private manner" and necessarily "reactive," requiring "the contrast" of the public as a shared "inherited" base from which it can assert its novel difference, "something from which to be alienated" (*CIS* 87–8). Here (as elsewhere) Rorty's entire project avowedly "turns on a firm distinction between the private and the public" (*CIS* 83).

This sharp "public–private split" (*CIS* 85) involves not only separating the language of consensus from the language of creation. It also means separating the political realm of "social organization" from the aesthetic realm of individual autonomy (which he wrongly equates with unique, distinctive self-creation).[15] Privileging the private and aesthetic as what gives meaning to life, Rorty advocates political liberalism as merely a means to provide the necessary stability and negative liberty for pursuit of our private aims. His "aim of a just and free society [is] letting its citizens be as privatistic, 'irrationalist', and aestheticist as they please so long as they do ... no harm to others" (*CIS* xiv).

But as many (including Habermas) have insisted, Rorty's "firm distinction between the private and the public" is simply untenable, since the private self and the language it builds on in self-creation are always already socially constituted and structured by a public field. Indeed, not only Rorty's particular privatized ethic of linguistic aestheticist self-styling but his whole notion of privatizing ethics clearly reflect the particular public and wider society that shape his thinking – the intellectual field and consumerist world of late-capitalist liberalism.[16]

Rorty's very idea of self-constitution and self-creation through language not only vitiates any strong public/private dichotomy; it also suggests a lurking linguistic essentialism that differs from the one he repudiates, but seems even more pernicious. His view that the self is nothing but a linguistic web or complex of narratives comes uncomfortably close to an essentialist view of human nature as exclusively linguistic. All that matters for selfhood and human being in the world is language: "human beings are simply incarnated vocabularies"; it is simply "words which made us what we are." Thus Nietzsche is praised as one who "by describing himself in his own terms ... created himself," since he "created the only part of himself that mattered by constructing his own mind. To create one's mind is to create one's language." For humans are "nothing more than sentential attitudes – nothing more than the presence or absence of dispositions toward the use of sentences phrased in some historically-constituted vocabulary" (*CIS* 27, 88, 117).[17]

The only nonlinguistic element of experience that Rorty is willing to recognize is brute physical pain. But in contrast to the essentially linguistic and human pain of "humiliation," it represents "the nonhuman, the nonlinguistic," what "ties us to the non-language using beasts" (*CIS* 40, 92, 94). The power of such brute suffering even drives the anti-metaphysical Rorty toward a seemingly metaphysical vision that pits human linguistic creation against a deeper, essentially cruel and inhuman ground reality of "just power and pain ... to be found 'out there'" (*CIS* 40).

In arguing that man is essentially mind and that mind is essentially linguistic, Rorty not only violates his anti-essentialism but endorses a mentalistic view of human nature against Nietzsche's own emphasis on the body's formative role and value. Such linguistic mentalism and somatic neglect is particularly pernicious in a philosopher intent on advancing the aesthetic, whose crucial connection with the bodily senses and pleasures should be obvious, if it were not for the discursive bias that has enthralled so much traditional aesthetic theory and still seems to ensnare Rorty's.

His aesthetic is thus hardly different from the rationalist modern aesthetic that Habermas advocates. He exhibits none of that Dionysian aestheticism of Bataille, Deleuze, or Foucault that Habermas condemns as postmodern. Nor does Rorty even seem to recognize the more moderate somatic aesthetics and pleasures that I recommend in certain forms of popular music and "body work."[18] He just likes to read books, and those he likes (notably Proust, Nabakov, Orwell and Forster) all belong to the refined modern canon of serious art rather than to mad Dadaism, savage surrealism, anarchistic postmodernism, or the hedonic works of popular culture. Moreover, he recommends his chosen forms of art not for the wild ecstasies they produce but because they may "help us become autonomous ... [and] less cruel" (*CIS* 141).

In short, Rorty's aestheticism is rationally melioristic, advocating art to improve the lifeworld by making the individual both stronger in himself and more tolerant in understanding others. How different is this from Habermas's strategy for continuing modernity's project of progress while overcoming its cultural fragmentation? Both seek to appropriate the achievements of our advancing, specialized high art tradition by translating its contents, through expert interpretive criticism, into the language and experience of our lifeworld.

IV

To sum up, both Habermas and Rorty see postmodernism as privileging the aesthetic over the Enlightenment tradition of reason, and both supply historico-philosophical narratives to explain this aesthetic turn. Moreover, both cherish the modernist aesthetic tradition of high art in its more formally disciplined and rational forms, prizing it for its useful contributions to the lifeworld. Finally, both identify this lifeworld with language, which thus becomes the essence of human nature and the battleground over which aesthetics and reason struggle for dominance. Here, in their contrasting privileging of the linguistic centrality of these terms, Rorty and Habermas at last show a real difference.[19]

But how momentous is it? Habermas clearly affirms language's important aesthetic dimensions: not simply "the world-creating capacity of language," its special "poetic-world-disclosive function," but also an "aesthetic–expressive" dimension that he recognizes in every speech act (*PDM* 313, 315). Conversely, Rorty readily admits the usefulness of the rational/irrational distinction within "the interior of a language game" and particularly within

175

the domain of "public rhetoric" (which Habermas, of course, would call "public reason," *CIS* 47, 87).

Rorty loves to shock old-fashioned rationalists by advocating aesthetic primacy even in "the language of theoretical science," which (like Mary Hesse) he sees as "irreducibly metaphorical." Metaphor, moreover, "is essential to scientific progress," since its innovative aesthetic imagination provides the necessary means to break out of the entrenched vocabularies of old scientific paradigms, thus paving the way for more productive new theories (*EHO* 166; *ORT* 162). But Habermas also recognizes that "the specialized languages of science and technology ... live off the illuminating power of metaphorical tropes," although these "rhetorical elements" are eventually submitted to argumentative and experimental disciplines of consensus-oriented discourse in the process of theory justification and in being "enlisted for the special purposes of problem-solving" (*PDM* 209; cf. *PT* 205). So if Rorty portrays the history of scientific progress "as the history of metaphor" (*CIS* 16), Habermas is simply objecting that this is not the whole story.

Yet Rorty clearly admits this as well. In defending Habermas against Lyotard's postmodern vision of science as pure innovational paralogy, he recognizes the useful regulative role of normal science, arguing that science no more aims "at piling paralogy on paralogy" than politics "aims at piling revolution on revolution" (*EHO* 166). Likewise, though preferring to highlight science's revolutionary moment as more interesting and inspiringly heroic through its creative difference and change, Rorty nonetheless shows great respect for normal science's language of consensus. Celebrating it as the expression of "unforced agreement" through the discussion of wide-ranging "suggestions and arguments," Rorty recommends it as an exemplary "model of human solidarity" (*ORT* 39). Finally, even the privileged aesthetic moment of novel difference must in some way gain validation through public discourse and its normative (albeit revisable) justificational procedures. This convergence of "private" fantasy with shared public language and the needs of a community is recognized even by Rorty as what distinguishes "genius" from mad "eccentricity or perversity" (*CIS* 37).

The limits of Rortian aesthetic sovereignty become still clearer when we turn to the realm of politics and the public sphere. *There*, as we saw, the "public rhetoric" of consensus must prevail; there we don't want idiosyncratic metaphors but shared norms, common categories, stable procedures and consistent rules of argument. There even universalism is affirmed – not in the Habermas sense as a foundational "idealizing presupposition of communicative action" (*PDM* 206), but as the goal of an ever wider, more inclusive community of reasonable, tolerant liberals. The aesthetic and its individualism dominate only in the private sphere, though this is the sphere that Rorty privileges in contrast to Habermas's championing of the public. The public/private split is crucial for Rorty's remapping of modernity's tripartite schema of science, art, and the ethico-political into a dualism of *public* discourse based on normality and consensus versus a *private* discursive sphere aimed at radical innovation and individual fulfillment. If normal science and politics can be fit into the former, the private ethics of personal lifestyles becomes aestheticized as part of the private realm of taste.

Yet Habermas's ideal of communicative reason seems procedural and liberal enough to accept for differences of taste in art and aesthetic lifestyles so long as this did not endanger the essential social norms of the public sphere. So if they share a taste for aesthetic modernism and the politics of liberal, social-welfare democracy, why does the Rorty–Habermas debate seem so urgent to us philosophers?

At stake in their question of privileging aesthetics or reason, the private or public, is our very conception of philosophy and our self-image as philosophers. For Rorty, philosophy gets aestheticized with ethics and is relegated to the private realm. It becomes an art of living one's own life with greater autonomy and fulfillment, and perhaps inspiring others to do like-wise. But it should never pretend to determine general norms for improving the direction of science or the public sphere. We should therefore "be more dubious about the social utility of philosophy than Habermas is" (*TP* 326). For Habermas, in contrast, reason's primacy over the aesthetic means keeping philosophy firmly with science in the public domain of consensus and knowledge. Philosophy remains the unifying discipline of the public sphere, integrating and legitimating its scientific, social, and even aesthetic norms. If no longer the authoritarian arbiter of culture, it remains the crucial "stand-in (*Platzhalter*) and interpreter," "the guardian of reason."[20]

Their debate between reason and aesthetics also seems momentous to the way philosophy aligns itself with other cognitive disciplines in our culture. Habermas is deeply committed to social theory and so has strongly linked philosophy to the social sciences, while Rorty is deeply critical of the very idea of general social theory and wants to link philosophy's utility with liter-ature. He thinks that general social science offers little help in promoting reforms that would reduce "the institutionalized infliction" of injustice in our society. Criticizing what he calls "large-scale German-style 'social theory,'" Rorty demands "concreteness" of description in making "specific kinds of pain and humiliation visible" along with specific proposals of change (*TP* 322, 326). He looks to creative literature as the greatest hope for performing the first useful kind of description, and perhaps inspiring the second. He therefore joins Harold Bloom in fearing that today's rising wave of cultural analysis in literary criticism is "converting the study of literature into ... one more dismal social science" and thus destroying its "inspira-tional value."[21]

But why should we believe that socially informed literary study destroys the inspiring power of literary works? To make that presumption we need to assume a dualism of aesthetic power versus knowledge, which is not only uncharacteristic of pragmatism but is also simply false. Great works usually gain power the better we know them. And just as we should not have to choose between knowledge and inspiration, there is no need to reject general social theory to affirm the value of particular descriptions, whether in novels, newspaper articles, or anthropological reports. Why can't we encourage both? Moreover, don't we need some degree of general theory to help us integrate these specific reports in a more comprehensive picture, if not also to help us generate ideas of what questions, sectors, and institutions in society we want descriptions about and how these institutions or sectors are to be individuated for our inquiry?

If Habermas seems to belittle the social utility of the aesthetic, he is right to insist that philosophy needs to work closely with social theory. Not only can this augment philosophy's social utility but it can even improve its own self-understanding by examining more carefully the social field that helps structure the agenda and directions that our philosophical thinking pursues.

Though Habermas is wrong to demonize the aesthetic as the other of reason, his fears do reflect an important point that pragmatism needs to embrace (as James and Dewey did) but Rorty sadly fails to: the crucial value of the nondiscursive dimension of the aesthetic. Language can neither always explain nor do justice to the meanings of aesthetic experience, some of which are deeply visceral and sensual. But to say that certain aesthetic dimensions cannot be reduced to reason and language does not imply that they are opposed to reason, or are devoid of intelligence or are not amenable to education by a combination of linguistic and nonlinguistic measures. When faced with such talk about the nondiscursive, Habermas is likely to pose the dialectical dilemma that to talk about the "other of reason" or "other of language" is already to inscribe that other within the ambit of reason and language. Indeed, he sees this as his trump card of performative contradiction against reason's critique by its other.

But surely one value of the aesthetic, through the intense pleasures and often overwhelming power of aesthetic experience, is to make us forget for a moment about language and reason, allowing us to revel, for a moment, in non-discursive sensual joy. This crucial sensual dimension is sadly neglected by Rorty because of his global linguisticism, rendering his aesthetic joylessly eviscerate. Of course, even if there is more to aesthetics than the discursive, there is no way to avoid language when talking about aesthetics. As T.S. Eliot's Sweeney complained, "I gotta use words when I talk to you." In one sense, this is a trivial sophism, but in another sense a deep truth. To discourse about the nondiscursive aesthetic is never enough to bring an adequately full recognition of its pleasures and powers. This is why the framework through which I treat them – a field I call somaesthetics – involves not merely theory but practice.[22] The discourse of theory is certainly needed to help clear the path of inquiry to allow room for more robust and more than discursive measures to heighten our sensuous aesthetic sensitivity. Unfortunately, theory's discourse (always inclined to privilege its own mode) has too often burdened that path with troublesome obstacles. Habermas's pragmatism remains an obstacle here, but then so does Rorty's.

Notes

1 An earlier version of this article appeared in my *Practicing Philosophy: Pragmatism and the Philosophical Life*, New York, Routledge, 1997, ch. 4.
2 Several of the papers given at that conference were later published in a book entitled *La modernité en question: de Richard Rorty à Jürgen Habermas*, eds François Gaillard, Jacques Poulain, and Richard Shusterman, Paris, Cerf, 1998.
3 See Richard Rorty, *Essays on Heidegger and Others: Philosophical Papers* vol. 2, Cambridge, Cambridge University Press, 1991; henceforth *EHO*. In that volume's introduction, Rorty retrospectively regrets his problematic usage of such a very broad and contested cultural term like "postmodernism" in defining his position as "Postmodern Bourgeois Liberalism" and more generally in characterizing contemporary philosophy. Instead he offers "Post-Nietzschean" as a more precise, uncontroversial label for philosophers (e.g. Heidegger, Derrida, Lyotard) earlier defended under the notion of postmodern (*EHO* 1–2). Since Habermas identifies the postmodern with Nietzsche, Rorty's terminological substitution does not affect the sense of their debate. Rorty's "Postmodern Bourgeois Liberalism" is reprinted in his *Objectivity, Relativism, and Truth: Philosophical Papers* vol. 1, Cambridge, Cambridge University Press, 1991; henceforth *ORT*.
4 Jürgen Habermas, *The Philosophical Discourses of Modernity*, Cambridge, Mass., MIT Press, 1987, 185–210. This book will be referred to in my text as *PDM*.
5 Richard Rorty, *Contingency, Irony, and Solidarity*, Cambridge, Cambridge University Press, 1989, pp. 44–5, 48, 53 (henceforth *CIS*). He glosses the notion of poeticized culture as "substitut[ing] the hope that chances for equal fulfillment of idiosyncratic fantasies will be equalized for the hope that everyone will replace 'passion' or fantasy with 'reason'" (53). See also his critique of Habermas's use of communicative reason to answer modern culture's "'need for unification' in order to 'regenerate the unifying power of religion in the medium of reason'"; in Richard Rorty, "Habermas and Lyotard on postmodernity," in *EHO* 169 (citing *PDM* 19, 20).
6 In an article of 1995, he confesses "my rather fragmentary treatment of aesthetic questions with the feeling that I am not yet up to the complexity of these questions (meiner eher fragmentarischen Behandlung ästhetischer Fragen mit dem Gefühl, dass ich der Komplexität dieser Fragen noch nicht gewachsen bin)". See J. Habermas, "Replik," Revue Internationale de Philosophie, 194 (1995), pp. 551–65, citation from p. 551; henceforth *R*.
7 This favored, circumscribed aesthetic of modernity is also described in a later, less polemical work in the same manner that emphasizes its compartmentalization. See "Handlungen, Sprechakte, sprachlich vermittelte Interaktionnen und Lebenswelt," in Jürgen Habermas, *Postmetaphysisches Denken: Philosophisches Aufsatze*, Frankfurt, Suhrkamp, 1988, pp. 63–104; henceforth *PD*.

> The aesthetic experiences are not admitted into forms of praxis; they are not referred to cognitive–instrumental skills and moral representations, which are developed from innerworld learning processes; they are tied up

[*verwoben*] with the world-constituting, world-disclosing function of language.

(*PD* 94, my translation)

This essay was not included in the English version, *Postmetaphysical Thinking:Philosophical Essays*, Cambridge, Mass., MIT Press, 1992; henceforth *PT*.

8 Jürgen Habermas, "Modernity – an incomplete project," repr. in Hal Foster, *The Anti-Aesthetic*, Port Townsend, Washington, Bay Press, 1983, p. 11.

9 For more detailed argument, see Richard Shusterman, *Pragmatist Aesthetics: Living Beauty, Rethinking Art*, Oxford, Blackwell, 1992; 2nd edition, New York, Rowman & Littlefield, 2000, ch. 2.

10 Habermas's theory of communicative reason does not limit the connection of validity and meaning to the standard notion of truth as the representation of facts, but concerns also the speech-act's dimension of "rightness" (in the sense of moral normativity) and "truthfulness" (in the sense of authenticity of expression). This tripartite analysis of validity is explicitly meant to parallel "the three fundamental functions of language" (representative, appellative-regulative, and expressive), but also clearly suggests modernity's division of spheres into representative science, regulative ethics and politics, and expressive art (*PDM* 313–15). Earlier, in *The Theory of Communicative Action*, vol. 1, Boston, Beacon Press, 1984, p. 335, he cites "works of art" as "exemplary" of the "rationality" of "expressive knowledge" which "can be criticized as untruthful." In short, modernity's tripartite differentiation of cultural spheres appears as the necessary rational development of the essential tripartite logic of language itself. Rorty is right to object that our cultural institutions and language are more contingent in origin. But given his own problematically vague and radical sense of contingency, Rorty's contrasting account of all language and culture as "sheer contingency" should likewise be resisted (*CIS* 22). Habermas returns to this tripartite analysis of the validity dimension of all speech acts in *PT* 76–9. But the conclusion of that book's essay "Philosophy and science as literature?" presents a seemingly different suggestion for artworks: that validity claims, though still present in fictional texts or utterances, are only binding for the people in the fiction, "not for the author and the reader" (pp. 223–4). This seems to challenge or at least greatly constrain the role of expressive truthfulness for the validity of aesthetic discourse.

11 Through a critical reading of Calvino's experimental novel, *If on a Winter's Night a Traveler*, Habermas tries to show how the leveling of the aesthetic-fiction/everyday-real world distinction will not succeed even in aesthetic practice. His central point is that "Everyday life [with its discourse to solve problems] continues to place limits around literary texts" that are essential for the differentially determined identity and proper functioning of these artworks. See "Philosophy and science as literature?" in *PT* 205–27, especially pp. 218, 223.

12 For a pragmatist critique of this metaphysics, see *Pragmatist Aesthetics*, pp. 79–82.

13 See Richard Rorty, "Habermas, Derrida, and the functions of philosophy" in *Truth and Progress: Philosophical Papers III*, Cambridge, Cambridge University Press, 1999, pp. 323, 325; henceforth *TP*.

14 Citations in this paragraph are from *CIS* pp. 105, 118, 125. Rorty's plea that philosophy become privatized and avoid all claims to general authority over others can be read as a confession of his own choice not to presume the role of a dominating major philosopher whose views claim to be definitive and generally binding, preferring instead what he calls a style of "weak thought" (*EHO* 6).

Such a position dovetails neatly not only with anti-foundationalism but with his liberalist pluralism.

15 For detailed argument against this conflation, see *Pragmatist Aesthetics*, pp. 253–5.

16 For more detailed argument of this point see *Pragmatist Aesthetics*, pp. 255–7.

17 Though Rorty always insists on the primacy of the propositional or sentential, he is forced by his privileging of the private and the idiosyncratically creative to admit the presence and value of associations and images of words below the level of propositional attitudes. These nevertheless depend for their possibility on sentential meaning (*CIS* 153)

18 See *Pragmatist Aesthetics*, chs 7, 8, 9; and my "Die Sorge um den Korper in der heutigen Kultur," in A. Kuhlmann (ed.) *Philosophische Ansichenten der Kultur der Modern*, Frankfurt, Fischer, 1994, pp. 241–77.

19 This, of course, is not the only difference between them. There are also some technical differences, for example, like Habermas's critique of Rorty's naturalization of reason to evolutionary coping and his alleged dissolving of the distinction between truth and justification. In contrast Habermas insists on the possibility of "unconditional validity" and "an unconditional truth claim that aims beyond what is justified." See Jürgen Habermas, "Richard Rorty's pragmatic turn," *On the Pragmatics of Communication*, Cambridge, MIT Press, 1999, pp. 358–9.

20 See Jürgen Habermas, "Philosophy as stand-in and interpreter," in *Moral Consciousness and Communicative Action*, Cambridge, MIT Press, 1990, pp. 3, 4. His linking of philosophy with science as opposed to the aesthetic is underlined in "Philosophy and science as literature?" where both the former (as opposed to the latter) cannot "give up the orientation to questions of truth" (*PT* 225).

21 Richard Rorty, "The inspirational value of great works of literature" in *Achieving Our Country*, Cambridge, Mass, Harvard University Press, 1998, pp. 125, 127; henceforth *AC*.

22 See Richard Shusterman, "Somaesthetics: a disciplinary proposal," in *Pragmatist Aesthetics*, 2nd edition, ch. 10; and *Performing Live*, Ithaca and London, Cornell University Press, 2000, chs 7–8.

Part IV

COMPARATIVE STUDIES

9

IS OBJECTIVITY PERSPECTIVAL?

Reflexions on Brandom's and Habermas's pragmatist conceptions of objectivity

Cristina Lafont

Among all the similarities and differences that immediately strike a reader of Brandom's and Habermas's approaches to communicative practices, those related to the conception of objectivity that both entail probably are the most intricate and hardest to establish. This is so not, as it happens in other cases, because they are too dissimilar to be compared, but rather the exact opposite. In some respects they are virtually identical, but in others almost directly opposed. Thus, it is not completely clear in advance whether the differences between them are merely stylistic or more substantive. But, given the central role that the conception of objectivity plays in both enterprises, the mere attempt to shed some light on this issue seems to require first a perfect mapping of the differences and overlaps between both approaches. Since I do not intend to offer such a mapping in what follows, my attempt to explore the issue of possible substantial disagreements between both conceptions of objectivity is just a first approximation that does not aim to exhaust any of the possible answers.

For a first attempt at comparing Brandom's and Habermas's conceptions of objectivity, it may be useful to refer to a characterization that Brandom offers in *Making It Explicit*[1] of the minimal feature that a conception of objectivity should have within the frame of a general pragmatist strategy. He states this feature in the following terms:

> What determinate practices a community has depends on what the facts are and on what objects they are actually practically involved with ... The way the world is, constrains proprieties of inferential, doxastic, and practical commitment in a straightforward way from *within* those practices.
>
> (*MIE* 332; italics in original)

It is clear that within the general frame of a pragmatist strategy whatever constraints are taken to be connected with the notion of objectivity, they will have to be understood as internal and not as external ones, i.e. as a result of normative presuppositions anchored in the practices to be explained, and thus as operative from the practitioner's own perspective. In this respect Brandom's and Habermas' approaches follow the same general strategy in their respective accounts of objectivity. Moreover, it is also possible to find a strong similarity between both approaches not only as regards their strategy, i.e. the kind of *question* that they both would like to answer, but as regards their *specific answers* as well. Brandom characterizes his answer in a way that it seems also appropriate to describe Habermas' own. In *Making It Explicit* Brandom characterizes his approach as an attempt to reconstrue objectivity:

> as consisting in a kind of perspectival *form*, rather than in a nonper-spectival or cross-perspectival *content*. What is shared by all discursive perspectives is *that* there is a difference between what is objectively correct … and what is merely taken to be so, not *what* it is – the structure, not the content.
>
> (*MIE* 600; italics in original)

Depending on one's own philosophical assumptions, it may seem doubtful that such an attempt could provide anything recognizable as a notion of objectivity, even if it were successful. Although this is not the path that I will follow here, the plausibility of this kind of doubt forces any attempt to analyze a conception of objectivity with these characteristics to show which features traditionally associated with the notion of objectivity are supposed to be preserved by such a non-traditional conception, so that it can still justifiedly be called a conception of objectivity, rather than of something else.

This question is not only interesting in and by itself, but also for the purpose of comparing Brandom's and Habermas's approaches. For here again both approaches identify the very same features of the communicative practices as the product of the practitioners' sense of objectivity, i.e. as a result of their sharing the above-mentioned difference. According to both accounts of communicative practices, the consequence of sharing this difference is that participants who try to reach agreement about something in the world are constrained in their assertional practice by what Brandom calls "the presumption of heritability" of commitments and entitlements or, to put it in Habermas's terms, the presupposition of "a single right answer."[2] Thus, according to both authors, speakers share the assumption that "whenever two believers disagree, a diagnosis of error or ignorance is appropriate for at least one of them." (*MIE* 240) It is this feature of the assertional practice that, in turn, justifies the claim, also shared by both authors, that there is an internal connection between this practice and the game of giving and asking for reasons, between communication and discourse. For, of course, only if speakers assume that their assertions are objectively right or wrong regardless of their subjective attitudes towards them, can they see the point in asking for reasons to determine which ones are right and, thus, feel the obligation to endorse those that turn out to be right, irrespective of their prior attitudes toward them. In this respect both approaches offer a reconstruction of the assertional practice in very strong normative terms: as Brandom expresses it, assertions are *knowledge* claims (cf. *MIE* 203). If their attempt is successful, they will be able to provide an account of objectivity at least in the sense that their reconstruction of our communicative practices will be clearly incompatible with a relativist one.

Given all the mentioned similarities between both conceptions of objectivity, the main task for a comparison should be to analyze how all the mentioned features and presuppositions involved in our communicative practices are explained or accounted for according to each approach and, in particular, how they are connected with "the difference between what is correct and what is taken to be correct." This explanation, in turn, should clarify what is the rationale of presupposing such a difference, what makes it intelligible for the practitioners, etc.

However, it is not easy to identify what Brandom's explicit answers to these questions are. For Brandom's discussion of his "perspectival account of objectivity" seems targeted to answer a quite different kind of question. He seems mostly concerned with the question of the origin of such a difference, or, as he puts it at one point, with the question of "where do norms come from?" He explains the importance of this question for his approach in the following terms:

> One of the central challenges of an account of conceptual norms as implicit in social practice is accordingly to make sense of the *emergence* of such an *objective* notion of correctness or appropriateness of claims and applications of concepts.
>
> (*MIE* 594; italics in original)

His answer to the question of where the notion of objectivity, built into our practices as a structural feature (i.e. as the distinction between normative statuses and attitudes), comes from is that "the normative statuses in terms of which deontic score is kept are creatures *instituted by* the (immediate) normative attitudes whose adoption and alteration is the activity of scorekeeping" (*MIE* 597; my italics). However, the question of origin is not the only (or even the most) relevant question to ask of an account of objectivity. It seems more than plausible that if "the distinction between claims ... that are objectively correct and those that are merely taken to be correct is a structural feature of each scorekeeping perspective" (*MIE* 595), it is in this sense a creature instituted by the scorekeeping practice. But still one would like to know not just where the feature originally came from, but rather what makes it intelligible, in virtue of what practitioners consider it rational to have their scorekeeping practices constrained by such a feature, etc.

In particular, for our purposes here of characterizing the specific features that distinguish Brandom's and Habermas's conceptions of objectivity, we cannot focus on the question of its emergence or origin. For just out of methodological reasons, both accounts presuppose an identical, pragmatist answer to the question of origin: objectivity has to be explained from within the communicative practices and thus as a result of the normative presuppositions (i.e. the norms) shared by the practitioners.

However, although both approaches share a general pragmatist strategy in explaining communicative practices, their explanations do not look at these practices from the same perspective. First, the "scorekeeping perspective" with the help of which communication is explained in *Making It Explicit* is characterized by Brandom as a kind of third-person perspective, whereas the "participants perspective" that Habermas aims to reconstruct in his *Theory of Communicative Action* is understood by him as explicitly opposed to any observer or third-person perspective. In addition, the perspective from which *Making It Explicit* is written is characterized by Brandom as "methodological phenomenalism" and, in this sense, is a third-person perspective. Although it is not completely clear how exactly this phenomenalism should be understood[3], at the very least the term suggests some discrepancy between the phenomenalist interpreter and those interpreted.[4] There is no such phenomenalist perspective in Habermas's approach. Thus, although the overall claim implicit in both approaches is to be able to give a correct account of the communicative practices they describe, all the mentioned differences may turn out to be responsible for different accounts of objectivity on the part of both authors.

Habermas's account of objectivity

With these preliminary considerations in the background, we can now try to give a characterization of Habermas's account of objectivity using the above-mentioned similarities as a starting point. Habermas's conception of objectivity can indeed be understood as an attempt to explain the sense in which "the way the world is" constrains communicative practices from within. It also offers an explanation based on the idea that what is shared by all discursive perspectives is *that* there is a difference between what is objectively correct and what is merely taken to be so, not *what* it is; what they share is *formal* and, thus, it is not a cross-perspectival *content*.

This characterization fits very well with Habermas's account of the conditions of possibility of discourse, i.e. of the reflexive kind of communication in which speakers discuss validity claims that are controversial and try to reach an agreement about them. It is clear that this reflexive kind of communication requires that the participants share a sense of objectivity, for otherwise they would not see the need for deciding about the disputed validity claims one way or another. In this sense, an explanation of the conditions of possibility of discourse is at the same time an explanation of what this sense of objectivity consists in within the Habermasian approach.

In the *Theory of Communicative Action*[5] Habermas introduces his analysis of the conditions of possibility of discourse in the context of an explicit comparison between the mythical and the modern worldviews. He focuses on a feature of mythical worldviews that he considers helpful for the attempt to understand, by way of contrast, the conditions of possibility of discourse, namely the relative lack of differentiation between nature and culture, between language and the world. In Habermas' opinion this characteristic of mythical worldviews implies that "a linguistically constituted worldview can be identified with the world order itself to such an extent that it cannot be perceived *as* an interpretation of the world that is subject to error and open to criticism" (*TCA* 50). The contrast with this situation explains at the same time what is the minimal condition for a reflexive communicative practice such as discourse to be possible at all. As Habermas points out "actors who raise validity claims have to avoid *materially prejudicing* the relation between language and reality, between the medium of communication and that about which something is being communicated [my italics]." This alone makes possible that "the contents of a linguistic worldview [become] *detached from the assumed world-order itself*" (*TCA* 50–1; my italics) Obviously, if participants in communication are to evaluate whether things are the way they think or rather as someone else believes, they cannot at the same time dogmatically identify their own beliefs with the way the world is. This is precisely the sense in which discourse is a reflexive kind of communication. It requires that the participants intuitively (and counterfactually) distinguish between everyone's (incompatible) beliefs and the assumed world-order itself. Put in Habermas's own terms they have to form "a reflective concept of world". Based on this idea Habermas can thus make explicit what the conditions of possibility of discourse are in the following terms:

> Validity claims are in principle open to criticism because they are based on *formal world-concepts*. They presuppose a world that is identical for *all possible observers*, or a world intersubjectively shared *by all the members of a group* and they do so *in an abstract form freed of all specific content*.
>
> (*TCA* 50–1)

The presuppositions of a single objective world, of a social world shared by all the members of a group, and of the plural subjective worlds of the different participants build a formal system of coordinates that makes possible the "access to the world through the medium of common interpretative efforts, in the sense of a cooperative negotiation of situation definitions" (*TCA* 69). In this sense

> the function of the formal world-concepts ... is to prevent the stock of what is common from dissolving in the stream of subjectivities repeatedly reflected in one another ... Every action oriented to reaching understanding can be conceived as part of a cooperative process of interpretation aiming at situation definitions that are intersubjectively recognized. The concepts of the three worlds serve here as *the commonly supposed system of coordinates* in which the situation contexts can be ordered in such a way that agreement will be reached about what the participants may treat as a fact, or as a valid norm, or as a subjective experience.
>
> (*TCA* 69–70; my italics)

In this sense the system of coordinates of the three concepts of world should not be misunderstood as some kind of beliefs that speakers happen to share. They are not beliefs with specific contents, they are structural features of the communicative practices that force themselves upon the participants by virtue of the constraints of the different kinds of discourse. The presupposition of *a single objective world* is a built-in feature of the assertional practice oriented towards the validity claim "truth" – a practice constrained by the *binary* distinction true/false[6]: if assertions are claims about how things are in the world and the world is one and the same for all of us, our beliefs about it can only be either true or false; and, for the very same reason, if someone else's beliefs are true, one should believe them oneself. Thus, within the Habermasian framework, the presupposition of a single objective world is what makes intelligible "the presumption of heritability" of commitments and entitlements that, according to Brandom, *specifically* characterizes the assertional practice. It also makes intelligible why this presumption is operative only in the case of doxastic commitments but not in the case of practical commitments in general,[7] as Brandom also points out.[8]

With this very brief characterization of the relationship between formal concepts of world and discourse we can establish some similarities and differences between Habermas's and Brandom's conception of objectivity. On the one hand, Habermas's approach seems to fit very well under Brandom's characterization of objectivity. For his approach shows us in precisely which sense what speakers share is *that* there is a difference between what is objectively correct and what is merely taken to be so, not *what* it is; what they share are *formal* presuppositions and not a cross-perspectival *content*. On the other hand, however, the presuppositions anchored in the system of coordinates of the three world-concepts *are cross-perspectival* precisely in virtue of being *formal*. Habermas's approach can account for the (essentially)[9] perspectival nature of our systems of beliefs just to the extent that it relies on a *cross-perspectival* system of shared formal presuppositions. In this sense at least it does not seem appropriate to characterize Habermas's approach as a "perspectival account of objectivity." But, of course, the pressing question is whether this terminological difference translates into a substantial one.

A prima facie difficulty in trying to answer this question by means of a straightforward comparison of both accounts is that, unfortunately, one issue that is not made explicit at all in Brandom's *Making It Explicit* is what notion of reality (if any) Brandomean speakers share. Moreover, it is far from clear that, if they were supposed to share one, Brandom would like to concede to it any role whatsoever in *explaining*[10] why the communicative practices described in scorekeeping terms look the way they do, as Habermas does.

On the one hand, Brandom's explicit goal of reversing the order of explanation from traditional representationalism clearly suggests the opposite. But, on the other hand, the appeal to reality (or, in Brandom's terms, to "nonperspectival facts") of traditional representationalism, of which Brandom explicitly disapproves, has no direct equivalence with the Habermasian appeal to a system of formal worlds anchored in the communicative practices of speakers in the form of normative presuppositions. It is clear that the primary target of Brandom's revisionary project is not an approach of Habermasian characteristics. Neither Brandom's nor Habermas's theories appeal to anything *external* to the communicative practices that they describe (and, *a fortiori*, to anything like "nonperspectival facts"). But, of course, this still leaves space for the question of whether *realist* presuppositions of *the speakers themselves* play an irreplaceable role in configuring the specific features of their communicative practices, as they do according to the Habermasian model.[11]

One indirect way of trying to answer this question is to see whether the specific features that Brandom has pointed out as structural characteristics of the assertional practice, in particular the "presumption of heritability" of commitments and entitlements (which is at the very core of the speakers' sense of objectivity), can be accounted for according to Brandom's approach without any appeal to realist presuppositions of the practitioners. If this were possible, we would have identified a crucial difference between Brandom's and Habermas's conceptions of objectivity. Moreover, the question whether a perspectival account of objectivity is possible would have to be answered in the affirmative.

Brandom's account of objectivity

As is well known, Brandom's approach to discursive practice is based on the notions of *commitment* and *entitlement* which are taken as primitives. The relation between these two primitive notions, in turn, allows Brandom to get a grip on a notion of *incompatibility*: *two claims are incompatible with each other if commitment to one precludes entitlement to the other*. With the help of these notions Brandom develops a scorekeeping model for describing communicative practices. The core of this explanation is Brandom's analysis of the linguistic game of assertions in terms of knowledge claims. As mentioned before, this allows Brandom to claim that there is an internal connection between the game of assertions and the game of giving and asking for reasons.

It seems clear that the notions introduced by Brandom as primitives do not have any *realist* content. They are basically *social* categories that scorekeepers use to assess other scorekeepers' attitudes. The notion of incompatibility is trickier in this respect, though. Understood as incompatibility-between-commitments-and-entitlements, it may seem equally unrelated to any kind of realist presupposition.[12] However, from the point of view of the content of such incompatibilities, the situation looks a little bit different. Taking into consideration that, as Brandom points out, the relations of incompatibility that hold between doxastic and practical commitments and entitlements are *different* according to the practitioners, it seems clear that the notions of commitment and entitlement themselves cannot suffice to explain this difference. This opens up the question whether the differences in material incompatibilities to which practitioners find themselves constrained in each case may be due to *realist* presuppositions on their side. According to the Habermasian approach, doxastic claims are understood by all speakers as constrained by the presupposition that they are about *one and the same* objective world – a world that is thus logically *independent* of any practical attitudes. This makes intelligible that the discourse about these claims is constrained by the presupposition of "a single right answer" or, to express it in Brandom's terms, by the presumption that commitments and entitlements can be inherited (i.e. that it makes sense to infer from someone else's doxastic commitments and entitlements to our own). On the other hand, given the plurality of speakers (i.e. subjective worlds), their practical claims about their own intentions, desires, commitments, etc., are trivially not seen by them as so constrained. This makes *intelligible*[13] that all scorekeepers consider commitment to the claim "snow is white" incompatible with entitlement to the claim "snow is not white" for any other scorekeeper, whereas they consider commitment to the claim "I am going to the theater" not incompatible with entitlement to the claim "I am not going to the theater" for any other scorekeeper; the very same consideration applies to the particular case of practical claims about who is entitled or committed to what.

It is clear that Brandom recognizes these differences in material incompatibilities among the different kinds of claims. Moreover, he considers a criteria of adequacy for any account of objectivity that it be able to preserve these differences (in particular the differences between ordinary empirical claims and claims about who is committed or entitled to what). However, even if they are indeed preserved in Brandom's approach, it is not entirely clear whether they are also *accounted for*.[14] It is simply not clear *in virtue of what* practitioners find it meaningful to establish these differences between incompatibility relations according to Brandom's official approach.

This question can be seen from two different angles. On the one hand, the question is whether the *practitioners themselves need* to share realist presuppositions in order for their communicative practices to have the specific structural features they do, as described by Brandom (i.e. the asymmetries between doxastic and practical commitments, their different incompatibility relations, etc.). On the other hand, a different version of the same question is whether within Brandom's reconstruction of these communicative practices in scorekeeping terms the above-mentioned features can be motivated independently of any appeal to realist presuppositions of the practitioners. That they are versions of the same question follows from the fact that the answers to them cannot fall apart. If an account of the scorekeeping social practices can be given without appeal to any kind of realist presuppositions on the side of the practitioners, this means *eo ipso* that practitioners do not *need* such presuppositions; even if they happen to share them, they should be considered as by-products of independently motivated features of their practices rather than as necessary conditions for them.

A passage in *Making It Explicit* suggests this second possibility. In the interesting context of discussing to what extent his approach is compatible with "methodological phenomenalism" Brandom shows how it is possible to translate presuppositions of the practitioners from the internal to the external, phenomenalist perspective. He starts with the distinction between attitudes and statuses as it is understood from the practitioners' own perspective:

> From the vantage point of any particular scorekeeper, what one is *really* committed to by an acknowledgment ... what *really* follows from the claim (and hence its objective content) is to be assessed by conjoining it with truths – that is, *statement of facts* [my italics].
>
> (*MIE* 596)

Here Brandom is pointing to a kind of situation in the scorekeeping practices where differences in material incompatibilities are generated through the distinction between attitudes and statuses. Brandom describes this distinction from the internal point of view of the practitioners as one based on *realist* presuppositions. When scorekeepers ascribe incompatibilities between commitments and entitlements that outrun those in fact recognized by the immediate attitudes of the speakers judged, they are presupposing a distinction between attitudes and statuses according to which *statuses depend on the obtaining of some states of affairs over and above the attitudes* actually held

193

by the speakers assessed. Then Brandom adds: "But what plays this role for a scorekeeper is the set of sentences by the assertion of which the scorekeeper is prepared to acknowledge, and so undertake, doxastic commitment" (*ibid.*).

The admissibility of the translation proposed by Brandom here, of course, depends on what "plays this role" is supposed to mean. It seems clear that it cannot mean that the distinction between what other speakers believe and what I believe can play the role of the distinction between what a speaker believes and what happens to be the case – at least, it cannot mean this *for the practitioners themselves*. For they are two logically independent distinctions (i.e. out of a grasp of the first practitioners would never get a grasp of the second). The most that Brandom can claim is that, from a external perspective and as regards their content, what a speaker will consider to be the facts that obtain will necessarily coincide with what he is willing to acknowledge commitment to. But, unless an alternative explanation is given for this necessary coincidence, it seems precisely to be a consequence of speakers' having grasped the realist sense implicit in the distinction between statuses and attitudes, and not the other way around.

Brandom explains further this intricate translation with the help of other examples. He continues:

> What from the point of view of a scorekeeper is objectively correct – what from that perspective another interlocutor is actually committed to by a certain acknowledgment – can be understood by us who are interpreting the scorekeeping activity entirely in terms of the *immediate attitudes*, the acknowledgments and attributions, of the scorekeeper. What appears to the scorekeeper as the distinction between what is objectively correct and what is merely taken to be or treated as correct appears to us as the distinction between what is acknowledged by the scorekeeper attributing a commitment and what is acknowledged by the one to whom it is attributed. The difference between objective normative status and subjective normative attitude is construed as a social-perspectival distinction between normative attitudes. In this way the maintenance, from every perspective, of a distinction between status and attitude is reconciled with the methodological phenomenalism that insists that all that really needs to be considered is attitudes.
>
> (*MIE* 597; italics in original)

However, if one looks carefully to the different translations that Brandom proposes to account for the different distinctions involved in this passage, it is not clear that they are all equally licit. The translation that Brandom proposes for the first distinction does not seem problematic: it is just an expression of the "essentially perspectival" (*MIE* 649) character of scorekeeping attitudes. As regards the differences between the *contents* of what the respective scorekeepers consider correct in cases of disagreement, Brandom's translation from a third-person perspective seems correct, i.e. it seems to be the *same* translation that the practitioners themselves would make from a third-person perspective: what each scorekeeper in case of disagreement considers correct is (trivially) whatever they believe to be correct. However, the next distinction that Brandom mentions in this passage has nothing to do with the respective *contents* of the scorekeepers' commitments. It is "the distinction between what is objectively correct and what is merely taken to be correct". In this case, Brandom's proposed translation does not preserve the sense of the original distinction. For, if scorekeepers have grasped the sense of this distinction at all, they know that it has nothing to do with the one subsequently offered by Brandom, namely the distinction between what is acknowledged by one scorekeeper and what is acknowledged by another. Of course, once this translation is admitted, once we are only concerned with the different beliefs acknowledged by different scorekeepers, then it is possible to claim that the difference between objective status and subjective attitude can be correctly construed as a social-perspectival distinction between attitudes and, thus, that "all that really needs to be considered is attitudes." It is clear that from a third-person perspective and as regards their content all beliefs look the same; they are just acknowledged by someone or other. But the fact of mere differences in beliefs cannot suffice for a scorekeeper to grasp the meaningfulness of distinguishing between what is correct and what is taken to be correct. This is especially the case if we take into consideration that scorekeepers *only in some cases* find it mean-ingful to qualify what from the third-person perspective are *incompatible* beliefs as cases of *disagreement between what is correct and what is taken to be correct*.[15]

We can try to get a better grip on the problem by focusing on Brandom's explanation of this specific case, namely the assertional practice in which speakers raise *knowledge* claims. For this is obviously a case in which speakers find it meaningful to distinguish between what is correct and what is taken to be correct. The core of Brandom's explanation is what he calls a "phenom-enalist reconstruction of the classic justified-true-belief account of knowledge" (*MIE* 297). As its name already suggests, Brandom's reconstruc-tion is based in the very same kind of translations between the internal perspective of the practitioners and the external perspective of the phenome-nalist that we found before. However, in this specific case, it may be easier to see what exactly gets lost in the process of translating. For, as I will try to argue in what follows, the specific *social-perspectival* feature that is described in this context from the phenomenalist, third-person perspective is a direct consequence of a *realist* presupposition of the practitioners that *itself cannot be accounted for in social-perspectival terms*. If this were the case, this would also help to answer our prior question about the relationship between the speakers' sense of objectivity and their realist presuppositions within

Brandom's approach. The answer would take the form of an alternative. If the external, phenomenalist perspective does not collapse into the internal one (i.e. does not incorporate any realist presupposition of the practitioners) the account offered remains *idiosyncratic*: that is, *it describes a feature of a practice without being able to make any sense of it*. If the external perspective is really meant to collapse into the internal one, then the account offered would have to make explicit the realist presuppositions of the practitioners that make intelligible the social-perspectival features of the practices described.

Brandom's account of knowledge

In "Knowledge and the social articulation of the space of reasons,"[16] Brandom characterizes his analysis of knowledge by the following features. According to his approach, knowledge is constructed "as a standing in the space of reasons" (p. 907), and the general question his analysis aims to answer is "What *must* I be doing in order to take you to have that standing?" (*ibid.*) The crucial claim behind Brandom's specific answer to this question is that

> what is expressed by locutions such as "knows" *can all be understood* as standings in a socially articulated space of reasons: standings that incorporate what are with respect to individual knowers internal and external epistemic considerations in the form of *the distinct social perspectives of attributing and undertaking commitments*.
>
> (*Ibid.*; my italics)

According to the general question, Brandom's analysis aims to provide an explanation of what a speaker is doing when she properly assesses that another speaker knows something. From a methodological point of view this explanation is articulated from the third-person, scorekeeping perspective. However, according to the general claim, it is supposed to capture at the same time all that is understood when speakers use locutions such as "knows." Thus, an important adequacy condition for Brandom's explanation is whether the third-person analysis of what he calls the "distinct social perspectives of attributing and undertaking commitments" also provides a correct account of "what is expressed by locutions such as 'knows'" from the participants' own perspective.[17]

In *Making It Explicit* Brandom characterizes his phenomenalist analysis of assessments of knowledge in the following terms:

> According to a phenomenalist reconstruction of the classic justified-true-belief account of knowledge … in taking someone to know something, one first of all attributes a commitment, that is, takes someone to believe. One further attributes entitlement to that

commitment, that is, takes the committed subject to be justified. What, then, is the function of the truth condition on knowledge? Conventionally, treating taking the claim that the subject is committed to as true is understood as attributing some property to it, characterizing it or describing it. But it has already been pointed out that the pragmatist's account of taking the claim to be true is as acknowledging or undertaking a commitment to it. The truth condition does not qualify the entitled commitment that is attributed but simply indicates that the attributer of knowledge must endorse it. This is a deontic attitude that differs in its social perspective. Attributions of knowledge have the central linguistic status that they do because in them commitment to a claim is both attributed and undertaken. This phenomenalist distinction of social perspective, between the act of attributing and the act of under-taking a commitment, is what is mistaken for the attribution of a descriptive property (for which an otiose metaphysics then appears to be required).

(*MIE* 297)

Thus, taking one of Brandom's examples, his explanation of assessments of knowledge seems to be the following:

S_1 assesses that S_2 knows that the swatch is red iff

1   S_1 attributes to S_2 a commitment to the claim that the swatch is red;
2   S_1 attributes to S_2 an entitlement to the claim that the swatch is red;
3   S_1 undertakes a commitment to the claim that the swatch is red.

This explanation raises different questions. Does it reproduce what a speaker means (i.e. is committed to) by attributing knowledge to someone? Does this explanation provide the circumstances and consequences of application of the expression "knows" as speakers use it? If we were to give this explana-tion to a speaker who does not know what "knows" means, would this speaker be able to use the expression as we do? All these questions are just variations of the above-mentioned methodological issue, namely to what extent this third-person account of knowledge is compatible with a first-person perspective.

In "Knowledge and the social articulation of the space of reasons," Brandom offers a similar account of knowledge from the first-person perspective, when he writes:

The key question is what I must be doing in order to take you to have that standing. And the answer is, in line with the JTB account of knowledge, that corresponding to the belief condition ... I must *attribute* a propositionally contentful commitment, that corresponding to the justification condition I must *attribute* also entitlement to that commitment ... and that corresponding to the truth condition I must also myself *endorse* or *undertake* the same propositionally contentful commitment.

(p. 907; italics in original)

Thus, according to this explanation,

I assess that S knows that the swatch is red iff

1'   I attribute to S a commitment to the claim that the swatch is red;
2'   I attribute to S an entitlement to the claim that the swatch is red;
3'   I myself undertake a commitment to the claim that the swatch is red.

However, this explanation seems counterintuitive in two respects. On the one hand, the inclusion of condition (3) suggests that the question of *whether a speaker knows something could somehow be a function of someone else's deontic attitudes*. How can the question of whether S knows something or not be a function of what I (or any other speaker, for that matter) endorse? This does not seem to be what we mean when we assess that someone knows something (or, to put it in Brandomian terms, this does not seem to be the norm we mean to follow in our assessments).[18] On the other hand, regardless of whether the three conditions taken together are sufficient or not, condition (3) does not seem to be even a necessary one. If anything, it seems to be a *consequence* rather than a *condition*.[19] The rationale behind Brandom's inclusion of condition (3) is the fact that, if I assesses that S knows that p, I am thereby committed to this claim and, thus, obviously, to believe p myself (i.e. to endorse the interpersonal intracontent inference: from the commitment attributed to S to the one I undertake myself). But this can hardly be understood as a *condition* for the correctness of my assessment; at the most it can be a *consequence* of it. However, it cannot be a consequence just of conditions (1) and (2). For given the sense in which Brandom uses the notions of commitment and entitlement,[20] it is clear that under conditions (1) and (2) the possibility that the swatch is not red is not excluded. But if this possibility is not excluded from my own perspective, it is not clear why my assessment should have as a consequence what is expressed in condition (3).[21] Matters do not get any better if one interprets condition (3) as a constraint on the assessment of knowledge rather than as a consequence. For, as regards the three conditions taken together (and leaving Gettier problems aside), *it is not at all excluded that someone knows that the swatch is red but the swatch is not red.*

If this is the case, then Brandom's analysis seems unable to capture "what is expressed by locutions such as 'knows'" (i.e. what we are doing when we assess that someone knows something). For it does not preserve the correctness of the following conditional:

1   If S knows that the swatch is red, then the swatch is red.

In the sense implicit in this conditional, speakers understand "knowledge" as a very strong deontic status (i.e. a truth-entailing one). Of course, one could adopt a revisionary strategy and settle for a more "modest" notion of knowledge than the one speakers use in natural languages.[22] However, no matter how else such a modest notion could look in general, in our context the issue would be an all-or-nothing affair: either it preserves the correctness of the above-mentioned conditional or it does not. If it does not, the new notion would amount to the notion of entitlement as used by Brandom, according to which it is perfectly possible that

> S is entitled to the claim that the swatch is red, but the swatch is not red.

However, it is clear that I could not possibly make this assessment (based on my collateral commitments) and endorse the very same claim that S is committed to (namely, that the swatch is red). This is why in Brandom's own approach ascriptions of entitlement to a claim do not entail that the ascriber undertakes commitment to this very claim. Thus, no matter whether Brandom would in general admit the possibility of a revisionary strategy as regards the notion of knowledge, it seems clear that he would not want to exclude the correctness of the above-mentioned conditional. For this conditional is precisely what justifies his *specific* explanation of the conditions for ascriptions of knowledge *vis-à-vis* ascriptions of other deontic statuses, namely the incompatibility between assessing that someone knows that p and not being committed oneself to the claim that p.[23]

Given these constraints, it seems clear that the only way to correctly render assessments of knowledge from the first-person perspective is the following:

I assess that S knows that the swatch is red iff[24]

1"   I attribute to S a commitment to the claim that the swatch is red;

2" I attribute to S an entitlement to the claim that the swatch is
     red;
3" The swatch is red.

Only *this* understanding of the truth condition[25] explains why, from the
speaker's own perspective, it is trivially the case that:

1   If S knows that the swatch is red, the swatch is red;

and thus,

2   If S knows that the swatch is red, I must myself undertake commitment
    to the claim that the swatch is red.

However, there seems to be no way of capturing condition (3") in terms of
the different social perspectives of the speakers, as we did before. For, as
Brandom explicitly recognizes, from the speaker's own perspective the
conditional:

3   If I am now committed to the claim that the swatch is red, then the
    swatch is red;

is not one that ought to be endorsed.[26] However, speakers can only grasp the
wrongness of this conditional if they understand the real significance of the
truth condition. The truth condition does not indicate that the attributer of
knowledge must endorse the claim that the swatch is red, as Brandom
asserts. It indicates that the swatch must be red. Thus, in order for speakers
to be able to capture what the actual constraints are supposed to be, the
truth condition *cannot be expressed in terms of social perspectives.*[27] Actually, to
recognize this is nothing more than to recognize Brandom's own criterion of
adequacy for any account of objectivity, namely that "the contents of ordinary claims, such as 'Snow is white' ... are not equivalent to those of any
claims about who is committed to what" (*MIE* 606).

If this is correct, the central claim of Brandom's approach should be
modified in the following way. On the one hand, it seems correct to say
(against what Brandom calls Gonzo reliabilism) that "what is expressed by
locutions such as 'knows' can all be understood as standings in a socially
articulated space of reasons." However, the "distinct social perspectives of
attributing and undertaking commitments" which characterize our assertional practices have the specific features that Brandom ascribes to them
precisely because such "standings incorporate ... internal *and external* epistemic
considerations," and not the other way around. Or, to put it in other terms,
in order for these practices to have the specific characteristics that Brandom's
analysis correctly describes, the notion of knowledge built into them has to

contain realist elements that *cannot be traded in for social-perspectival ones*. Only in virtue of these realist elements can such a notion of knowledge play the role that Brandom ascribes to it when he claims that "the ... deontic status of knowledge defines the *success* of assertion" (*MIE* 203).

Are knowledge claims perspectival?

Brandom's social-perspectival account of knowledge tells us something interesting about the linguistic game of assertions, namely that if the point of this game is the inheritance of commitments and entitlements (i.e. the exchange of information), whenever speakers assert that p, they cannot claim less than that they know that p in the strongest possible sense of "to know." For if they were to claim less than that, their claim would never have the consequence that speakers could get *information* out of each other's speech acts. However, this is so because of the *realist* sense of the assertional practice.

Assertions, as opposed to other speech acts (such as questions or commands), belong to the linguistic game of saying how things are in the world. This is the *point* of asserting. Thus it is a structural feature of this practice that one cannot claim less than that one is saying how things are. But given that things can be otherwise, if one wants to claim that things are thus and so, one has to be able to show that one knows it, and thus that one could justify that this is so. On the one hand, the point of exchanging assertions is to inherit commitments, i.e. to obtain information the audience did not have before. On the other hand, in order to count as information, it is not sufficient that speakers *purport* to say how things are. They also have to be *successful*. This explains the internal connection between the game of assertions and the game of giving and asking for reasons. By virtue of *purporting* to say how things are, speakers are subjected to the assessment of their audience as to whether or not they succeed. In this sense, the claim of saying how things are is a complex one. It can be analyzed into different components regardless of whether they are explicitly stated by the speaker or not: in claiming that things are so *and not otherwise* speakers are not only claiming that their statements are *true* (i.e. happen to be true) but also that they *know* it, and thus that they could, if necessary, *justify* that it is so. It is in this sense that "asserting is making a knowledge claim" (*MIE* 203).[28]

As with any other game, on the basis of its given point the possible outcomes can be sorted into the successful and the unsuccessful cases. With regard to the statement asserted, the two possible outcomes are designated with the distinction true/false: if things are as asserted, the statement is true, otherwise it is false. With regard to the speaker's reasons,[29] the two possible outcomes are designated with the distinction justified/unjustified: if the speaker's reasons are correct (i.e. establish the truth of the statement), the statement is justified; if they are not, it is unjustified. However, the *success* of the outcome is not the only relevant issue for our assertional practice. It may also be interesting to assess the *attempt* as such. We may want to distinguish objectionable from unobjectionable attempts, regardless of success. If the attempt was unobjectionable, the speaker is justified (i.e. epistemically responsible); otherwise she is not. The distinction between attempt and success is responsible for two different senses of justification (or entitlement). One is the achievement sense of "justified" that implies success, i.e. implies that the justification *happens to be correct*; the other is the task-sense of "justified" that implies only that the attempt was done according to the corresponding (epistemic) rules.[30] The notion of justification in the second sense is used to qualify the *speaker's* attempt and not the *content* of her justification (or her capacities), as it is in the first sense. Accordingly, "knowledge" is the deontic status that we use to designate the successful case, i.e. the case where nothing goes wrong. If the speaker's statement is true, her justification is correct and she was epistemically responsible, she knows; otherwise she does not. It is in this sense that, as Brandom expresses it, the status of knowledge "*defines* the *success* of assertion."[31] Thus, it is clear that if one just *purports* to assert that p, one cannot claim less than that one knows that p, and also that if one *succeeds* in asserting that p according to the others, they have to endorse p themselves.

But there is no way to understand the rationale of these two correlative features without presupposing that they belong to *the specific game of saying how things are in the world* – a world that is one and the same for all practitioners and, thus, independent of their respective attitudes. This minimal notion of reality implicit in our knowledge claims is *neither perspectival nor reducible to any other kind of notion*. It is just the notion that practitioners have to share in order to understand that "the way the world is, constrains proprieties of inferential, doxastic and practical commitment in a straightforward way from within those practices" (*MIE* 332). It is at least in this sense that an account of objectivity cannot be perspectival all the way down.

Notes

1 R. Brandom, *Making It Explicit*, Cambridge, MA: Harvard University Press, 1994. (Hereafter quoted as *MIE*.)

2 Habermas's expression of this assumption is ambiguous. In its weaker sense it means that for any clearly stated question about a truth claim, its answer can only be either true or false. It is in this sense that it coincides with Brandom's presumption of heritability and this is the sense intended here. However, it can also be interpreted in the stronger sense of implying not just that claims of truth can only have "a single right answer" but also that there can only be "a single correct interpretation" or description of it. In this sense it goes far beyond Brandom's own assumptions. For this latter assumption is incompatible with Brandom's view of doxastic attitudes as essentially perspectival. Habermas himself oscillates between the two interpretations, but it seems possible to interpret Habermas's approach as implying only the weaker assumption and, thus, as also compatible with conceptual relativity (cf. Note 9).

3   It is hard to get a clear grasp as to what exactly is meant by "normative phenomenalism" in *Making It Explicit*. The very term "phenomenalism" suggests some kind of reductive perspective, but Brandom stresses over and over again that the task of *MIE* is not reductive but expressive. The official version of what it is that makes *MIE* a kind of phenomenalism is that in some sense "all that really needs to be considered is attitudes" (*MIE* 597) for "deontic statuses" are just creatures instituted by the scorekeeping practices. On the other hand, Brandom will explicitly point out later on that "the work done by talk of deontic statuses cannot be done by talk of deontic attitudes actually adopted or relinquished ... Talk of deontic statuses can in general be traded in only for talk of proprieties governing the adoption and alteration of deontic attitudes" (*MIE* 626). It is hard to see how this claim can be compatible with the prior one according to which "all that need to be considered is attitudes", for "proprieties governing the adoption ... of attitudes" is precisely what deontic statuses are; they are "scorekeeping devices for identifying and individuating deontic attitudes" (*MIE* 648). And if one also insists, as Brandom does in a different context, "on the irreducibly normative character of the metalanguage in which norm-instituting social practices are specified" (*MIE* 626), then it is not clear at all in which sense it is a kind of phenomenalism. The question of what exactly are the entities about which *MIE* defends a kind of phenomenalism does not receive much clarification from the official explanation that Brandom offers a page later, when he writes: "The scorekeeping account incorporates a phenomenalist approach to norms, but it is a normative phenomenalism, explaining having a certain normative status in effect as being properly taken to have it." (*MIE* 627) This is not one of the most illuminating claims of *MIE*. If all that is meant by a phenomenalist approach to norms is just that norms do not exist like trees, i.e. that they do not exist independent of the human practices who institute them, then every reasonable philosopher is a phenomenalist about norms. However, the suggestion throughout the book is that Brandom's phenomenalist claim is stronger than that.

4   However, one of the crucial claims at the end of MIE is also that the external perspective from which the book is written collapses into the internal one (so that "the norms turn out to be ... here" *MIE* 649).

5   J. Habermas, *The Theory of Communicative Action*, Boston: Beacon Press, 1984. (Hereafter quoted as *TCA*.)

6   The binary distinction true/false can be traced back to the equally binary distinction between real/unreal (whether it be in the form of the distinction exists/does not exist at the subsentential level or in the form of the distinction is the case/is not the case at the sentential level).

7   Brandom contemplates the possibility that the constraints in the specific case of moral commitments may turn out to be more similar to the doxastic case than the other practical cases of prudential and institutional commitments, although he does not attempt to offer an explanation. Within Habermas's approach the specific features of the moral case can be explained along the following lines: the presupposition of *a single social world* shared by all human beings is a built-in feature of the discursive practice oriented towards the validity claim "moral rightness" – a practice constrained by the *binary* distinction just/unjust. But there is no such presupposition in the case of ethical–political discourses, which admit of a plurality of social worlds (i.e. political communities) and, thus, also of different outcomes (this is why in these discourses we use expressions such as "good for me" or "good for us" that do not have a binary use).

8 Brandom's own official account of this difference is not very satisfactory. He explains why there is no "presumption of heritability" of commitments and entitlements in the practical case in the following terms:

> That there is no implicit normative commitment that plays the same role with respect to desire (and therefore intention and action in general) that truth plays with respect to beliefs consists simply in the absence (in the structure according ᴧo which entitlements to practical commitments are inherited) of anything corresponding to the interpersonal dimension of testimony and vindication by deferral.

(*MIE* 240)

However, this can hardly count as an explanation as long as the absence of "vindication by deferral" in the practical case is not itself explained. The possibility of vindication by deferral is a *consequence* of the "presumption of heritability" and, thus, it is part of what has to be explained if one wants to understand the rationale of the asymmetries between the two cases. However, in the very same context Brandom offers an "inofficial" explanation to the reader that seems to point to the same distinction that we find in Habermas's approach, namely that doxastic commitments are constrained by "an implicit norm of commonality", so that "whenever two believers disagree, a diagnosis of error or ignorance is appropriate for at least one of them", whereas in the case of practical commitments just the very fact that "we come with different bodies ... ensures that we will have different desires" and, thus, intentions, actions, etc. Expressed in Habermas's terminology, in the first case speakers presuppose a single objective world, whereas in the second case they (trivially) presuppose plural and different subjective worlds.

9 Although Habermas's own interpretation of his theory does not *include* conceptual relativity as an explicit claim, it is possible to interpret his theory as *compatible* with such a claim, so that systems of beliefs can be considered essentially perspectival in a very similar way as in Brandom's own approach. I have argued in this direction in my *The Linguistic Turn in Hermeneutic Philosophy* (Cambridge, MA: MIT Press, 1999).

10 In his reply to Habermas ("Facts, norms, and normative facts," *European Journal of Philosophy*, forthcoming), Brandom explicitly points out that his talk of an independent reality in *MIE* is not supposed to do any explanatory work. He argues as follows. Within the framework of his social-perspectival account of objectivity

> the acknowledgment of the existence of conceptually structured facts to which our practices (according to us) answer comes cheaply. It is not meant to have any explanatory value except what can be cashed out in terms of the deontic and social-perspectival articulation of our discursive practices. In particular, it is not intended to explain so much as the possibility of that articulation – rather, the other way around.

(p. 5)

Thus, "the recognition of an independent, conceptually structured objective reality is a *product* of the social (intersubjective) account of objectivity, not something that is either prior to or a substitute for that account" (*ibid.*; my italics). But, unfortunately for our purposes, the option that Brandom is excluding here is not the one that we are discussing in our context. Brandom is denying that his reconstruction of communicative practices requires something like the postulate of the existence of an independent reality *on the side of the theorist* to explain these practices. Given the general pragmatist strategy pursued in *MIE*, Brandom's claim seems obviously right. But in this respect Brandom's and Habermas's approaches are precisely on the same (pragmatist) boat. The question that we are trying to answer here as regards the possible differences between both approaches is whether the presupposition of an independent reality *on the side of the practitioners themselves* is an *irreducible* element that has to be acknowledged by any attempt to explain the structural features of their practices or whether it is possible to explain these very same features without taking into consideration any kind of realist presuppositions that the practitioners may share. As far as I am aware, Brandom does not address this issue explicitly anywhere. To the extent that this is not a self-posed question (but rather a question that arises in the context of comparing his approach with Habermas's) we cannot appeal here to any explicit claims of Brandom. We will rather try the indirect way of arguing that either realist presuppositions of the practitioners are recognized from the very beginning as an irreducible component of their normative attitudes or they cannot be obtained as a product of any combination of non-realist presuppositions.

11 So much so, according to Habermas's approach, that they can be used as a key to account for the asymmetries between different linguistic games which otherwise would appear as mere idiosyncrasies. (For a particular example, cf. Note 8.)

12 In some sense this is not correct, though. For such incompatibilities include also those generated through the distinction between attitudes and statuses, and this is a distinction that involves realist presuppositions. According to Brandom's own account, the difference between an attitude and a status from the practitioners' perspective is precisely that the latter depends on the obtaining of some state of affairs over and above the given attitudes to which a status is attributed (cf. *MIE* 596). I will discuss this later on.

13 The inclusion of the realist presuppositions linked with the system of coordinates of the three formal worlds in Habermas's approach do not serve an *explanatory* purpose in any strong sense of the term. Rather, it only implies acknowledging the *irreducibly* hybrid nature of the normative presuppositions operative in the communicative practices described: they are not only concerned with speakers' attitudes but equally with the world they purport to talk about. Thus, the question is not whether realist presuppositions are more explanatory than epistemic ones, but rather that if they are not recognized from the very beginning as an irreducible component of the normative attitudes of the practitioners, they cannot be obtained as a product of any combination of presuppositions of a different kind.

14 Moreover, as I will show later, recognizing the non-equivalence of these kinds of claims (empirical versus epistemic ones) may turn out to be a crucial difficulty for Brandom's attempt to explain the notion of knowledge in social-perspectival terms.

15 This is not only the case as regards the difference between doxastic and practical commitments, it is also the case within doxastic commitments depending on whether they are related to the objective world or to the different subjective worlds of the speakers (assertions of the first kind such as "snow is white" or "it is raining" are seen by the practitioners as cases of disagreement about what is correct and what is taken to be correct, whereas assertions of the second kind, such as "ground meat tastes horrible" or Brandom's own example "cows look goofy," are not).

16 In *Philosophy and Phenomenological Research* 55, 4 (1995), pp. 895–908. (Hereafter quoted as *KSSR*.)

17 Sometimes Brandom characterizes his third-person analysis as a way to get a "closer" view of the practices so described, for example when he claims that "looking at the practices a little more closely involves cashing out the talk of deontic statuses by translating it into talk of deontic attitudes. Practitioners

take or treat themselves and others as having various commitments and entitlements" (*MIE* 166). However, in this sense, the metaphor of "looking more
closely" at such practices does not mean looking at them "the way the practitioners do" (i.e. from the practitioners' own perspective). For it is clear that
precisely for the practitioners a matter of status cannot be equated to a matter of
attitudes.

18 The idea of a hybrid deontic status seems very fruitful for explaining assessments of reliability. For, although such assessments (like any assessment) will
depend on the assesser's own commitments, (1) reliability is nonetheless
ascribed to the very same speaker to whom knowledge is ascribed and (2) the
assessment is based on a hypothesis about *characteristics and circumstances* of the
assessed speaker and not about anyone's deontic attitudes (specifically not those
of the assessed speaker; this is the interesting feature of Brandom's explanation).
However, in the case of assessments of knowledge, the kind of hybrid deontic
status that Brandom proposes is implausible, for (1) it suggests that the question of whether a speaker knows something or not can be somehow a function of
what happens to other speakers and, moreover, (2) it is supposed to be a function
of what commitments another speaker has, i.e. a function of deontic *attitudes*
(and not of what happens in the world, as in the case of reliability). Thus,
whereas in the case of assessments of reliability the externalist element is
preserved as such in Brandom's own explanation, in the case of assessments of
knowledge his explanation transforms an externalist element into an internalist
one. This is what produces the difficulties that I will try to show in what
follows.

19 Of course, the other option is that it is a coincidence (i.e. a contingent
constraint) but this will only make matters worse (see Note 8).

20 See Note 17.

21 Brandom offers an example of this kind of situation in *KSSR*:

> If you are standing in a darkened room and seem to see a candle ten feet in
> front of you, I may take you to have good reason for believing that there is a
> candle ten feet in front of you, and so to take you to be entitled to your
> commitment. But that may be my attitude even if I know, as you do not,
> that there is a mirror five feet in front of you and no candle behind it, so
> that I am not in a position to endorse or commit myself to what you are
> committed to.
>
> (p. 903)

22 In this context it may be important to mention that Brandom does not want to
be committed to explaining the notion of knowledge used in natural languages.
In a footnote in his book *Articulating Reasons* (Cambridge, MA: Harvard
University Press, 2000, p. 212; hereafter abbreviated as *AR*), he suggests that
the best strategy in epistemology as regards the notion of knowledge may turn
out to be a revisionary one. For, as he argues, it may well be the case that the
notion of knowledge that speakers use in their natural languages is implausibly
strong and, in such a case, it should be traded in for a more modest one.
However, Brandom does not specify exactly in which respects the strong notion
should be deflated. In the context of the above-mentioned comments he is
talking about the possibility of excluding as a condition for S knowing that p
that S knows that he knows that p. In my opinion this would be a very wise
move. But, obviously, this would exclude only a specific sort of internalist but
no externalist constraint. The question here is whether Brandom would like to
exclude (or transform in the epistemic terms of deontic attitudes and statuses)
some of the externalist conditions, specifically the so-called truth condition
(which, given the insights of deflationism, perhaps should rather be called the

206

reality condition). However, it is hard to imagine that he would like to exclude as a condition for S knowing that p that it be the case that p. For, as I will argue in what follows, such a new notion would not bear out Brandom's own analysis of assessments of knowledge in scorekeeping terms, specifically the consequence of the "presumption of heritability" of commitments based on condition (3). This feature, though, is not just an optional component of Brandom's approach but is at the very core of his explanation of the game of assertions (and thus of communication in general).

23 Of course, this incompatibility could be understood as a stipulation about our use of the locution "knows." It is not impossible to think along revisionary lines that we could introduce a locution in our language – let's call it "fnows" – that we would use whenever someone is committed and entitled to a claim and, because we happen to be also so committed, we want to signal agreement as well. (I am grateful to Michael Williams for pointing out this hypothetical line of thought to me.) In this case, the problem would appear only if we also wanted this locution to substitute for the locution "knows." For in such a case assertions would turn out to be merely "fnowledge" claims. Accordingly, what a speaker would be claiming by claiming that the swatch is red would be only that "I am committed and entitled to the claim that the swatch is red; you should commit yourself to it." However, if we accept with Brandom that the following conditionals ought not to be endorsed, namely, that

If I am committed to the claim that the swatch is red, the swatch is red; and

If I am entitled to the claim that the swatch is red, the swatch is red;

the consequence seems to be that the speaker's assertion *would never amount to the claim that the swatch is red*. Given that Brandom's own criterion of adequacy for an explanation of the assertional practice is that ordinary empirical claims are not to be equated with claims about who is committed and entitled to what, it is clear that we cannot obtain claims of the first kind out of any combination of claims of the second kind. If we want to play the game of asserting empirical claims, thus if we want the success of asserting that the swatch is red to be dependent on whether the swatch is red, then the deontic status that "defines the success of assertions" (whatever we want to call it) would have to entail that the swatch is red. If we call it "knowledge", then the following conditional ought to be endorsed, namely:

If I know that the swatch is red, the swatch is red.

Taking into account that Brandom considers the "heritability" of commitments and entitlements as a matter of *inference* (from someone else's claims to my own) it seems clear that the incompatibility that we are discussing here is understood by him as a *consequence* rather than as a coincidence (or stipulation). I do not mean to suggest that the hypothetical line of thought discussed here is Brandom's own.

24 For the purpose of discussing Brandom's approach I avoid considerations pertaining to the Gettier problem here, since they are not directly relevant for my argument. In a footnote in *KSSR* (pp. 904–5), Brandom points out that it may be possible to give an account of the Gettier problem within the social-perspectival framework. This seems very plausible. For once it is recognized that the satisfaction of the justification condition should be endorsed by the assesser of knowledge (and not only by the one to whom knowledge is ascribed), one cannot get the Gettier problem off the ground. Gettier examples are grounded on situations where it is stipulated that we have a collateral commitment regarding the correct justification for the belief at issue (p) that is incompatible with the commitment of the speaker whose knowledge we have to assess. As

long as we have this commitment and take it to be correct, we cannot concede that the speaker knows that p. However, if it is along these lines that Brandom would try to handle the puzzle of the Gettier examples, a problem similar to the one that I am discussing here with regard to the truth condition will arise with regard to the justification condition. For what the assesser of knowledge in those cases does not endorse is not S_2's epistemic responsibility (i.e. his entitlement in the weak, non-truth-entailing sense of the term), but that S_2's justification is in fact correct, i.e. does track the truth. This means that the assesser of knowledge is presupposing the strong notion of entitlement (as truth-entailing) that Brandom does not want to include in his approach (see *KSSR* 899; *AR* 201). It is because S takes her own entitlement to p to be *the correct one* (and incompatible with S_1's own) that she cannot accept S_1's commitment to p to amount to knowledge *despite S_1's epistemic responsibility* (i.e. her entitlement in the weak sense of the term). I discuss this issue later (see Note 30).

25 In this context it is interesting to note that this understanding of the truth condition just follows from Brandom's prosentential account of truth, which is supposed to preserve the validity of the equivalence schema "P" is true iff p (see *MIE* 299).

26 See *AR* 199.

27 What seems to be awkward in the general strategy is the claim that

> the normative expressive resources made available by distinguishing the status of being assertionally *committed* from that of being *entitled* to such a commitment are *sufficient* [my italics] to distinguish ... between the content of ordinary empirical claims and the contents of any claims about who is committed or entitled to what.
>
> (*AR* 199–201; italics in original)

It seems doubtful that out of a grasp of the notions of commitment and entitlement speakers can get a grasp of the notion of something that is independent of any commitments or entitlements. It seems rather that it is by grasping the notion of *status* itself that they grasp the notion of the independence between the obtaining of some states of affairs and others (e.g. ordinary empirical facts and facts about attitudes). But, if this is the case, then the distinction between the status of being committed and being entitled is sufficient to distinguish between empirical and epistemic claims only if it already presupposes it.

28 As Brandom points out, it does not matter whether with their assertions speakers explicitly claim to know or not. For this claim is rather a structural feature of the practice of asserting: "the complex hybrid deontic status of knowledge defines the *success* of assertion" (*MIE* 203; italics in original). The same holds for the other claims: truth and justification. Assertions that make *explicit* reference to these claims actually signal a transition from the ordinary context of communication about how things are in the world to the reflexive context in which the epistemic status of assertions is evaluated. Once our assertions about the world are called into question, we need to explicitly say things like "I know that 'p'," "'p' is true," or "'p' is justified" (and their opposites: "you do not know that 'p'", "'p' is false", etc.).

29 Or, in general, the mechanism of belief formation. The speaker's justification may be the result of her explicit reasoning or just of her reliability.

30 Brandom uses the notion of "entitlement" exclusively in the task sense of justification as epistemic responsibility. Moreover, in *KSSR* Brandom points out that a notion of justification as truth-guaranteeing "is not to be had" (p. 899). This claim can be interpreted in two different ways, though. If "truth-guaranteeing" is understood in the achievement sense that we are referring to here, as meaning just "truth-entailing", this notion cannot be excluded from our understanding

of justification for the very same reason that it cannot be excluded from our understanding of any other activity that can succeed or fail. Given the internal connection between the task sense and the achievement sense of any expression used to qualify these kinds of activities, it does not make any sense to have a notion for evaluating the correctness of an attempt, if one does not also have a notion to qualify its possible outcomes, i.e. its success or failure. And one cannot have a notion to qualify a success that is not success-entailing. However, the expression "truth-guaranteeing" may be understood as implying more than "truth-entailing" and I think that it is against this understanding that Brandom's claim that such a notion "is not to be had" should be interpreted. As G. Ryle explains in *The Concept of Mind* (Chicago: University of Chicago Press, 1984), the distinction between achievement and task words is precisely that the first imply that "some state of affairs obtains over and above that which consists in the performance ... of the subservient task activity" (p. 150). This is the externalist sense of achievement words: they express *that* a certain state of affairs obtains, but they do not also specify *how to tell* whether this is the case on any particular occasion – as do the corresponding task expressions that we use to qualify the correctness of the attempt to obtain the achievement. For if the meaning of achievement words cannot depend on anything concerning the activity at issue other than its outcome, these words *have to be criterially empty*. In this sense, achievement words can be "success-entailing" precisely because they are not "success-guaranteeing", they do not provide internalist cues as to how to guarantee success through the correct performance of the activity. Taking all this into consideration, the notion that is not to be had is a notion of justification that will give us (internalist) epistemic criteria sufficient to *guarantee* the success of the activity (i.e. the achievement of knowledge). But we can only know that such a notion is not to be had *because* we have grasped the externalist sense of the achievement itself as expressed by the "truth-entailing" notion of justification: we can be fallibilist only after having grasped that whether our justifications happen to be correct is not only a function of our epistemic responsibility. (I offer a more detailed analysis of this issue in Chapter 6 of my book *The Linguistic Turn in Hermeneutic Philosophy*, Cambridge, MA: MIT Press, 1999.)

31 This is why this deontic status (trivially) has only an achievement sense: if the notion of knowledge is supposed to designate the *successful* case, the case in which *nothing* goes wrong, it cannot at the same time be made *compatible with failure*. For if it were (i.e. if it were equated with the task sense of the notion of justification as epistemic responsibility), one would have to invent another notion to be able to indicate what the successful case of assertions is supposed to be.

10

HABERMAS, DEWEY, AND THE DEMOCRATIC SELF

Sandra B. Rosenthal

The conceptual alternatives in which democratic theory has been couched, far from offering a pathway for resolving the dilemma of balancing the features of individual freedom and communal solidarity, too often announce their ultimate irreconcilability. This problem is starkly exhibited in Alasdair MacIntyre's view that the United States may well be founded on incompatible moral and social ideals: on the one hand, a communitarian vision of a common "telos," and on the other hand an ideal of individualism and pluralism. Thus, he holds that "We inhabit a kind of polity whose moral order requires systematic incoherence in the form of public allegiance to mutually inconsistent sets of principles."[1] And, indeed, what we are offered by the litany of frameworks is too often a forced choice between the extremes of the "grand melting pot" and the "grand accumulator of fragmented parts."

Both Habermas and Dewey are concerned with community solidarity within the context of pluralism and diversity, avoiding the extremes of the homogeneity of the communitarian vision and the fragmented, heterogeneous pluralism of the libertarian vision. In developing their respective alternatives, both incorporate perspectivalism and fallabilism, view political deliberation as beginning in concrete problematic situations, and believe the way communication functions in contemporary society is of vital concern, for the resolution of social problems requires free and open communication within a self-corrective process.

In connection with this, Habermas draws on John Dewey for support of his political theory, quoting from Dewey with the following:

> Majority rule, just as majority rule, is as foolish as its critics charge it with being. But it never is merely majority rule ... The means by which a majority comes to be a majority is the more important thing: antecedent debates, modification of views to meet the opinions of minorities ... The essential need, in other words, is the improvement of the methods and conditions of debate, discussion, and persuasion.[2]

Yet Habermas's interest in pragmatic philosophy focuses on Peirce and Mead, with a glaring and regrettable neglect of Dewey.

Part of the reason for this is perhaps to be found in the context of his reconstruction of Mead's understanding of the self. Habermas rejects Mead's early writings, which he correctly views as "under the naturalistic presuppositions of John Dewey's functionalist psychology."[3] In fact, however, Mead remained a naturalist functionalist similar to Dewey throughout his career. Habermas's understanding of Dewey's position explains his virtually wholesale rejection of it, as can be seen in his claim that

> Mead can explain the phenomenon and emergence of conscious life only after he has given up Dewey's model of an isolated actor's instrumental dealings with things and events and has made the transition to the model of several actors' interactive dealings with each other.[4]

This characterization, however, is far removed from the actual Deweyan vision of the self, a pragmatic, naturalist, functionalist vision which is virtually indistinguishable from, though less developed than, that of Mead's.[5] Thus, Habermas's analysis and reconstruction of Mead's position to accommodate his own framework can equally be directed to Dewey's pragmatic understanding of the self. And it is here that the seeds of the differences between the political theories of Dewey and Habermas are to be found.

Habermas's reconstruction of Mead moves from the prelinguistic to the linguistic level in the formation of self-consciousness. As he states,

> Mead believes he must redirect his analysis to the prelinguistic level of gestural communication ... Nonetheless, an internal reconstruction of the conditions that make original self-consciousness possible can be based upon a prior understanding of linguistic communication.[6]

And it is to the linguistic level that Habermas moves in his theory of democracy. The ensuing discussion will first turn to a brief sketch of Habermas's position as it relates to his reconstruction of the Dewey–Mead view of the self to accommodate his own political theory.

Habermas develops a position of discursive proceduralism, the norms of which assure that reasonable consensus will emerge. Discourse is rooted in acceptance of a quasi-transcendentally grounded ideal speech situation which is fundamentally universalistic and a-historical and which is at once the normative basis of agreement and constitutive of the conditions of rational communication. The discursive principle is given more specificity as a democratic principle, which is institutional, and presupposes the validity of moral norms which are true irrespective of any particular political framework. The democratic principle promises that "only those statutes may claim legitimacy that can meet with the assent of all citizens in a discursive process of legislation that in turn has been legally constituted."[7] It "lies at another level than the moral principle," because of its specificity.[8] The democratic principle lies at an institutional level.

The solidarity that grows out of discourse occurs through a common recognition of the terms of fair discourse and is not, Habermas emphasizes, the "thicker" solidarity of communitarian positions, which cannot adequately take account of pluralistic societies. The linguistic bond occurring within intersubjective speech is the source of solidarity in a democracy, a solidarity not found in libertarian individualism.

Basic rights, for Habermas, are intersubjective ingredients of a system of laws founded in mutual recognition and self-legislation. These rights guarantee both private autonomy and rights to political participation, ensuring that law "preserves its connection with the socially integrative force of communicative action."[9] The system of rights should "contain precisely the basic rights that citizens must mutually grant one another if they want to legitimately regulate their life in common by means of positive law."[10]

Habermas makes a distinction between moral norms, which can be justified universally, and the ethical, which is locally pluralistic and involves competing claims of particular interests or what he later called existential/ethical commitments. The former involves the impartial character of consensus and the latter the strategic character of compromise. While parties can agree to working a compromise for various reasons, discursive consensus must be based on identical reasons that are capable of convincing all the parties in the same way.[11] The moral perspective, which concerns the rightness of procedures and their outcomes and carries moral obligation, is on a different level than that of competing ethical perspectives concerning the nature of the good life. Habermas, borrowing from Michelman's terminological distinction, refers to these in terms of the dialogical and the instrumental respectively.[12]

The moral point of view, as opposed to the ethical, demands impartiality, "the unforced conviction of a rationally motivated agreement," which requires that we "concentrate on those questions that are amenable to impartial judgment ... We must ask what is equally good for all."[13] This impartiality of discourse is presupposed by any practical discourse. In the move from what is good locally to what is good for all, practical reason can reach a level of intersubjectivity and can be ultimately translated into law. Channels of public influence allow the flow from the informal sphere of morality to the formal system.

Habermas holds that institutional paths should be established for the communication scattered throughout the public realm. Because so scattered, it is "subjectless" or "anonymous," giving rise to a subjectless public opinion. "The self of the self-organizing legal community disappears in the subjectless forms of communication." In short, popular sovereignty, as it "retreats into democratic procedures becomes anonymous."[14] This is perhaps to be expected, for the loss of the prelinguistic origins of selfhood has lost with it the relevance of any sense of agency, of a thick, dynamic embodied center of creativity which underlies and overflows the confines of language. The seeds of this willingness in Habermas to introduce the "subjectless" and "anonymous" can be seen in a commentary on Mead's understanding of the self from the perspective of his own linguistic position. Habermas attempts to capture Mead's sense of concreteness which goes beyond particular roles through the distinction between role identity and ego-identity, holding that this lies in the distinction between past and future: what kind of a person I have become as opposed to what kind of a person I want to be.[15]

The very sense of the question as to "the kind of person I want to be," or "the kind of integration of roles I want to achieve," however, seems to require not only more than the exercise of a series of specific roles, but also more than any integration of roles, the "thickness" of a living reality which takes, integrates, and changes roles but which can never be exhausted through this expression. This is solidly established by Mead in his too frequently overlooked, albeit brief, references to the biological dimension of the self, which is not lost once the reflective level emerges but rather pervades its activity,[16] and the sense of which is captured in Mead's early writings – dismissed by Habermas as "too Deweyan" – as the prelinguistic, vague sense of thick agency.[17] This dimension can be expressed by a sense of what Dewey calls "impulsion," though this term is used by him in a some-what different context.[18] While Dewey and Mead would agree with Habermas that "original self-consciousness is not a phenomenon inherent in the subject but one that is communicatively generated,"[19] communication for Habermas is understood solely as linguistic communication. Thus "the performative meaning of the 'I'" becomes, for Habermas, "Mead's 'me,' which must be capable of accompanying all my speech acts."[20]

On a different but closely interrelated issue, Habermas finds a problem with Mead in that he blurs the difference between "the epistemic self-relation of the knowing subject and the relation-to-self of the acting subject."[21] Mead makes this mistake, Habermas continues, because "he comprehends 'knowing' as problem-solving practice and conceives of the cognitive self-relation as a function of action."[22] He further traces the source of this "problem" to the fact that Mead explains both of these "on the basis of a reorganization of the stage of prelinguistic, instinct-steered interaction."[23] Reconstructing the pragmatic position to provide for such a distinction allows him to make a dichotomy between the way institutionalized forms of social intercourse are put into question by "split-off motives and repressed interests" on the one hand, and "revolutionarily renewed language" on the other.[24] Through his concern with discourse and ideal speech he severs discourse from action, the "thick" subject as a decision- and action-oriented individual from "the sovereignty of the people" as "a flow of communication."

Procedural democracy is limited to rational argumentation and the impartial character of consensus, and consensus becomes the criterion of truth and objectivity. It is a purely discursive process from which values are excluded, as is the "strategic" process of negotiation and compromise. Again, Habermas garners support for this position from the development of a social self, viewing Mead's universalizing ideals, necessary for self-development, as a return to the "Peircean concept of a consensus achieved in an unlimited communication community, or an 'ultimate opinion.'"[25] Thus in developing his path beyond the libertarian–communitarian extremes, he views individualism as the "flipside" of a Peircean type of universalism,[26] a view which is contradicted by the very primal dynamics of the perspectival nature of the pragmatic self, as will be discussed shortly.

Habermas maintains that the technological sciences follow their own set of rules, and the system which constitutes the technical sciences is immune to democratic transformation. This position is intertwined with his sharp distinction between instrumental or technological or purposive rational action, and meaning-enriching communicative action or symbolic interaction,[27] a dichotomy which he attempts to strengthen in the context of a critical analysis of Mead by noting the distinction between types of sentences that do and do not require communicative intent.[28] But it will be seen that for Mead and Dewey alike, the meanings incorporated into language embody both experimental activity and communicative intent by the very dynamics of the primal activity in which the social self emerges.

Habermas, then, dichotomizes discursive, procedural democracy and transformative human action; communicative or symbolic interaction and technological, purposive action as modes of human activity; experimentalism and meaning enrichment; and concomitantly, facts and values. It is precisely the rejection of all of these dualisms which structure Dewey's understanding of democracy and the nature of selfhood it involves.

For Dewey, the primal origins of the self are to be found in interactions among conscious organisms. Individuals take the perspective of the other in the development of their conduct, and in this way there develops the common content which provides community of meaning and the social matrix for the emergence of self-consciousness. This process is inherently technological–experimental,[29] for perspectives are tools for, serve the purpose of, organizing experience, and the adequacy of any perspective can be judged only by experimental method, by testing its workability in directing the ongoing course of experience. This process is also inherently communicative and meaning-enriching, for these tools are utilized to resolve problematic or potentially problematic situations by being productive of consequences which lead to contextual integration through reconstruction of the situation or the infusion of experience with enriched meaningfulness.

This activity pervades, and partially constitutes, human experience in general. Technology as a distinctively human enterprise emerges with the emergence of the interrelated features of symbolic and reflexive activity, or in other terms, the emergence of shared meanings and selfhood, and is infused with the human purposes which direct it and with the social and cultural values in which it is embedded. Experimental–technological-meaning enriching activity is the very matrix within which selfhood emerges and this pervasive mode of human action is embedded in the internal dynamics of the self.

Habermas's dualism of instrumental and communicative action mentioned above is anchored in a view of experimental–technological activity as a "straight-line instrumentalism," concerned only with "facts" and geared toward domination and control, while the human sciences involve communicative action or symbolic interaction and are emancipatory and enriching and expansive of meaning.[30] This narrowing of purposive experimental action with its resultant divorce from communicative action is reflected in his distinction between the impartial character of consensus and the strategic character of compromise, which, as indicated earlier, he refers to in terms of the dialogical and instrumental respectively. It also accounts for his understanding of the system of science as beyond the reach of democratic transformation. He agrees that experimental method can be traced to the development of selfhood, but views it as leading to a paradox misleadingly resolved through a temporal dimension. A "transformed and reflexive consciousness of time" provides "the imputation that present action will be placed under premises that anticipate future presents."[31] This, he believes, may in turn "explain tendencies toward a certain existential burdening and moralizing of public issues," a "normative congestion."[32]

Experience and knowledge as perspectival are also inherently pluralistic. Any self incorporates, by its very nature, both the conformity of the group perspective and the creativity of its unique individual perspective.[33] Freedom does not lie in opposition to the restrictions of norms and authority, but in a self-direction which requires the proper dynamic interaction of these two poles within the self.[34] Because of this dynamic interaction constitutive of the very nature of selfhood, the perspective of the novel, "liberating" pole always opens on to a common, "conserving" perspective. These same dynamics are operative in community. The novel perspective of the individual is an emergent because of its relation to institutions, traditions, and patterns of life which conditioned its novel emergence, and it gains its significance in light of the new common perspectives to which it gives rise. In this continual interplay of adjustment of attitudes, aspirations, and factual perceptions between the common perspective as the condition for the novel emergent perspective and the novel emergent as it conditions the common perspective, the dynamic of community is to be found. The act of adjustment – which is not assimilation or fusion into one but can best be understood as accommodation – between the novel perspective and the common perspective is the essential communicative dynamic of community. A free society, like a free individual, requires both the influencing power of authority as embodied in institutions and traditions and the innovative power of individual creativity as contextually set or directed novelty in an ongoing, inseparably intertwined process.[35]

The adjustment of incompatible perspectives at any level requires not an imposition from "on high" of abstract principles but a deepening to a more fundamental level of human rapport. The understanding of a radically diverse way of life, or way of making sense of things, is not to be found from above by imposing one's own reflective perspective upon such diversity, but rather from beneath, by penetrating through such differences to the sense of the various ways of making sense of the world as they emerge from the essential characteristics of beings fundamentally alike confronting a common reality in an ongoing process of change. Such a deepening does not negate the use of intelligent inquiry, but rather opens it up, frees it from the products of its past in terms of rigidities and abstractions, and focuses it on the dynamics of concrete human existence.

To understand one's own stance on any issue is to understand its inherently perspectival approach and the illuminating light which other perspectives can rightfully cast upon it. The development of the ability both to create and to respond constructively to the creation of novel perspectives, as well as to incorporate the perspective of the other, not as something totally alien, but as something sympathetically understood, is at once growth of the self. This involves more than Habermas's ideal of a "universalistic form of life" of "reciprocal recognition";[36] it involves an ongoing process of learning from and restructuring one's concrete self – in the fullness of its emotions, drives, desires, beliefs, purposes and aspirations – in the process of adjusting to the other. Growth of self incorporates an ever more encompassing sympathetic understanding of varied and diverse interests. It involves as well the concomitant reconstruction of the institutions and practices which become incorporated within the self's conserving dimension, and at times demands also a reconstruction of the very organs of adjustment of the community which ground such reconstructive dynamics. Rationally directed change leads to growth both for the individual and the community, but for Dewey rationality cannot be isolated from the concrete human being in its entirety.[37]

This "thickness" of existence (which outruns the concerns of Habermas) is reflected in the issue of rights. Dewey agrees that ongoing community adjustments must be understood not as pitting the individual armed with rights against the common other that limits these rights; there are no absolute individual rights of "free," atomic individuals. But neither are rights merely the result of government legislation or contractual agreements, for freedom of the self in a general sense lies in the proper relation between the two dimensions of novelty and conformity constitutive of its very nature. Individual rights are also social rights, although responsible social rights are not possible without individual freedom. A free society, like free individuals, requires this balance. In this way, the good of the whole is not the good of the common or group other over against the absolute rights of the individual. The good of the whole is the proper relation between the individual and the common other, because the whole is community and community encompasses the individual and the common other in an ongoing process of adjustment.

What this indicates is that humans *qua* humans are born into implicit arrangements that embody in their very nature reciprocity, accommodation, and proper balance or justice; indeed, as indicated above, these dimensions are built into the very internal dynamics of the free self. This position grounds autonomy, solidarity, and fairness more deeply than is allowed by Habermas's position by rooting these features in the primal communal nature of the thickness of concrete human existence. It is the two dimensions of freedom and constraint, rights and obligations, self and other, all embedded in the nature of the self and community alike, which give rise to the situational and relational nature of rights. Both freedom and rights and responsibilities are "thick," overflowing the confines of law or system or language, just as the subjects within democratic procedures are "thick" action-oriented individuals overflowing the confines of discourse.

Moreover, the human organism and the nature within which it is located are both rich with the qualities and values of our everyday experience, and thus experimental method as operative in the process of living must serve the qualitative fullness of human interests. The dynamics of experimental method, which embody "the fundamental principles of the relationship of life to its surroundings,"[38] is the vehicle by which concrete growth, achieved through the expansive integration or harmonizing of novelty and continuity, leads to the aesthetic–moral enrichment of human experience. Thus science is "operative art." Human experience is through and through both experimental–technological and moral–aesthetic. This dual function becomes a problem only if one separates, explicitly or implicitly, facts and values or truncates human experience.

The unity of experimental–technological purposive activity and communicative, meaning-enriching activity, as discussed earlier, is embedded in the very primal constitution selfhood. For Dewey, the answer to the problems of technology is not less technology but more and better technology. And, though advanced technology requires increased technical skills, this is far from enough, for it must be guided by an attunement to the aesthetic–moral richness of experience which it must ultimately serve and subject to ongoing guidance by transformative collective intelligence. Indeed, attunement to the aesthetic–moral richness of existence is itself a tool for guiding the direction of ongoing experimental–technological activities and hence productive of the types of consequences to which these give rise. Perhaps a way of briefly summarizing all of the above is to say that the artful functioning of experience cannot be truncated into isolatable skills, for it is holistic through and through, a character of experience which is lost in the truncations of Habermas's framework.

All of the various features discussed thus far are embodied in Dewey's understanding of democracy. As Habermas expresses this point from his own perspective, the "paradox" of experimental activity as intertwined with the development of selfhood, discussed above, is "the source from which the radically democratic perspectives of Mead and Dewey derive their own internal consistency."[39]

Dewey stresses that democracy is not a particular body of institutions or a particular form of government, but the political expression of the functioning of experimental method. Any social structure or institution can be brought into question through the use of social intelligence guided by universalizing ideals, leading to reconstructive activity which enlarges and reintegrates the situation and the selves involved, providing at once a greater degree of authentic self-expression and a greater degree of social participation. In this way, democracy provides for a society which controls its own evolution, and participation in this process is "necessary from the standpoint of both the general social welfare and the full development of human beings as individuals."[40]

Dewey, then, can point out that growth itself is the only moral "end," that the moral meaning of democracy lies in its contribution to the growth of every member of society,[41] and that growth involves the rational resolution of conflict.[42] In this way, the moral import of democracy for Dewey lies in the fact that it is the ideal of community life itself.[43] Any authentic organization involves a shared value or goal, and the overreaching goal of a human society is precisely this control of its own evolution. Thus, the ultimate "goal" is growth or development, not final completion.

This in turn indicates that neither democracy nor the working ideal of universality can imply that differences should be eliminated or melted down, for these differences provide the necessary materials by which a society can continue to grow. Though society indeed represents social meanings and social norms, yet social development is possible only through the dynamic interrelation of this dimension with the unique, creative individual. The creative perspectives of individuals offer the liberating possibilities of new reconstructions. The liberating is also precarious. But the liberating, the precarious, the novel, occurs within the context of tradition, stability, continuity, community. The demands of adjusting the old and the new, the stability of conformity and the novelty of creativity, "is inherent in, or a part of, the very texture of life." [44]

A true community, as by its very nature incorporating an ontologically grounded temporalism and perspectival pluralism requiring ongoing growth or horizonal expansion, is far from immune to the hazardous pitfalls and wrenching clashes that provide the material out of which ever deepening and expanding horizons are constituted. Dewey's understanding of democracy, however, does not merely allow a place for inherent pluralism with the accommodation, negotiation, and compromise it requires, but positively demands it. As he points out, life itself "grows when a temporary falling out is a transition to a more extensive balance of the energies of the organism with those of the conditions under which it lives."[45] While Habermas's position, like Dewey's, incorporates perspectivalism, his consensus theory of democracy cannot accommodate the radical perspectivalism required by the Dewey–Mead view of the self and which is present in Dewey's understanding of community.

When there is lacking the reorganizing and ordering capabilities of creative intelligence, the imaginative grasp of authentic possibilities, the vitality of motivation, or sensitivity to the "felt" dimensions of existence, all of which are needed for ongoing reconstructive horizonal expansion, then instead of growth the result is irreconcilable factionalism. For Dewey, the skills of experimental inquiry are needed not just for the adequate exploration of specific subject matter but for the possibility of the interrelated ongoing reconstruction and expansion of the self, values, and the institutions and practices of the community, including the very organs of adjudication for the communicative adjustments which make possible such ongoing reconstructions and expansions. Experimental inquiry or "the method of intelligence," as it functions to further the enrichment of the fullness of concrete human existence involves, in Dewey's words, "wide sympathy and keen sensitiveness, and persistence in the face of the disagreeable," all which in turn allow for the "balance of interests" needed for intelligent analysis and decision.[46] What will solve present problems and provide the means for ongoing growth of the self and the community is human intelligence with its creativity, sensitivity, imagination, and moral awareness geared to the human condition in all of its qualitative richness.

Thus, Dewey's understanding of democracy and the nature of the democratic self is inextricably intertwined with his ongoing stress on the pressing need for both universal education – which means education not just of all individuals but also of collective social intelligence – and holistic education or education of the whole person, a need with which Habermas would agree. The absence of this dimension from Habermas's discussions of democracy and its ramifications, then, is both noticeable and surprising. Further, one might wonder whether Habermas's understanding of education for democracy, which seemingly would not focus on either the thickness or holistic nature of human experience in a Deweyan manner, would ultimately be compatible with Dewey's rich analyses of the educational process in its intertwining with democracy.

Dewey stresses that to have "anything that can be called a community in

219

its pregnant sense there must be values prized in common."[47] But he is not seeking common values as a type of common content which infringes on individualism and pluralism, which erodes freedom or melts down differences, a situation which he disparages as "a factitious sense of direct union and communal solidarity," [48] an artificial "moral consensus."[49] These values prized in common are values which foster aesthetic and moral sensibility and a concomitant attunement to the other, creative intelligence, imagination, and a healthy common sense rooted in the cultivation of these qualities. These qualities promote an atmosphere in which one can develop one's values and talents, promote the development of individuals who can engage in dialogue in such a way that society can continually reconstruct itself in a manner that will lead to the ongoing thriving of individuals and communities alike through a process of participatory self-government requiring the vitality of the essential community dynamics of pluralistic perspectival accommodation.

This participatory self-government is directed by the dynamics that direct growth in all areas of human activity – that is, the dynamics of experimental method and the transformative nature of human action that are embedded in the very life process and its development within the emergence of selfhood. And the life process and its development within the emergence of selfhood are inherently fused with the indefinitely rich moral–aesthetic dimension of concrete human existence which can be left behind only by truncating experience. It is this pervasiveness of the moral throughout the thickness of concrete existence to which Deweyan philosophy is constantly attuned, which Habermas views as the "existential burdening and moralizing of public issues," the "normative congestion" which, as discussed earlier, he attributes to the seeds of experimental method within the development of selfhood and the resulting paradox.

It can be seen, then, that Dewey's naturalist, functionalist view of the self, which locates its primal origins in pre-linguistic experimental–technological-meaning enriching activity, provides the matrix for democratic theory far removed from that of Habermas, though they have many goals in common. For Dewey, in opposition to Habermas, "truth" is the outcome of experimentation rather than consensus; negotiation, adjustment, accommodation and compromise for different reasons are all an integral part of democracy, indeed of the democratic self, by which individuals and communities alike can grow by learning from and taking the perspective of others; and no system, institution, or type of endeavor is immune from the inherently experimental, cooperative, transformative democratic process by which "thick" individuals organize to bring about the reconstruction of beliefs, values, institutions, and the very organs of adjudication that allow for the ongoing process of perspectival growth.

While Habermas and Dewey, then, are engaged in the common endeavor of resolving the dilemma of balancing individual freedom and communal solidarity, a dilemma which has plagued past understandings of democracy, there are numerous diverse, often contradictory, deeply embedded and pervasive differences in their respective solutions. And both the depth and pervasive significance of these differences are inextricably intertwined with the diverse understandings of the origins and nature of the democratic self as developed in the writings of Habermas and Dewey respectively.

Notes

1 A. MacIntyre, "Is patriotism a virtue?" *Lindley Lecture*, Kansas, University of Kansas, 1984, pp. 19–20.
2 J. Habermas, *Between Facts and Norms*, Cambridge, MIT Press, 1996, p. 306.
3 J. Habermas, *Postmetaphysical Thinking: Philosophical Essays*, trans. William Hohengarten, Cambridge and London, MIT Press, 1996, p. 171.
4 *Ibid.*, p. 174. See also p. 173.
5 This claim is developed by me in some detail in *Speculative Pragmatism*, Amherst, Massachusetts, University of Massachusetts Press, 1986. Paperback edition, Peru, Illinois, Open Court Publishing, 1990.
6 J. Habermas, *Postmetaphysical Thinking*, p. 175.
7 J. Habermas, *Between Facts and Norms*, p. 110.
8 *Ibid.*
9 *Ibid.* p. 111.
10 *Ibid.* p. 118.
11 *Ibid.* p. 411.
12 J. Habermas, *The Inclusion of the Other: Studies in Political Theory*, ed. C. Cronin and P. De Greiff, Cambridge, MIT Press, 1998, p. 245.
13 Habermas, "Morality, society, and ethics: an interview with Torben Hviid Nielson," in *Justification and Application*, Cambridge, MIT Press, 1993, p. 151.
14 J. Habermas, *The Inclusion of the Other*, p. 251.
15 J. Habermas, *Theory of Communicative Action*, vol. 2, *Lifeworld and System: A Critique of Functionalist Reason*, trans. Thomas McCarthy, Boston, Beacon Press, 1987, p. 106.
16 This position is developed by me in some depth in *Speculative Pragmatism*, Chapter 4, *passim*.
17 See "The definition of the psychical," *Mead, Selected Writings*, ed. Andrew Reck, New York, Bobbs-Merrill, 1964, pp. 25–59.
18 This concept is explored by me in *Speculative Pragmatism*, pp. 186–91.
19 J. Habermas, *Postmetaphysical Thinking*, p. 176.
20 *Ibid.* p. 189.
21 J. Habermas, *Postmetaphysical Thinking*, p. 178.
22 *Ibid.* p. 178.
23 *Ibid.*
24 *Ibid.* p. 180.
25 *Ibid.* p. 184.
26 *Ibid.* p. 186.
27 *Toward a Rational Society*, trans. Jeremy Shapiro, Boston, Beacon Press, 1970, pp. 91–2.
28 J. Habermas, *The Theory of Communicative Action*, vol. II, p. 28.
29 The way in which the experimental and the technological are inextricably intertwined yet cannot be conflated is discussed by me and co-author Rogene Buchholz in *Rethinking Business Ethics: A Pragmatic Approach*, Oxford and New York, Oxford University Press, 2000, Chapter 7.

30 J. Habermas, *Knowledge and Human Interests*, trans. Jeremy Shapiro, Boston, Beacon Press, 1970, pp. 309–10.

31 J. Habermas, *Postmetaphysical Thinking*, pp. 187–8.

32 *Ibid.* p. 188.

33 J. Dewey, "Authority and social change," *The Later Works*, ed. Jo Ann Boydston, Carbondale and Edwardsville, University of Southern Illinois Press, vol. 11, 1987, p.133.

34 *Ibid.* Thus, "the principle of authority" must not be understood as "purely restrictive power" but as providing direction.

35 J. Dewey, *The Public and Its Problems*, *The Later Works*, vol. 2, 1984, pp. 330, 332.

36 J. Habermas, *Postmetaphysical Thinking*, p. 186.

37 J. Dewey, *Human Nature and Conduct*, *The Middle Works*, ed. Jo Ann Boydston, Carbondale and Edwardsville, University of Southern Illinois Press, vol. 14, 1983, pp. 136–7.

38 J. Dewey, "Affective thought," *The Later Works*, vol. 2, 1984, pp. 106–7.

39 *Ibid.* p. 188.

40 J. Dewey, "Democracy and educational administration," *The Later Works*, vol. 11, 1987, pp. 217–18.

41 J. Dewey, "Reconstruction in philosophy," *The Middle Works*, ed. Jo Ann Boydston, Carbondale and Edwardsville, University of Southern Illinois Press, 1976–1983, vol. 12, 1982, pp. 181, 186.

42 J. Dewey, *Ethics*, *The Middle Works*, vol. 5, 1978, p. 327.

43 Dewey makes a distinction between democracy as a social idea and political democracy as a system of government, but holds that the two are connected and ultimately that they are inseparably intertwined; *The Public and Its Problems*, p. 325.

44 J. Dewey, "Authority and social change," p. 133.

45 J. Dewey, *Art As Experience*, *The Later Works*, vol. 10, 1987, pp. 19–20.

46 J. Dewey, "Reconstruction in philosophy," pp. 173–4.

47 J. Dewey, *Freedom and Culture*, *The Later Works*, vol. 13, 1988, p. 71.

48 *Ibid.* p. 176.

49 *Ibid.* p. 157.

POSTSCRIPT

Some concluding remarks

Jürgen Habermas

Response

I am grateful to Mitchell Aboulafia and his co-editors, Myra Bookman and Catherine Kemp, for having invited distinguished colleagues to contribute to the present volume. I owe a great debt to the contributors themselves who took pains in addressing problems they have faced in reading one or another of my publications. All parts of the volume would deserve a much more detailed response. I must apologize for not being able to meet the obligation to respond in proper detail within given time constraints.

I have learned most from the essays which, following the suggestion of the editors, compare some strands in the thought of American Pragmatism with corresponding elements of my philosophical work. David Ingram's careful analysis makes me aware of the underestimated complexity of the rich tradition of Legal Realism. In their interesting comparison between Dewey's and my own strategies to conceptualize "actions" and "the self" of social actors, Lenore Langsdorf and Sandra B. Rosenthal pursue, each in her own way, illuminating lines of argument. Their criticisms take a similar direction to objections with which Hans Joas has confronted me in a different context. I also appreciate Richard Shusterman's Pragmatist Aesthetics from the perspective of which Dick Rorty and I are perceived walking side by side. Myra Bookman gives a sensitive account of how I have received, and tried to digest, Jean Piaget's ideas in a pragmatist spirit. And Cristina Lafont follows her own agenda of defending realism all the way down.

Sometimes discourses are too distant from one another to allow a fruitful exchange. This was my first impression when I looked at the large picture of late twentieth-century philosophy as painted in broad strokes by Joseph Margolis – and then faced the charges that he raised against what he takes to be my understanding of "egalitarian universalism": if even Rorty comes out as just another "Cartesian," I don't mind the label. With regard to Tom Rockmore's worries, I regret that the English translation of *Wahrheit und Rechtfertigung* (Suhrkamp, 1999) has not yet been published. It is, indeed, a central question whether or not the kind of "Kantian pragmatism" that

Putnam and I both defend is a reasonable epistemological project. This issue should perhaps not be judged by the accuracy of how I (in a deliberatively selective way) appropriated Peirce's pragmatist conception of knowledge in a book written three and a half decades ago.

There are two essays to which I would like to respond at greater length. Karl-Otto Apel hits a weak point in the architectonics of my legal philosophy. In the third chapter of *Between Facts and Norms* I apparently failed in my attempt to distinguish a "discourse principle" – that is, to explain the requirements for the rational acceptability of propositions in general – from the "moral principle" explaining the procedure of "universalizing" norms of action. A certain confusion may be due to the fact that the normative content of the discourse principle overlaps with that of the moral principle, but the meaning of the latter is much more specific. Only the moral principle explains what it takes *for supposedly all-inclusive norms* of actions to meet post-conventional justification requirements (while "all-inclusive" points to the idealized range of addressees, unlimited in social space and historical time).

Frank Michelman challenges my conception of constitutional democracy from a different angle. We have different conceptions of "reasonable pluralism" in legal interpretation. How far must the community of constitutional interpreters remain divided by reasonable disagreements? Are the gaps so deep and enduring that they could be bridged only by some infeasible sort of "constitutional essentialism" (smacking of doubtful apriorism)? We certainly cannot know a rule without knowing how to apply it to some cases. Nor can we know a case without a glimpse at the rule of which it may count as a case. But this does not prevent us from introducing and – if it comes to law and morality – justifying rules in advance of their application to *further* cases. We usually do this by appealing to *some* typical situations of possible conflict that are in need of regulation. The "typical" cases, in the light of which norms and principles can only be justified, reflect both the degree of abstraction of "rules" and the prima facie character of the "deontological force" or validity they may claim.

Justified norms remain open for application. Statutes, established by a legislature, wait for interpretations by a court or a public administration. The separation of powers mirrors, at an institutional level, the division of labor between discourses of justification and of application, each of which, according to a different pattern of argumentation, obeys a logic of its own.[1] An appropriate application needs a specifying interpretation, and some interpretations do not leave the meaning of the applied rule untouched. This becomes obvious in "hard" cases when a judge has to solve the problem of a prima facie collision of competing norms or principles. Over time constitutional principles are also "developed" by legal interpretation, when their meaning is not only further explicated, but changed in the light of strikingly new and unprecedented cases. But even such a "change" in meaning must be justified. The interpreter must "get it right" by having recourse to ideas that connect the present generation of citizens with the founders and the generations in between. What binds them together is the performative meaning of the very practice of constitution making. The "purpose" of this practice is supposed to be understood in the same way as the founding, development, and preservation of a voluntary association of free and equal citizens governing themselves by means of modern, i.e. positive and legitimate, law. It is the availability of, and the persisting possibility of an appeal to, this same point of reference that spans, in the last instance, reasonable pluralism, however deeply it continues to split the community of constitutional interpreters.

Reflections on pragmatism

Instead of going into more detail I will now turn to the six questions Mitchell Aboulafia asked me to answer:

When did you first encounter thinkers who have been called pragmatists?

As a high school student I got interested in philosophy. During that postwar period (from 1945 to 1949, when I finished gymnasium) it was quite difficult to buy books. I basically depended on three sources – the wellstocked library of my uncle, a philosophy teacher; the rather cheap supply of the communist bookstore; and the not so opulent bookcase of my parents. It was there that I happened to find, among my father's books from the time of *his* studies, an introduction to philosophy by a Viennese philosopher who was, as I learned later on, the first translator of William James. His name was Wilhelm Jerusalem.[2] He not only dedicated the whole of § 26 to an explanation of Charles Sanders Peirce's "pragmatic maxim," but throughout the book he kept referring to William James, John Dewey and F.C.S. Schiller side by side with Ernst Mach. This naturalist approach to an evolutionary conception of mind and culture appeared to fit with the Historical Materialism of Marx and Engels, whose small paperbacks I read at about the same time.

I had forgotten this first encounter with pragmatism until recently, when I remembered Jerusalem at an occasion of taking some autobiographical notes. I searched for his book on my shelves and found it in the right place – among the secondary literature to the collection of pragmatist authors that has continued to grow since I first bought the seven-volume edition of Peirce in the early 1960s.

Did any of your teachers or fellow students have knowledge of pragmatism?

As far as I remember, none of my philosophy teachers, during my university studies between 1949 and 1954, ever mentioned either the school or one of its prominent members. But in the course of my studies I came upon Max Scheler's sociology of knowledge, first published in 1925.[3] The essay "Erkenntnis und Arbeit. Eine Studie über Wert und Grenzen des pragmatischen Motivs in der Erkenntnis der Welt" contains a thorough discussion and criticism of William James's epistemology. In the same context Scheler introduced his own famous tripartite classification of "forms of knowledge" – *Erlösungs-, Bildungs- und Leistungswissen*. As you can gather from the conception of "knowledge-guiding interests" that Apel and I developed during the 1960s, that early encounter with Scheler has left deep traces (even though I failed to make an explicit reference to Scheler in *Knowledge and Human Interest*, as I should have done).

Apel was the one who directed my attention to Peirce in the early 1960s. First I read those well-known epistemological essays from his middle period. The Peirce chapter in *Knowledge and Human Interest* came out of a lecture that I had delivered at Heidelberg in 1963. A little earlier, Morton White's *Reunion of Philosophy* had provided me with a perspective from which I could defend the rational continuum between descriptive, evaluative and normative propositions against Popper, whose theory was one with which I was struggling during the so-called "dispute on positivism." From Morton White came the reference to Dewey's *Logic of Discovery*. Somewhat later I brought two more books of Dewey home from my first visit to the US – *The Quest for Certainty* and *Reconstruction in Philosophy*. After moving from Heidelberg to Frankfurt, I started teaching G.H. Mead's *Mind, Self, and Society* in my sociology classes. (On my recommendation the book was translated and published by Suhrkamp in 1968.) By that time I had probably become more familiar, and also more in agreement, with pragmatism than most of my American colleagues.

I was, in any case, surprised by their reactions when I first visited American universities in 1965 – Ann Arbor, Berkeley and some other places. The philosophy departments were still under the spell of either Carnap's theory of science or Wittgenstein's linguistic phenomenology. When I mentioned pragmatism as "the" great American tradition, I was always met with shrugging shoulders. Peirce was perceived as "odd" at best, Dewey as a "fuzzy thinker." Dick Bernstein, who in 1972 invited me to deliver a lecture at Haverford College, was the first "real" pragmatist that I had met, and the one who ever since has kept pushing me in the direction of a more intense detranscendentalization of Kant. Dick Rorty gave me the same advice, of course, when I came to his seminar at Princeton two years later. Besides these two, and also with an academic education at Chicago,

Larry Kohlberg became another friend whom I came to admire as a very impressive embodiment of the pragmatist spirit.

What have you found most valuable in the pragmatic tradition for your own work?

The impact on my intellectual development was threefold. In epistemology – and the theory of truth – Peirce had the strongest influence, from my Frankfurt inaugural lecture on *Knowledge and Human Interest* (1965) onwards up to *Wahrheit und Rechtfertigung* (1999). Since Apel and I had remained in contact, it was his interpretation that at first guided my reception. Our early familiarity with, and leaning towards, philosophical anthropology and the analytic of *Dasein* in *Being and Time* (Heidegger's analysis of "being in the world" in particular) had prepared us for a pragmatist epistemology. Peirce's style of analysis was more up to date and hence more appropriate for a defense of the *internal* relations between forms of knowledge and types of action, as opposed to the limited view of the logical empiricists and their focus on the semantic dimension. For Peirce, reason and understanding were from the start embodied in the research activities of a community of investigators. We perceived Peirce's pragmatist approach as a promise to save Kantian insights in a detranscendentalized yet analytical vein. That promise also pertained, for me more than for Apel, to a reconciliation between Kant and Darwin, between a transcendental and an evolutionary perspective. My studies of Schelling's philosophy of nature, and the reception of Marx, had made me more open towards a "soft," non-scientist naturalism.

The second influence, almost as strong as that of Peirce, came from Mead's theory of social interaction. The conceptual frame of what Mead's students were later to call *Symbolic Interactionism* served me as guide towards a *Theory of Communicative Action* that was to connect the Hegelian Marxism of Critical Social Theory with both the methodology of the hermeneutic tradition (from Schleiermacher and Dilthey to Gadamer) and a dialogical conception of language and communication that Apel and I had initially learned from Wilhelm von Humboldt. It was only later that I also discovered the ethical implications of Mead's mutual "perspective-taking" – a dynamic working towards Piaget's "decentration of perspectives." This view was again reminiscent of the ethical theory already implicit in Humboldt's analysis of the first and second person roles of participants in dialogue.

It was a lucky historical coincidence for us young Germans, the first generation of post-war philosophy students, that streams of "our" sources in German Idealism (including Humboldt and Marx) – from whom the great pragmatists themselves had once taken off – were again flowing together with what we then discovered were the results of an earlier and overwhelmingly productive American–German encounter.

One would expect the third influence of pragmatism obviously to be in the field of political theory. And it is true that I was attracted most strongly by the progressivist mentality of a communitarian-inspired modernism so beautifully expressed in the pathos of Walt Whitman's great hymns. Remember also the lines of William James, inscribed in James Hall at Harvard: *"The community stagnates without the impulse of the individual, the impulse dies away without the sympathy of the community."* The anti-elitist, democratic, and thoroughly egalitarian *attitude* that shapes and penetrates the work of all the pragmatists was far more important than the *contents* of any particular essay on politics or democracy.

Since Robert B. Westbrook's study, *John Dewey and American Democracy* (1991), everybody thinks of Dewey as also a great political theorist. And with his *Public and Its Problems* (1927) Dewey could have been a major source for my *Structural Transformation of the Public Sphere* (1962). In fact, he was not. I came across Dewey's writings only after finishing that first book. And even after that I did not pick up his political or ethical writings for several decades. Naturalizing Hegel, Dewey remained for me an anthropologically minded epistemologist rather than a political thinker. He figured as the philosopher who anticipated major arguments of both Arnold Gehlen's *Der Mensch* and Richard Rorty's *Philosophy and the Mirror of Nature*.

At some time in the late 1980s, perhaps, I discovered from hindsight the convergence in our views on the discursively structured public sphere as a requirement for democracy. This circumstance does not, of course, diminish the political role that pragmatism has played in the formation of my ideas of democracy and the constitutional state. Pragmatism constitutes, besides Marx and Kierkegaard, the third Young Hegelian tradition, and the only one that convincingly develops the liberal spirit of radical democracy.

What are the greatest strengths of pragmatism?

The combination of fallibilism with anti-skepticism, and a naturalist approach to the human mind and its culture that refuses to yield to any kind of scientism.

What are its greatest weaknesses?

The message that only differences that make a difference should count is often mistaken for advice to blur even relevant distinctions. And just as often, the anti-Platonic distrust in an ideological misuse of abstract ideas is misunderstood as the denial of the transcending force and unconditional meaning of claims to truth. There is an empiricist undercurrent in Dewey's and an emotivist undercurrent in James's thought. Both threaten the Kantian heritage that is saved, in pragmatist translation, by Peirce – and, by the way, by Brandom. My friend Dick Rorty is most Kantian in the seriousness of his ambition to turn those weaknesses into philosophical strengths.

*What do you see as the most lasting contribution of pragmatism
to the tradition of Western philosophy and social thought?*

The pragmatists would have rejected a question suggesting that each of the great philosophers accomplishes one characteristic thought of his or her own. In contrast to this false Heideggerian pretense, Peirce and Royce, James, Mead and Dewey felt the obligation to solve problems, one by one, just in the local context where they actually faced them. But equally, they would have objected to a false generalization of this honest attitude in terms of a contextualism that cheers the local provincialism of our problem-solving capacities. Alongside Marx and Kierkegaard, again, pragmatism emerges as the only approach that embraces modernity in its most radical forms, and acknowledges its contingencies, without sacrificing the very purpose of Western philosophy – namely, to try out explanations of who we are and who we would like to be, as individuals, as members of our communities, and as persons *überhaupt* – that is, as man.

On John Dewey's *The Quest for Certainty*

The following piece by Habermas on Dewey appears for the first time in English. Habermas recommended its translation for this anthology.

On John Dewey's The Quest for Certainty[4]

Translated by Robert Metcalf

In looking back upon the century now coming to a close, the 1920s turned out to be the most fruitful decade for German philosophy – with Wittgenstein's *Tractatus*, Lukács' *History and Class Consciousness*, Cassirer's *Philosophy of Symbolic Forms*, Scheler's *Forms of Knowledge and Society*, Plessner's *Stages of the Organic and Man*, and, of course, Heidegger's *Being and Time*. Shortly thereafter, in 1929, a book of similar rank appeared in the US: *The Quest for Certainty*, the most influential work of John Dewey, who, then seventy years old, stood at the high point of his fame. It has taken a long time for this classic of pragmatism to now become available in the German translation of Martin Suhr. Today Dewey is a household name. In the intervening years, the word "pragmatism" has risen from an expletive to an honorific term. The delay in reception certainly brings to mind the asymmetrical relation between Dewey and his philosophical colleagues in Germany.

While Dewey was a young college student in his home town of Burlington, Vermont, he had already become well acquainted with Kant, Fichte, Schelling and Hegel in this stronghold of the transcendentalists. By contrast, in the native land of German idealism, the seed of what was to become Dewey's own "naturalized" Hegelianism began to sprout only generations later. It was not until a decade or two after the Second World War that pragmatism was taken seriously here as a long-misjudged variant of young Hegelianism and as a source of kindred themes. As can be seen from the dates when the texts appeared in translation, this process of appropriation focused at first, in the early 1960s, more heavily on Charles Sanders Peirce and George Herbert Mead than on Dewey and James. Today pragmatism, in its diverse readings, builds a transatlantic bridge for vital philosophical exchange in both directions. Whoever reads *The Quest for Certainty* with an interest in the history of its reception discovers therein an explanation of the tensions and misunderstandings between Dewey and those three traditions which, in this country, are still closest to him, though in different respects for each.[5]

Dewey directs attention to the everyday praxis in which people must "cope with" reality and "get along with it." With this move the category of "action" (*Handeln*) attains an unprecedented philosophical status. Above all else, Dewey directs his attention, informed by the history of philosophy, to the seam between knowing and acting in order to assign to philosophy a new role. Eschewing the way in which classical theory withdraws from the world, he propagates the turn toward being engaged in the world. Science and technology irresistibly hasten the processes of mastering nature and developing industry. Here it is shown how knowledge can become practical, since it is aimed at praxis from the very beginning. However, politics and education, the civilizing of social intercourse and the cultivation of taste, and above all the self-organization of society, find themselves in a deplorable state for lack of a comparably intelligent guide – and philosophy fails to provide guidance. Instead of fortifying the gap between the higher and the lower, between the lofty height of ideas and the profane, philosophy ought to abandon the pretended certainty of pure theory. It must face the challenges of the contingent world and join in cooperation with the sciences instead of operating in a fundamentalist opposition to them. Only in this way can philosophy articulate the horizons of certain possibilities for the "forms of social and private action." With this revolutionizing of philosophy's self-understanding Dewey set himself apart from all other stances.

Dewey's front against the logical empiricism of Carnap and Reichenbach is no less pronounced than his opposition to the philosophical idealism of Scheler and Heidegger, or to the anti-scientific view of Horkheimer and Adorno. In the course of the 1930s, Dewey's philosophy was to some extent already superseded in the US by the analytic type of philosophy of science exported from Austria and Germany. The emigrés had great sympathy for the "scientific spirit" that they found in the pragmatist camp, and they endeavored to involve Dewey in their project of a unified science. But by 1939, when the eighty-year-old was to be honored with the first volume of the *Library of Living Philosophers*, the voices of the empiricists had already become quite critical – as Hans Reichenbach's contribution shows. There were two essential differences.

In *The Quest for Certainty*, Dewey criticizes the empiricist "spectator-model of knowledge," according to which elementary sensations provide a firm basis for experiences. In fact, experiences are gained only in interaction with a reality against which behavioral expectations may run aground. For this reason reality is disclosed not through the receptivity of the senses, but rather in a constructive manner in the context of projecting and performing actions that succeed or fail. Objects are not "conceived" independently of the controlled outcome of deliberately performed actions. Therein lies the significance of scientific experiments. Furthermore, Dewey criticizes empiricist ethics, where value-judgements are reduced to emotions, attitudes or decisions. Dewey is convinced of the cognitive content of value-judgements. According to his conception, judgements on praiseworthy and desirable things gain objectivity due to the fact that they are connected with an awareness of the consequences they entail for a praxis whose aims we can achieve.

With these views Dewey was not able, at the time, to satisfy the growing theoretical demands of a younger generation. In the leading American departments he remained a "nonentity" (*ein toter Hund*). This situation only began to change when, in 1979, Richard Rorty identified Dewey, along with Wittgenstein and Heidegger, as one of the "three most important philosophers of our century." In Germany, on the other hand, Dewey was, to be sure, not even present in the past – with the exception of the field of education and of Gehlen's anthropology. Certainly Scheler had treated some important themes of pragmatism in his sociology of knowledge. Nevertheless, he held fast to a hierarchy of forms of knowledge, according to which knowing by way of "mastery" or "performance" – the only way that counted for Dewey – remained subordinate to knowing by way of "intellectual formation (*Bildung*)" and "salvation." Scheler himself is an example of the Platonism that satisfies the quest for certainty through the metaphysical surrogate of taking flight into the realm of ideas. Idealism embraces contemplation as the way to salvation for philosophers. Dewey thinks that it thereby misses the way to the only certainty that we can actually achieve. The intelligent mastering of a risky environment is possible only along a practical pathway of coping.

Heidegger, too, drew tacitly upon the insights of pragmatism in *Being and Time*, in the analyses of "equipment," the "ready-to-hand," and "context of involvement." With the concept of "being-in-the-world," Heidegger also participated in the anti-Platonic thrust of pragmatism. On the other hand, Heidegger's thought aimed to disclose, beyond the everyday world that he dismisses as "ontic," the ontological dimension of the authentic. By the late Heidegger, the Platonic ideas have been drawn into the whirlpool of enownings (*Ereignisse*)[6] in the history of being. But the ontological difference preserves – now with a vengeance – that *chorismos* between the extraordinary and the customary that Dewey levels out. Heidegger binds the privileged access to truth, reserved by him for poet and thinker, to the submissive posture of "commemorating" the destinings of a higher power. In contrast, Dewey begins his investigation with the bifurcation of two paths along which man "seeks certainty in a world full of dangers." Opposite the "praying suppliant," who is brought to mind by the fatalistic thinking of being, Dewey posits the activity of inventors: "The other path consists of inventing arts and with their help making the powers of nature useful."

This confidence in the civilizing power of mastering nature also finally separates Dewey from those with whom he is allied in criticism of divorcing theory from praxis, though not in criticism of "instrumental reason." The operationally conceived natural sciences were from the beginning aimed at the acquisition of technologically useful knowledge. And technological success makes them for Dewey an unquestioned model of problem-solving behavior. Of course, Dewey is expecting too much from the "application of experimental activity to every question of praxis," if he thinks that moral or political value-judgements are also to be justified by reference to the consquences of an instrumental praxis of implementing values (*Werteverwirklichung*). In his approach to moral philosophy, the views of his friend George Herbert Mead on mutual perspective-taking in interaction would have been able to lead him further.

Still, Dewey exposed the cognitive roots of a lifeworld praxis that is up to coping with the contingencies and frustrations of a surprising reality. The quest for certainty is the flipside of being conscious of risk, aware that appropriate habits of action develop and maintain themselves only by productively working through failures and mastering challenges. What distinguishes human beings as essentially capable of action is this problem-solving behavior: knowing how to clarify a problematic situation, and knowing that in this activity one can rely on no authority other than one's own intelligent effort.

At any rate, Dewey is immune to any kind of tragic solemnity over, or existential revalorization of, this *situation humaine*. He does not play off the profound against the superficial, the extraordinary against normality, the enowning against what is customary, or the aura against what is trivial. Dewey doesn't inflame, he ignites.[7] As a democratic thinker, Dewey is egalitarian through and through. For this reason he was able to find a sensitive reception only as the Bundesrepublik – the "old one," as they say today – separated itself from the young-conservative sentiments of a tumultuous past. For the Berliner Republik, too, he would be the better patron.

Notes

1   K. Günther, *The Sense of Appropriateness. Application Discourses in Morality and Law*, Albany, State of New York University Press, 1993.

2   Wilhelm Jerusalem, *Einleitung in die Philosophie, siebentes bis neuntes Tausend*, Wien und Leipzig, Wilhelm Braunmüller, 1913.
3   Max Scheler, *Die Wissensformen und die Gesellschaft*, Bern und München, Francke Verlag, 1960.
4   Originally published in *Die Zeit*, 23 July 1998. Translated and reprinted by permission of the author.
5   These three traditions are the ones I deal with subsequently: logical empiricism (Carnap), anthropological phenomenology (Scheler and early Heidegger), and Western Marxism (in particular Horkheimer and Adorno).
6   Translator's note: Although *Ereignis* might be rendered, in more ordinary contexts, by the English "event," the peculiar significance of this word for Heidegger's thought justifies its translation as "enowning." See the translators' preface to Martin Heidegger, *Contributions to Philosophy (From Enowning)*, translated by Parvis Emad and Kenneth Maly, Bloomington, Indiana University Press, 1999.
7   In the original: "Dewey regt nicht auf, er regt an."

INDEX